FREEING THEOLOGY

FREEING THEOLOGY

THE ESSENTIALS OF THEOLOGY IN FEMINIST PERSPECTIVE

EDITED BY
CATHERINE MOWRY LaCUGNA

HarperSanFrancisco
A Division of HarperCollinsPublishers

Text design by Jaime Robles.

FIRST EDITION

Library of Congress Cataloging-in-Publication Data:

Freeing theology : the essentials of theology in feminist perspective
/ edited by Catherine Mowry LaCugna. — 1st ed.
    p.   cm.
Includes bibliographical references and index.
ISBN 0-06-064935-6 (pbk. : alk. paper)
1. Feminist theology. I. LaCugna, Catherine Mowry.
BT83.55.F744 1993
230′.082—dc20   92–56129
                                                              CIP

95 96 97 RRD(H) 10 9 8 7 6 5 4 3 2

This edition is printed on acid-free paper that meets the American National Standards Institute Z39.48 Standard.

Contents

Introduction

THIS IS NOT a book *about* feminism or *about* the Christian tradition but an example of doing theology from a new perspective. It explores recent developments in Catholic theology by analyzing the ways in which traditional doctrinal areas within Catholic theology have been challenged and transformed by feminist scholarship. The ten chapters demonstrate what it means to recover, challenge, and, indeed, create tradition through reinterpretation.

The feminist critique of the androcentric bias of religion and theology redefines the themes that properly belong within different areas of specialization, recasts the meaning of basic terms (for example, *natural law*), highlights new images and metaphors for both God and human experience, and revises the way we use theological and religious language. This critique has had a far-reaching effect on the methods and procedures of Christian theology, particularly in Catholicism. Hundreds of Catholic women have now been trained in all the fields of theology. One wants to attribute this development to the Holy Spirit, but a more readily verifiable reason for the high number of Catholic theologians who are women is due, at least ostensibly, to the policy of the church that forbids the ordination of women to presbyteral ministry. The majority of strong advocates and theologians within the Christian feminist movement have been Catholic, again probably because the institution that forbids female ordination invites the most vigorous critique. There is also the fact that Catholic theology today is increasingly lay rather than clerical.

But much more lies behind Christian feminism than the prohibition of ordination. Across the denominations, Christian feminism is a far-reaching critique of the fundamental sexism of the Christian tradition inasmuch as it has valued men over women, has seen masculine experience as normative for women's experience, has imaged God in predominantly masculine metaphors, or has used the Christian message to support violence against women.

The presence of women theologians not only has changed the sociology of who is doing theology today, it has fundamentally changed the way of doing theology. Along with retrieving the forgotten contributions of women who were mystics, theologians, and saints, feminist theologians have rendered a devastating critique of the patriarchal dimensions of theology, notably, the vaunting of the male above the female—which the tradition presents as reflecting the mind and purpose of God. A fundamental principle of feminism is that both women and men share fully in human nature and that neither is superior to the other. Neither men nor women can claim to be closer to God or more perfectly created in God's image without vitiating the truths of the Christian faith and the authenticity of biblical revelation.

Theological feminism has a distinctive contribution to make to the life of the church. Feminism did not originate in the academy, nor is its lifeblood primarily there. It draws its strength of conviction from women whose experience tells them that the kingdom of God preached by Jesus promises a different order of relationship among persons than what prevails today. Feminism derives from an authentic *religious* insight inasmuch at it manifests the desire for the genuine communion between women and men in Jesus Christ. In its theological form, Christian feminism exposes the idolatry of projecting onto God false dualisms or hierarchical arrangements between men and women, spirit and matter, and so forth. It also exposes the profoundly harmful effects of patriarchy on the humanity of both women and men and rejects the part played by Christian piety and theology in sustaining patriarchy's hold upon society and church.

These essays are marked by the Catholic concern to be in continuity with the Christian tradition as much as possible, indeed, to search to the fullest possible extent for liberating elements within the Christian tradition. While the contributors to this book share a remarkable consensus, they also illustrate theological differences that result from different methodological choices concerning, for example, the extent to which the tradition should be or can be normative for contemporary theology. Feminism is not a monolithic discipline or approach; there are now many kinds or degrees of feminism, though all feminists, women and men, share the basic conviction of the equality of women and men.

The discussion is shaped by two bodies of learning: Catholic theology and feminist scholarship. Each chapter examines a major doctrinal topic or area within theology, beginning with the way the subject matter was approached and understood within the Catholic tradition and then showing how feminist principles transform the theological treatment of the subject matter, often down to its most basic concepts and methods. The result is a presentation of a basic theme in theology from a Catholic as well as consciously feminist theological point of view.

The chapters are not meant to present "*the* feminist theology of topic *x*." Not all topics covered in this book are at the same point of development in terms of current scholarship, feminist or otherwise. A great deal more has been written about feminist biblical hermeneutics than about feminist sacramental theology. But in both cases, the chapters evaluate developments that have taken place and aim to come to greater clarity about future directions.

Contemporary theology is still dominated to a large extent by the "tract" approach—the arrangement of the main topics within dogmatic theology into discrete sections and according to an order derived from Scholasticism. The chapters in this book are arranged according to this scheme, even though this very arrangement is called into question by doing Christian theology in a feminist mode. Here one learns that the barriers separating, for example, Trinity and theological anthropology are far more permeable than the scholastic arrangement allows. At the same time, since this book is intended for use in the classroom, the order of chapters is consistent with the way that many theological syllabi and curricula are arranged. The reader is encouraged to read the chapters in the order that makes the most sense to her or him.

The annotated bibliographies alert the reader to basic resources pertinent to each topic. Some entries are repeated, since certain works emerge time and again as classics of Christian feminist theology and are therefore essential to each area. As with any annotation, the bibliographies are by no means complete but give a representative sampling of important works in each area.

This project was initiated by John Loudon, Executive Editor at Harper San Francisco, and could not have been completed without him. Our thanks go also to Mimi Kusch, Production Editor, and Karen Levine, Editorial Assistant. My own special word of gratitude goes to the authors who worked diligently to make my work of editing a pleasure and a welcome exercise in collegiality.

Catherine Mowry LaCugna
The University of Notre Dame

CHAPTER ONE

THE NEW VISION
OF FEMINIST THEOLOGY

— Method —

ANNE E. CARR

A VOCIFEROUS ARGUMENT took place in my church recently when a woman charged the visiting preacher with being insensitive to the women in the congregation. He protested that his sermon was simply an attempt to offer a theological understanding of the biblical passages of the lectionary in a way that was faithful to the texts and to traditional teaching. She argued that his approach should use inclusive language, take account of feminist understanding, and that his way of theologizing should incorporate the insights of women about the patriarchal and misogynist character of the Christian tradition. She claimed that she and other women in the congregation were faithful Christians but that their personal integrity demanded fidelity to their own deepest convictions about themselves as fully human participants in the church. His theology, she said, should use the methods of feminist theology to give a sermon that was helpful to women. "What methods?" he asked. Indeed.

What methods have feminist thinkers developed in recent years, and how are they different from those that the preacher learned in seminary? In this chapter, after laying out the contours of theological method in general, I sketch questions of method in feminist theology through the work of two of its most influential representatives. I examine the thought of Rosemary Radford Ruether and Elisabeth Schüssler Fiorenza, both Catholic theologians, to delineate some of the methodological issues they raise. I also explore some of the critiques their work has received by other theologians. Although Mary Daly, one of the first feminist academicians, warned against "methodolatry" as a rigid traditional framework that considers women as nondata and their questions nonquestions,[1] the issue of an appropriate method for *feminist* theology has recently come to the fore. It has been raised in different ways by both Catholic[2] and Protestant[3] feminist theologians, as twentieth-century Christian feminist theology moves into its second generation.

THE NATURE OF THEOLOGICAL METHOD

Theology, as knowledge or discourse about God and all things in relation to God, has long been done in different contexts, within many traditions, and with various implicit and explicit methods of approach. Within the wide Christian tradition, the many theologies can be distinguished by their methods. This is so even within the books of the Bible itself, the originating and core document of Christian faith, recognized now as entailing a variety of theological orientations. And it is so in the theologies associated with particular geographical areas or historical periods or with different groups of thinkers or individuals whose writings found their way into the stream of the tradition of the church. Thus biblical, medieval, Thomistic, Lutheran, and Calvinist theologies, Protestant, Orthodox, Catholic, Anglican, and Methodist theologies display the different starting points, sources and norms, implicit or explicit theoretical assumptions, and interpretive strategies that comprise their methods. In turn, these methods shape and even determine the content or emphases of their discourse about God and God's revelation in Jesus Christ.

As the broad set of Christian traditions developed and the work of theological reflection became more refined, it was always marked by its historical and geographical setting and by the social location and experience of the theologians involved, just as it was marked by the cultural, ecclesial, and personal experience of its intended readers. Changes in theological method often occurred in relation to transformations in the wider culture, in philosophical thinking, and in other fields of human thought.[4] As theological reflection proceeded throughout Christian history, there were increasingly explicit efforts to achieve systematic consistency in its propositions, that is, internal coherence within the various topics and categories of explanation and external coherence with other knowledge and with the cultural and personal experience of its listeners or readers. Thus the question of method today has become a theological topic in itself, as thinkers debate whether Christian thought should, or necessarily does, accommodate itself to its particular cultural time and language while remaining faithful to the whole of Christian tradition[5] or whether it should strive rather for faithful presentation of the grammar and narrative patterns of its originating sources in the Bible and the rules of the classical doctrines.[6]

Only in later times were the categories of Scripture, tradition, reason, and experience explicitly differentiated as sources for theological reflection. For the most part, previous theologians assumed these elements in their work, appealing to the central authority of the Bible as it was interpreted in their times, to the authority of earlier theologians or philosophers, to church councils or the pope, to rational argumentation, or to common experience, both cultural and personal. More recent theology is characterized by the conscious attempt to proceed with both consistency and coherence to demonstrate and to argue for the rationality and truth of its assertions about God and all things in relation to God.

Roman Catholic theological methods are clearly outlined in a recent essay by Francis Schüssler Fiorenza.[7] Acknowledging the historical variety of theologies in the ascetic, spiritual, and monastic traditions, he describes three classic academic models that have been most influential—those of Augustine, Thomas Aquinas, and neoscholasticism—and several contemporary methods. Augustinian and Thomist methods were concerned to relate revelation (known chiefly in the Scriptures but also in the Christian writings of the past) to current philosophy: Neoplatonism in Augustine's thought and Aristotle in Aquinas's synthesis. Neoscholasticism responded to the challenges of the Protestant Reformation, the

Renaissance, and the rise of the natural sciences with a return to Thomist categories, but understood in a rationalistic and Cartesian framework. The three classic ways share a common emphasis on Scripture and tradition, the scientific character of theology, the centrality of the church community, and the role of experience. They differ in that Augustine emphasized the role of personal purification in the right interpretation of the Bible, whereas Thomas stressed *sacra doctrina* as a rule-governed procedure with its own authorities, and neoscholastic theology emphasized church teaching.

Elements of the three classic models can still be discerned in Catholic thought, but recognition of the historical character of theology and the realization that philosophy is not simply its instrument led to the shift from classical to contemporary approaches. These Fiorenza describes as transcendental, hermeneutical, analytical, correlational, and liberational. Feminist theology is usually understood as a form of liberation theology, but in fact it employs a variety of different approaches within that broad rubric.

THE NEW VISION OF FEMINIST THEOLOGY

While it is logical to raise the question of theological method as a first issue in this treatment of feminist theology, the question has arisen only recently, after several decades of discussion in which feminist thinkers have been productively engaged. That discussion has entailed the creation of song, poetry, spirituality, ritual, dance, liturgy, and prayer as well as the more formal but still broadly understood "theology" that comprises biblical and historical interpretation, ethical studies, and analyses of doctrinal themes. Perhaps it is only after such wide engagement, when there is a substantial body of material, different ways have been tried, and the results assessed, that the more theoretical issue of method can be fruitfully explored.

Catholic feminist theology derives from the emergence of feminist consciousness among large groups of Roman Catholic women in the last three decades.[8] This consciousness, touching the depths of women's personal identity and integrity, occurred for some as a result of the wider, international movement of women for liberation, equality, respect, and influence. But the specific Catholic awareness was itself a catalyst and a source of leadership in the wider movement. As women's studies—the academic arm of the women's movement—developed, religion and its reflective discourse in theology were perceived early on to legitimate patriarchy and sexism in society's institutions. In this way religion and theology

elicited feminist analysis and critique. When home and family life, education, the churches and synagogues, and the various professions (law,
medicine, business) all came under feminist academic scrutiny, scholars
pointed out that religious and theological views of women had helped
to shape subordinating social structures and women's own negative self-
perceptions. But even before these detailed analyses appeared, the question of women had been raised in the Roman Catholic context.[9] The
obvious situation of women in the Catholic church, with its explicit patriarchy and sexism, may have fueled the development of feminist awareness
among Catholic women and so spurred Catholic leadership in feminist
theological reflection.

Critique of Tradition

The emergence of feminist consciousness has been described as a
blinding flash of light. It blinds in that it disorients and disturbs the
viewers; it is light in the way it vividly illumines the whole landscape. In
the initial disorientation and illumination experienced by Catholic feminist theologians, their first task was to critique the tradition itself from a
feminist perspective. Their awareness that women's voices were absent
through the centuries of tradition as well as in the present and their recognition that women were envisaged theologically as naturally inferior and
a source of sin and pollution led feminist scholars simply to make that
point: in Catholic theology, a male-centered and male-authored perspective, derogatory of women, was so pervasive that the entire tradition was
skewed and needed to be righted. From the first, this sense that a terrible
wrong needed righting, whether that meant a minor correction or a full-
scale transformation, gave feminist theology its early designation as advocacy theology. Like liberation theologies generally, feminist theology is
an involved and engaged enterprise, so that its "objectivity" as a neutral
and "disinterested" search for truth is sometimes challenged as being a new
ideology. It is now a principle of contemporary hermeneutics that all
interpretation is conditioned by the presuppositions and prejudgments of
the interpreter and feminist thinkers usually identify their social locations
and presuppositions. This move is taken in an effort to be as clear as possible about the perspectives that govern particular lines of thought and
argument.

While as baptized members of the church, women had surely been
present and active in its life, including its reflective life, this presence and
activity had been either effectively erased in the texts of the past or

denigrated in assertions of women's ontological, moral, intellectual, bodily inferiority and supposedly natural subordination to men. In centuries of biblical interpretation and theological construction, women were viewed as property, objects, tools, or minors, as dangerous temptresses (Eve) or paragons of virtue (Mary), and women were taught to obey fathers and husbands in a pattern of supposedly benevolent domination/submission. Women were seldom understood as simply fully human and fully Christian. So the initial feminist critique of Catholic tradition analyzed these distortions and urged the need to right the historical record.[10]

Recovery of Women in Christian History

The second move in feminist theology, both logically and chronologically, was the recovery of women's history in the Catholic and wider Christian traditions. Feminist theologians searched for aspects of the Christian past of women that were hidden, unnoticed, or devalued yet available for retrieval if the right questions were asked and the right sources uncovered. While the first task of critique had exposed the position of women as victims of oppression and exploitation in biblical stories and the interpretation of these stories in the preaching and reflection of the men who were the church's leaders, theologians, and reformers, the recovery of women's history showed that women were not simply victims but agents in the church and in its spiritual and theological reflection.

Feminist thinkers demonstrated that in both testaments of the Bible and in the historical development of Christianity, women's activities were significant. By reading the available texts and reinterpreting the stories they disclose, feminist theologians were able to recover some of the lost or concealed history of women in the Bible and in Christian tradition.[11] As women discovered the fuller contours of the historical legacy, the question was raised of the real difference women's thought would make to theology in the present.

Theological Reconstruction

Beyond critique and historical retrieval, then, there emerged the third task of feminist thinkers, the incorporation of both the newly understood historical material and the contemporary insights of the now plural feminist community into the constructive work of theology. This meant reshaping the doctrine or teaching about revelation, the Bible, God, creation, anthropology, the Holy Spirit, grace, sin, redemption, the church, the sacraments. By the time women in sufficient numbers had achieved the training, skills, and positions in seminaries and universities that enabled a broad contribution to formal theology, the women's movement itself had expanded beyond the white, Western, middle-class framework of its origins. Today feminist scholarship includes the voices of many races, classes, and ethnic groups, registering the important differences among the women of the world. Thus feminist theology is ecumenical, global, and plural in its approaches, understanding each effort as a partial and limited contribution to a wider conversation.

Only when the threefold task of critique, historical retrieval, and theological construction—the work of several decades—was fully present did the question of theological method arise as a significant issue in its own right. While it is a first topic logically, it is one of the last to emerge historically. Feminist theologians plunged into the task at hand, experimented with diverse ways of exploring a new terrain, and put forward innovative and often collaborative approaches. There is now a vast literature of feminist biblical interpretation, historical studies, and feminist theology and spirituality available in what is already a global and plural venture.

Feminist theology values this diversity of approaches, acknowledging the manifold social locations of its different participants and seeing richness in its own pluralism. Feminist theology has been ecumenical from its origins, as the discussion has included Christians of many denominations, Jewish feminists, and feminists of other traditions or of no tradition at all. Catholic thinkers have borrowed images and ideas from the wider Christian tradition, from its marginal strands, from Judaism, and from ancient, prebiblical texts. They use models borrowed from feminist studies in other disciplines, such as history, psychology, anthropology, sociology, and natural science. Scholars in these areas offer helpful theories that analyze the historical denigration and devaluation of women as well as the androcentrism of much scholarship. The incorporation of general or secular feminist theory has characterized the ongoing life of Catholic feminist theology. This wide-ranging use of source materials and interpretive strategies has resulted in a diversity of feminist theological approaches, so that it is more accurate to speak of feminist *theologies,* especially today when black or womanist and Hispanic feminist theologies are integral to the discussion.

Some of the first Catholic feminist scholars to discuss the question of method in an explicit way were biblical scholars. Trained in both

European and American universities, these women brought their feminist awareness to the work of interpretation. They used historical-critical, literary, and rhetorical methods to approach the overall message of the Bible or its various books, the Bible's images of women, and its themes and stories about women. After the initial attempts to bring a feminist angle of vision to the biblical material, the diversity and fruitfulness of this work engendered conferences, symposia, and collections of essays that explored not only specific approaches to the ancient texts but also the various feminist and theological stances operative in exegesis and interpretation.[12]

A helpful overview of this pioneering work is provided by Carolyn Osiek's typology. Using the word *feminist* in a broad sense as "concern for the promotion and dignity of women in all aspects of society,"[13] she lists five responses of women who recognize both the Bible's major role in the oppression of women in patriarchy and women's own situation in a patriarchal church. These responses include rejection, loyalty, revision, sublimation, and liberation. The rejectionist simply refuses to acknowledge any authority or usefulness in the Bible or in the entire religious tradition it represents. The loyalist, at the opposite extreme, insists that the Bible, as the Word of God, cannot be oppressive but is the source of a divine plan of true human freedom. Within this perspective, one may either counter a text that blatantly enjoins female submission with another that enjoins female liberty or perhaps argue that the scriptural submission theme applies only to leadership in the family, not to society generally.

The revisionist holds that the patriarchal framework of the Jewish and Christian traditions is a historical fact but is not theologically necessary. The male supremacist, androcentric, and sexist elements of the Bible are not intrinsic to its message but can be sifted from it by means of exegetical method and analysis of cultural context.

The sublimationist option is based on the "otherness" of the feminine as witnessed in the imagery and symbolism of culture. Either the feminine is seen as innately superior to the masculine, or the life-giving and nurturing qualities of woman are considered to be of such a different order that any crossing of sex roles runs counter to nature itself. In this option the typically feminine characteristics of Jesus and the Spirit are emphasized.

The liberationist alternative proposes that the central message of the Bible is human salvation as liberation, either as found in the prophetic tradition (freed from its patriarchal contexts) or in those texts that transcend androcentrism and patriarchy and point to the conversion and transformation of society today and in the future.

THE CONTRIBUTION OF ROSEMARY RADFORD RUETHER

Osiek points out that these various approaches to the Bible arise from different experiences and assumptions of feminist thinkers. These assumptions are really theological positions. In fact, Osiek uses the ground-breaking work of Rosemary Radford Ruether to set up her typology. Ruether's *Sexism and God-Talk* (1983) is probably the first full-scale attempt to lay out a Christian and Catholic feminist systematic theology. She follows the traditional list of theological topics (God, creation, anthropology, sin, redemption, Christ, church, and so forth), but discusses these from a feminist point of view. She formulates her point of view this way: "The critical principle of feminist theology is the promotion of the full humanity of women. Whatever denies, diminishes or distorts the full humanity of women is, therefore, appraised as not redemptive." This principle translates theologically to "the affirmation that whatever diminishes or denies the full humanity of women [which has never really existed] must be presumed not to reflect the divine or an authentic relation to the divine, or to reflect the authentic nature of things, or to be the message or work of an authentic redeemer or a community of redemption."[14]

Ruether was one of the first Christian feminist theologians to reflect explicitly on methodological issues. In *Sexism and God-Talk*, she proposed a general theory of religious tradition (and theology) as codified experience, using this theory as a backdrop for her argument that the uniqueness of feminist theology is the use of *women's* experience. This experience, shut out of supposedly universal human experience in the past, shows that Christian theology has really been a construction of male experience. Feminist theology makes the social context of theological knowledge visible, since it demonstrates that traditional formulators of theology are men and, in the recent past, middle-class men in university and seminary contexts.

Ruether postulates that every great religious idea begins in a revelatory experience that provides powerful symbols for the whole of life. This revelation may be experienced by an individual, but it takes hold in communal consciousness and is collectively transmitted. The historical community mediates the revelatory experience through integrating the revelation with existing cultural or religious symbols and traditions to

illumine and disclose new meaning in unexpected ways. Such new codification is first oral, then written, and soon it requires teachers and leaders
to channel and control the process, to separate alien elements and devise
criteria that determine the correct interpretive line. A canonical body of
writings or teaching structures develops that necessarily marginalizes or
suppresses heterodox interpretations. As the canon is formed, those who
maintain power and leadership in the community are the winners, while
the losers simply disappear. Once such a canon or structure is present, all
interpretation becomes reflection on (or of) past codification.

Yet the present experience of the community cannot be ignored.
There is a constant process of revision in which the interplay of originating
pattern with logic and new ideas forms an intellectual tradition. But it is
a tradition that remains vital only if it is in touch with the depth experience of its time, only so long as its revelatory pattern continues to provide
meaning. Thus the interpretive circle goes from revelatory experience to
current cultural or personal experience. Crises occur when the tradition
itself is understood to contradict contemporary experience or when institutional structures are perceived as self-interested or corrupt. While
in some cases the whole religious heritage may be understood to be false,
in others the earlier pattern is still seen to be authentic. But since a simple
return to the past is not possible, the past is used as a place from which
to criticize later tradition, to suggest a radicalization that encompasses new
experience. This general theory, Ruether holds, especially characterizes the
authority structures of communities like Catholicism, Judaism, and
Orthodoxy, while more scripturally based communities appeal to the
Bible or some part of the Bible.

In a Christian context, the critical principle of the promotion of the
full humanity of women is the ancient principle of the *imago dei* or Christ
as the goal of human destiny. What is new is that women are claiming that
principle, making themselves the subjects of authentic, full humanity.
The principle is perceived to have been corrupted in men's theology, in
which males are made the norm of humanity and women are scapegoated
for evil. Such perception implies, for Ruether, that the goal of feminist
theology cannot be simply to reverse the distortion by making men or certain classes and races or nonhuman creation subordinate. Rather, feminist
theology must search for a new mode of relation that is inclusive of all.

Ruether affirms that in this search there is no final definition of feminist theology. She describes her own work as a Christian, Western cultural
synthesis that includes selected material from the Hebrew and Christian

Scriptures and from marginalized or heretical traditions in Christianity. She employs the primary themes of classical theology but includes Near Eastern and Greco-Roman religion and philosophy as well as critical post-Christian worldviews. Admitting that all these traditions are sexist, she argues that each also contains inclusive alternatives. From the Hebrew biblical tradition, Ruether selects the prophetic principle, defining it as the refusal to elevate any social group over others as the agent of God or to use God to justify social domination and subjugation. Four themes from that tradition are central to the mission of Jesus: God's defense and vindication of the oppressed; criticism of dominating systems of power and of power holders; the vision of an age to come when present injustice is overcome; and critique of ideology or religion as it justifies an unjust social order.

Ruether maintains that the prophetic-liberating tradition is not static but serves as a plumbline for truth and justice according to particular contexts. While it too can be ideologically deformed, as in Israel's triumph over the Canaanites or Christianity's triumph over the Jews or in the sacralization of religious kingship or the servitude of subjected peoples, the prophetic principle maintains its edge when the focus is kept on identification with the poor and on the move from powerlessness to power. It is distorted when it is identified with existing power, convention, and the status quo. The more radical vision of Jesus transforms the revenge motives and reversal of domination in the Hebrew Bible; the false spiritualization of the kingdom of God is transformed by feminist interpretation of the nondualistic wholeness of Jesus' message. Ruether recognizes that the prophets were myopic in relation to women. Her point is that the idea of the Word of God in the prophetic-liberation tradition can be expanded to a new use where the focus is not just on past texts with their sociological limitations but on the liberated future.

Ruether uses countercultural, marginal, and heretical traditions in Christianity, including recent feminist interpretations of the Jesus movement as an early egalitarian tradition, the prominence of women in the Montanist movement, and the Gnostic gospels that privilege women and the Magdalene tradition over the Petrine. She studies women mystics, female communities, and popular movements like the Quakers and Shakers to discover fragments of a Christian feminist history. And in using the dominant theological framework to structure her feminist theology, she acknowledges that all the traditional doctrines are distorted by sexism. But when these are corrected by feminist critique of androcentric hierarchicalism, they are shown to disclose new possibilities. For example, the notion of sin is not the problem, but women blamed for sin. Thus in her constructive work she uses elements of the ancient Near Eastern and Greco-Roman background, often incorporated into Judaism and Christianity, that transcend both patriarchy and dualism.

Finally, Ruether uses the feminist versions of three streams of modern critical culture in the West: liberalism, romanticism, and socialism-Marxism. Liberal feminism accepts the model of current capitalist society and works to secure equality for women within it but offers little critique of the system itself. Liberal feminism fails to deal with classism and racism in its middle-class orientations. Socialist and Marxist feminisms analyze the political and economic frameworks of patriarchy to argue for the restructuring of both the productive and reproductive (family) systems of society as women's environment. Liberal and socialist feminisms stress the sameness and equality of women and men and work for the equal participation of women, traditionally confined to the private sphere of home and family, in the public sphere of life. Romantic feminism, by contrast, emphasizes the difference or superiority of women's sensitivity, creativity, intuition, interdependence, bodiliness, relationality, and connection to nature.

Ruether's own liberation feminism incorporates aspects of all three: the drive for social egalitarianism of liberalism, the aim of building a just society of socialist feminism, and the promotion of deeper human values of romantic feminism. In this way her synthesis transcends the limits of each. In its concern for the experience of the oppressed, her work avoids the middle-class complacency of liberal feminism. In its focus on a just society it deals directly with patriarchalism. In its attention to human values, it strives for the liberation of all persons, women and men, in a community of mutuality, and indeed the liberation of all creation in a harmony of ecological interdependence. This is the all-encompassing vision that Ruether develops in her feminist theology.

In a subsequent reflection on method (1985), Ruether describes her procedure as a method of correlating the feminist critical principle with the biblical critical principle of the prophetic-messianic tradition. The correlation between the two is both critique and renewal of vision in which the true Word of God emerges over sinful and unjust distortions. She maintains that the prophetic-messianic tradition does not mean a particular group of texts, a canon within the canon, but rather is the dynamic process by which biblical tradition continually reevaluates itself.

In new situations it proclaims the liberating Word of God in its contemporary setting over against its own past and against present deformations of society. Evidence of this renewing process can be discerned within the Bible itself and in every generation in which women have appropriated the prophetic hope as good news for themselves. Feminist theology must affirm such a theory of interpretation as "normative and indispensable" for faith today.

Yet within this process of correlation, or perhaps beyond it, Ruether argues in another place[15] that because women's experience is not itself at the center of the biblical or other traditional Christian texts, it is necessary to find and use new, extrabiblical, and extra-Christian texts that make that experience visible. When read in a feminist perspective, canonical patriarchal passages are denied their "normative status," and "a new norm" develops as the basis of "a new community, a new theology, eventually a new canon." This new norm places women at the center rather than the periphery so that their speech and presence become normative for feminist theology.

In her constructive work, Ruether builds on the conviction that there is an ultimately good divine reality that is reencountered in the "new midrash," the "third Covenant" of feminism. She calls this divine reality God/ess, an unpronounceable name that is neither male nor female but both, yet suggests the female as the "primal matrix" of all creation. Jesus, who continues the prophetic-liberating tradition of the Bible, is a political leader who challenges the status quo and whose leadership is built on service. It is not his maleness that is important but his message, his judgment on all exclusion and subordination. The Jesus of the synoptic Gospels, stripped of the masculine imagery of the Messiah and Logos, points beyond himself to "one who is to come." Thus he is distinguished from the Christ, the messianic humanity of the future. Jesus is one but not the only manifestation of the Christ who continues to be disclosed in history. A final or timeless revelation would breed anti-Semitism and prevent response to the action of the Holy Spirit in the present, the Spirit whose presence and action feminist theology prizes.

THE NEW BIBLICAL HERMENEUTICS
OF ELISABETH SCHÜSSLER FIORENZA

While her major work is in biblical studies, Elisabeth Schüssler Fiorenza understands herself as a theologian as well and has had enormous influence on feminist theology. In her many articles and her important book, *In Memory of Her: A Feminist Theological Reconstruction of Christian Origins* (1983), as well as her reflections on feminist method, *Bread Not Stone: The Challenge of Biblical Interpretation* (1984), she has awakened many women (and men) to the importance of feminist interpretation of the Bible and of feminist theology. She maintains that Christian self-identity is not just a matter of religious beliefs but is also a communal-historical identity. As the *ekklesia* of women, women today can "claim the center" in a process of transformation in Christian faith and community.

Schüssler Fiorenza acknowledges many types of feminist theology but sees her own as a critical theology of liberation. She distinguishes her biblical method from doctrinal, positivist-historical, and dialogical-hermeneutical approaches to the Bible. As liberationist, her theology is engaged rather than neutral scholarship and is concerned with empowering women. Arguing that the Bible itself is engaged, both in its pastoral, ecclesial contexts and in its wider cultural and political situations, she insists that biblical and theological interpretation has always taken an advocacy position, although not always consciously. Thus she begins with the experience of women who are struggling for liberation and sees her work as helping to overcome this oppression. She also privileges the theological judgments of this group of women. Schüssler Fiorenza refuses to relinquish the Bible to those who maintain its hierarchical character and reinforce patriarchy as Christian. Rather, she challenges this use because of the Bible's deep religious significance for many women and because of its continuing cultural and religious influence.

She uses four hermeneutical principles in her work. The first, a hermeneutics of suspicion, recognizes the patriarchy and androcentrism of many biblical texts and thus entails ideology critique, asking whose interests are served in particular passages. The second is a hermeneutics of proclamation that assesses which texts are suitable for liturgical use. The third, a hermeneutics of remembrance, searches the texts for traces of women's history in early Christianity to reconstruct the activity and centrality of women, which is the biblical heritage of women today. Finally, a hermeneutics of creative actualization helps women claim biblical history by the use of historical imagination and through ritual and art. She uses the historical-critical method and feminist analysis in her work. Thus she claims to move beyond the feminist methods that use an abstract theological principle or a prophetic norm that is often, in concrete biblical contexts, itself oppressive of women. A merely textual approach or an approach that touches only the individual mind but has no social-political effects is also judged inadequate. Her effort instead is to read the silences as well as the evidence in the New Testament as the "tip of the iceberg" to offer a feminist social history of early Christianity that places women, in their activity and *praxis,* at the center.

Schüssler Fiorenza questions not only patriarchal texts and traditions in the Bible and texts that centuries of exegesis, preaching, and theology have mistranslated or misinterpreted. In addition, she questions andro-centric *traditioning* in which a later writer has recorded in an androcentric way stories that were not originally androcentric. She points out that "the New Testament does not transmit a single androcentric statement or sexist story of Jesus, although he lived and preached in a patriarchal culture. . . . In the fellowship of Jesus, women apparently did not play a marginal role, even though only a few references to women disciples survived the androcentric tradition and redaction process of the gospels."[16] Those few references lead Schüssler Fiorenza to uncover the importance of women as apostolic witnesses of Jesus' ministry, death, and resurrection *and* the tendency of New Testament authors to downplay the role of women as apostles and witnesses of the Easter event. She analyzes traces of women's history in the New Testament to show the presence of a vigorous female ministry and participation in early Christianity. When the evidence about women is presented in a feminist perspective, there is a mass of data to show that Galatians 3:28 was not simply an abstract ideal but a political reality in the early communities.

Schüssler Fiorenza also challenges the interpretive models used by scholars whose understanding of history is androcentric. She moves beyond the thematic approaches of "women and the Bible" or "female imagery for God" to argue for an interpretive model of early Christianity that accounts for the data about women disciples, apostles, prophets, teachers, missionaries, patrons, founders, and leaders of congregations and the importance of women and the divine female principle in the Gnostic communities. It is a model that can account for the complaint of Tertullian in the second century, for example, that women dared to exercise leadership, even sacramental leadership. Thus she shows that the early Christian writings are not objective, factual history but pastorally engaged writings that disclose the agency of women in the origins of Christianity.

Schüssler Fiorenza notes that the orthodoxy/heresy framework of interpretation has already been surpassed by a theory that ecclesial patri-archalization occurred over centuries through the New Testament and patristic eras. While this process is understandable sociologically, some still argue that it was *necessary* for the early church's survival. In this way, "love-patriarchalism" is used to legitimate the historical subordination of women. In contrast, Schüssler Fiorenza offers an egalitarian model of early Christianity as a conflict movement, based on the discovery that Christianity was neither originally patriarchal in itself nor integrated into patriarchal society. That the Jesus movement and the early Christian missionary movement were countercultural, radically egalitarian, and inclusive accounts for the evidence about women (and other marginal people) in the Jesus traditions and in the early missionary traditions. She holds that her "egalitarian model" for the reconstruction of early Christianity accounts for both the traditions of women's leadership in the church and for the process of the church's practical adaptation to and theological legitimation of the patriarchy of its Greco-Roman cultural setting. Schüssler Fiorenza uses the important distinction in feminist theory between biological *sex* and socially constructed *gender* to argue that it is not sex (childbearing, for example) but gender (the *meaning* that a social or political framework ascribes to sex) that is the basis for the devaluation of women in the Bible and in later theology.

She is interested in history for its emancipatory impulses, and she tries to free these impulses for the future. Thus she holds that biblical texts must not be understood as presenting "archetypes," identified with revelation as timeless truths or unchangeable patterns for the church. Rather, Scripture offers "prototypes" that are open to the future, that suggest a continuity between past and present revelation. And, in one of her most theologically controversial affirmations, she asserts that "a biblical interpretation which is concerned with the *meaning* of the Bible in a post-patriarchal culture" must hold that "biblical revelation and truth about women are found . . . in those texts which transcend and criticize their patriarchal culture." That is, only those texts that transcend patriarchy can be accorded the status of revelation, and these can be used "to evaluate and to judge the patriarchal texts of the Bible."[17] Thus she argues that the fatherhood of God opposes patriarchal structures in the church and that Christ's lordship opposes relations of dominance and submission in the Christian community. For "according to the gospel tradition Jesus radically rejected all relationships of dependence and domination."[18]

Schüssler Fiorenza holds that many New Testament texts do not describe early practice but rather prescribe it and so indicate that behind the text an active struggle was taking place regarding women in the church's social and cultural setting, for example, in marriage and household arrangements. Rules governing the behavior of women in the family and in church order can instead show that women were important agents in the early church and that this agency was a locus of contention as Christianity gradually became integrated into patriarchal (and slaveholding) social structures. The household codes of "early Catholicism" are a rewriting of tradition, over against an earlier egalitarianism, that not only justify a patriarchal church and social order but also serve as a patriarchal metaphor for the relation of God and Christ to human beings. In her discussion of the Jesus movement as a reform within Judaism, she describes the "Sophia-God" of Jesus as the all-inclusive God of the outcasts, the poor, and the marginalized. "Divine Sophia is Israel's God in the language and *Gestalt* of the goddess," called sister, mother, beloved. Jesus is the prophet and child of Sophia whose death is the consequence of his all-inclusive praxis.[19]

These discoveries lead Schüssler Fiorenza to argue that the norm of feminist theology cannot be found in particular biblical texts, since all the texts are part of an androcentric tradition. Neither can it be found in an abstract, timeless theological principle or an ahistoric prophetic principle. In her view, both are more concerned with an apologetic for the authority of the Bible in Christianity. Instead, the only adequate criterion for feminist theology is the women themselves who struggle for liberation, transcendence, and selfhood in remembrance of their heritage. They are Women-Church, the *ekklesia* of women, the "movement of self-identified women and women-identified men" who judge theological claims according to whether they serve to oppress or liberate women. She writes, "The locus or place of divine revelation and grace is therefore not the Bible or the tradition of a patriarchal church but the *ekklesia* of women and the lives of women who live the 'option for our women selves.'" The aim of this church is women's religious self-affirmation and power, their freedom from "all patriarchal alienation, marginalization, and oppression."[20]

CRITICAL PERSPECTIVES

Several critics have questioned the theological views of Ruether and Schüssler Fiorenza, pointing out that while "women's experience" can be used as a source in feminist theology, it cannot be a norm. As normative, it fails to provide for self-criticism, and thus feminist theology would be open to self-deception and a new kind of oppression. Allusions to the immanent "mother God" or "primal Matrix," it is claimed, lead to a loss of the transcendence of the biblical God whose love, although compared to that of a mother, is nevertheless holy and other than anything or anyone in creation. Further, if all things and especially humans come from the being of God, as some feminists claim, the implication is a sharing in the divine that is ultimately idolatrous and narcissistic self-worship. Finally, theological critics express reservations about the replacement of the finality of Jesus Christ by the principle of full humanity and the reduction of the gospel that this entails, as well as the failure of feminist theology to distinguish between the judgment and promises of the Bible and personal experience.[21]

While acknowledging the wealth and significance of their contributions to feminist theology, especially in highlighting the historical and contemporary experience of women, Protestant theologian Pamela Dickey Young also questions the theological methods of these two thinkers. She asks whether the "eclecticism" of Ruether's new norm and Schüssler Fiorenza's "new magisterium" for theological judgment in the church of women struggling for liberation allow for a truly *Christian* feminist theology. As a committed feminist, she suggests that while one can bring a feminist perspective to theology and thus use women's experience, especially feminist experience, in the construction of a *feminist* theology, the norm of *Christian* theology must be found in a Christian source. Young's own suggestion for a Christian norm (like that of Schubert Ogden) is the earliest layer of apostolic witness in the New Testament as that can be determined by historical criticism. Through that scriptural "Jesus tradition," the earliest witness is thus connected to the central Christian symbol of Jesus. While this criterion affirms a traditional Protestant "canon within the canon" of the Bible, the Catholic framework generally includes (the selective use of) the *whole* of the Bible and Christian tradition. Nevertheless, Young's analysis of the use of the term *experience* in feminist theology and her distinctions among starting point or perspective, sources, and norm are helpful in thinking about the future of Catholic feminist methodology.

SOME CATEGORIES FOR FUTURE DISCUSSION

The *perspective* that informs a particular theological effort colors the whole discourse and is usually apparent in its starting point. In feminist theology, that starting point and perspective is often women's experience. Sometimes that may mean *bodily* experience, as when the theologian uses the biological experiences of women in menstruation, pregnancy, childbirth, lactation, childrearing, or menopause to draw out images, models, insights, and concepts that provide analogies for God or God's relation to the world.[22] Sometimes women's experience means *socialized experience,* what a particular culture teaches or has taught about women's roles, character, and virtues, as when a thinker questions cultural expectations or ecclesial rules about the appropriate "place" of women and their roles in society and church.[23] Sometimes the theologian means *feminist* experience, a response to socialized experience in an awareness of sexism and patriarchy or a consciousness of the exploited or marginal status of women in the systems of society, as when a feminist thinker argues against the theological distortions and injustice of patriarchy and sexism (Ruether). At other times, the word *experience* refers to women's *historical* experience, as when texts are studied to discover women's lives and activities in the past, in various geographical and ethnic contexts, and in both its negative and positive aspects (Schüssler Fiorenza). Or it can refer to women's unique, *individual* experiences, but usually as these are shaped by their social, political, ecclesial, and cultural context.[24] "The personal is the political" remains an enduring principle in feminist thought. Finally, one might add the specifically *Christian* experience of women in their varied responses to the language, liturgy, doctrine, and other practices of the church, some feminist, some not. Feminist theology, with its fundamental insight that women have been excluded, caricatured, or stereotyped in Christian tradition, can employ any of this experience in its effort to promote the flourishing of women in religious contexts. The perspective of women's experience characterizes most feminist theology and provides the lens (Johnson) or angle of vision for the whole of the discourse, although the category of experience has been challenged in some recent approaches.[25]

Most Christian and Catholic feminist theologians do not oppose experience to the Bible or to traditional theology but are concerned to find and highlight the experience of women in both Bible and tradition. Moreover, some speak of the *interpreted experience* of women, indicating the use of written or enacted sources that are not merely subjective or individual but publicly available in the cultural artifacts they employ. Thus the Word of God and the action of the Spirit are incarnate in the experience of Christians, just as they are in the Bible.

With regard to the *sources* of feminist theology, the Christian feminist theologian can use a variety of materials, historical as well as contemporary. That material does not need to be explicitly "theological," but it must have genuine relevance for the discussion at hand. Anything can be used as a source, provided that it fits coherently and consistently in the pattern proposed and that it illumines one or more aspect of a particular theological argument. Thus Christian feminist theologians use texts and religious symbols from the past, both Christian and extra-Christian, theories from other scholars in their own disciplines or from feminist scholars in other disciplines, as well as compelling stories, plays, poems, rituals, or liturgies as sources for theological reflection.

The question of a *norm* for Christian or Catholic feminist theology is difficult to describe. Letty Russell's principle of the partnership of humankind with God in the mending of creation is criticized as being too abstract, yet she argues that even an extra-Christian feminist norm is implicitly a principle of biblical eschatology. As a norm, feminism offers an interpretation of the whole Bible or of Christian tradition. In the Catholic context, Sandra Schneiders also uses the notion of a principle that demands new interpretation in new situations. It can be argued that most forms of Catholic theology accord primacy of place to the whole of Scripture and tradition but implicitly or explicitly offer an interpretation of the meaning of that whole (as in Karl Rahner's notion of the self-communication of God or Edward Schillebeeckx's understanding of the unity of past and present Christian experience as salvation from God in Jesus). In the transcendental, correlational, analytical, hermeneutical, and liberational orientations that Francis Schüssler Fiorenza discusses as the major contemporary approaches in Catholic theology and in his own suggested method, that norm is a given thinker's reconstruction of the integrity of the Christian tradition, an interpretation of its paradigm or essence. It is not easily formulated in a single phrase or sentence for, as he indicates, such judgment is a complex affair in which a plurality of criteria may be operative.

A specifically Christian norm in feminist theology might be found in trinitarian, relational understandings of God as love, the universal self-communication of God in Christ, the gospel of the passion and death of Jesus and the sending of the Spirit, or the inclusive commandment to love God and neighbor (both female and male) and all of creation. It might be found in a feminist rendering of divine and human love that explicitly includes justice or in an incarnational principle that emphasizes embodiment, mutuality, and reciprocity of relationship in every context. But it is clear that what distinguishes feminist theology is its women-centered approach, its treatment of traditional topics through the lens of feminism.

While different theologians offer different ways of understanding what serves as a norm in their proposals, the distinctive character of feminist theology is not a norm but the perspective of women, a specifically feminist angle of vision. Although the two feminist approaches we have examined are identified by their authors as liberationist, other methods (especially correlational and hermeneutical) have been used by feminist thinkers, and new ones may emerge in future discussion. A method is not a straitjacket, a way to be followed rigidly, but a path to insight and illumination, an approach that leads to the flourishing of life in individual and commual action as in the social structures that are their context. Nor can method be detached from the particular content of a given discussion, for the specific data or themes will suggest different methods of approach. Nevertheless, it is important that some criterion or criteria for judgment be laid out as part of each theological enterprise.

Adequate theological methods are necessary but not sufficient to ensure that feminist theology will not be dismissed as a passing fad by patriarchal theology but will be integrated into *all* Christian theology today and in the future. For, as Ruether observes, historians have discovered that feminist impulses emerged many times in the past, only to be marginalized, suppressed, and ultimately forgotten in the dominant patriarchy. And this could happen again if the institutional bases—schools, libraries, curricula—are not established to ensure that feminist theology will be taught, developed, and expanded in such a way that it redefines theology itself. Ruether warns that this redefinition will entail profound struggle. Part of that struggle is the intellectual work of feminist theology, a pursuit that is individual and collective, plural yet performed in global and inclusive solidarity. The task is to reclaim the center, as Schüssler Fiorenza names it, so that theology itself becomes and remains truly inclusive. Claiming the center will mean that feminist perspectives, if not feminist methods, are so incorporated into the whole of theology that theology itself is transformed. Only then will feminist consciousness become so universal that feminist theology—its perspectives, sources, and norms—will be taught in every school and seminary, and preachers in every local congregation will use the broad context of feminist thought, even some of its methods, in offering sermons that are helpful to women as well as to men.

NOTES

1. See Mary Daly, *Beyond God the Father, Toward a Philosophy of Women's Liberation* (Boston: Beacon Press, 1973), 11–12.

2. See Rosemary Radford Ruether, "The Future of Feminist Theology in the Academy," *Journal of the American Academy of Religion* 53 (1985): 703–13.

3. See Pamela Dickey Young, *Feminist Theology/Christian Theology: In Search of Method* (Minneapolis: Fortress Press, 1990).

4. Cf. Werner G. Jeanrond, "Theological Method," in *A New Handbook of Christian Theology*, ed. Donald W. Musser and Joseph L. Price (Nashville: Abingdon Press, 1992).

5. Cf. David Tracy, *Plurality and Ambiguity: Hermeneutics, Religion, Hope* (San Francisco: Harper & Row, 1987).

6. Cf. George A. Lindbeck, *The Nature of Doctrine: Religion and Theology in a Postliberal Age* (Philadelphia: Westminster Press, 1984).

7. Francis Schüssler Fiorenza, "Systematic Theology: Tasks and Methods," in *Systematic Theology: Roman Catholic Perspectives*, vol. 1, ed. Francis Schüssler Fiorenza and John P. Galvin (Minneapolis: Fortress Press, 1991), 1–87.

8. Mary Jo Weaver, *New Catholic Women: A Contemporary Challenge to Traditional Religious Authority* (San Francisco: Harper & Row, 1985).

9. Mary Daly, *The Church and the Second Sex* (New York: Harper & Row, 1968).

10. Rosemary Radford Ruether, ed., *Religion and Sexism: Images of Women in the Jewish and Christian Traditions* (New York: Simon and Schuster, 1974).

11. Elisabeth Schüssler Fiorenza, *In Memory of Her: A Feminist Theological Reconstruction of Christian Origins* (New York: Crossroad, 1983); Rosemary Radford Ruether and Eleanor McLaughlin, eds., *Women of Spirit: Female Leadership in the Jewish and Christian Traditions* (New York: Simon and Schuster, 1979).

12. See Adela Yarbro Collins, ed., *Feminist Perspectives on Biblical Scholarship* (Chico, CA: Scholars Press, 1985) and Letty Russell, ed., *Feminist Interpretation of the Bible* (Philadelphia: Westminster Press, 1985).

13. Carolyn Osiek, "The Feminist and the Bible," in *Feminist Perspectives on Biblical Scholarship*, ed. Collins, 97.

14. Ruether, *Sexism and God-Talk: Toward a Feminist Theology* (Boston: Beacon Press, 1983), 18–19.

15. Ruether, "The Future of Feminist Theology in the Academy," *Journal of the American Academy of Religion* 53 (1985): 703–13.

16. Elisabeth Schüssler Fiorenza, "Interpreting Patriarchal Traditions," in *The Liberating Word*, ed. Letty Russell (Philadelphia: Westminster Press, 1976), 52.

17. Schüssler Fiorenza, *In Memory of Her*, 32.

18. Elisabeth Schüssler Fiorenza, "You Are Not to Be Called Father," *Cross Currents* 29 (1979): 317.

19. Schüssler Fiorenza, *In Memory of Her*, 133ff.

20. Elisabeth Schüssler Fiorenza, *Bread Not Stone: The Challenge of Feminist Biblical Interpretation* (Boston: Beacon Press, 1985).

21. See the articles by Achtemeier, Doob Sakenfeld, and Stroup in *Interpretation* 42, no. 1 (1988).

22. Sallie McFague, *Models of God: Theology for an Ecological, Nuclear Age* (Philadelphia: Fortress Press, 1987), and *Metaphorical Theology: Models of God in Religious Language* (Philadelphia: Fortress Press, 1982); also Elizabeth Johnson, *She Who Is: The Mystery of God in Feminist Theological Discourse* (New York: Crossroad, 1992).

23. Judith Plaskow, *Sex, Sin and Grace: Women's Experience and the Theologies of Reinhold Neibuhr and Paul Tillich* (Washington, DC: Univ. Press of America, 1980).

24. Rebecca S. Chopp, *The Power to Speak: Feminism, Language, God* (New York: Crossroad, 1991).

25. Sheila Greeve Davaney, "The Limits of the Appeal to Women's Experience," in *Shaping New Vision: Gender and Values in American Culture,* ed. Clarissa Atkinson, Constance Buchanan, and Margaret Miles (Ann Arbor: Univ. of Michigan Research Press, 1989).

FOR FURTHER READING

Achtemeier, Paul, ed. *Interpretation: A Journal of Bible and Theology* 42, no. 1 (1988). Devoted to questions of feminist approaches to the Bible and theology. Especially helpful are the articles by Katherine Doob Sakenfeld, George W. Stroup, and Elizabeth Achtemeier.

Carr, Anne. *Transforming Grace: Christian Tradition and Women's Experience.* San Francisco: Harper & Row, 1988. Explores a number of feminist themes, using a method of correlation and contrast to argue for a tranformation of Christian theology and Catholic church practice from a feminist perspective.

Chopp, Rebecca S. *The Power to Speak: Feminism, Language, God.* New York: Crossroad, 1991. Suggests a new method in feminist theology that incorporates American pragmatism and postmodern thought.

Collins, Adela Yarbro, ed. *Feminist Perspectives on Biblical Scholarship.* Chico, CA: Scholars Press, 1985. Collection of theoretical and practical essays on feminist approaches to the Bible.

Daly, Mary. *The Church and the Second Sex.* New York: Harper & Row, 1968; rev. postchristian ed., 1975; new rev. ed. Boston: Beacon Press, 1985. The earliest Catholic feminist discussion; uses historical analysis to point to the contradictions in theology and church practice; current edition reflects author's postchristian position in its preface, introduction, and "afterwords."

Davaney, Sheila Greene, ed. *Feminism and Process Thought: The Harvard/Claremont Symposium Papers.* New York: Edward Mellen Press, 1981. A collection that integrates feminist issues with process thought, a metaphysical system that prizes relational themes.

———. "The Limits of the Appeal to Women's Experience." In *Shaping New Vision: Gender and Values in American Culture,* edited by Clarissa Atkinson, Constance Buchanan, and Margaret Miles. Ann Arbor: Univ. of Michigan Research Press, 1989. Suggests some postmodern questions about the category of experience.

———. "Problems with Feminist Theory: Historicity and the Search for Sure Foundations." In *Embodied Love: Sensuality and Relationship as Feminist Values,* edited by Paula

M. Cooey, Sharon A. Farmer, and Mary Ellen Ross. San Francisco: Harper & Row, 1987. Deals with the problem of historicity in feminist theology and proposes a non-ontological approach that avoids "foundationalism."

Fiorenza, Elisabeth Schüssler. *In Memory of Her: A Feminist Theological Reconstruction of Christian Origins.* New York: Crossroad, 1983. Discusses feminist hermeneutics and method in historical reconstruction of Christian traditions.

––––––. *Bread Not Stone: The Challenge of Feminist Biblical Interpretation.* Boston: Beacon Press, 1985. A collection of essays on method that have both biblical and theological significance.

Fiorenza, Francis Schüssler. "Systematic Theology: Tasks and Methods." In *Systematic Theology: Roman Catholic Perspectives,* edited by Francis Schüssler Fiorenza and John P. Galvin. Minneapolis: Fortress Press, 1991. Provides a thorough discussion of historical and contemporary Catholic theological methods and doctrinal topics.

Jeanrond, Werner G. "Theological Method." In *A New Handbook of Christian Theology,* edited by Donald W. Musser and Joseph L. Price. Nashville: Abingdon Press, 1992. A brief discussion of both historical and contemporary Christian theological methods.

Johnson, Elizabeth. *She Who Is: The Mystery of God in Feminist Theological Discourse.* New York: Crossroad, 1992. Situated in a liberationist framework but using an approach that "braids bridges" between feminist wisdom and the classic wisdom of the Christian tradition about the doctrine of God.

Kelly, Joan. *Women, History and Theory: The Essays of Joan Kelly.* Chicago: Univ. of Chicago Press, 1984. One of many volumes of secular feminist theory about the methods and insights of feminist history that provides insights relevant to theological discussion.

Lindbeck, George A. *The Nature of Doctrine: Religion and Theology in a Postliberal Age.* Philadelphia: Westminster Press, 1984. A widely used work that proposes a cultural-linguistic understanding of religion and a rule theory of doctrine that emphasizes intratextuality in theology.

Marks, Elaine, and Isabelle de Courtivron, eds. *New French Feminisms.* New York: Schocken, 1981. Provides an introduction to some postmodern feminist discourses in their women-centered diversity.

McFague, Sallie. *Metaphorical Theology: Models of God in Religious Language.* Philadelphia: Fortress Press, 1982. Suggests a theory of metaphor in theology that is especially significant for feminist thought.

––––––. *Models of God: Theology for an Ecological, Nuclear Age.* Philadelphia: Fortress Press, 1987. Experiments with feminist metaphors for God that are responsive to contemporary concerns.

Plaskow, Judith. *Sex, Sin and Grace: Women's Experience and the Theologies of Reinhold Neibuhr and Paul Tillich.* Washington, DC: Univ. Press of America, 1980. Offers an early analysis of women's "experience" as a theological category.

Ruether, Rosemary Radford, ed. *Religion and Sexism: Images of Women in the Jewish and Christian Traditions.* New York: Simon and Schuster, 1974. One of the earliest examples of feminist theological analysis and critique.

———. "The Future of Feminist Theology in the Academy," *Journal of the American Academy of Religion* 53 (1985): 703–13. Analysis of the history of the relation of feminist theology to patriarchal theology that proposes necessary steps for the genuine transformation of theology.

———. *Sexism and God-Talk: Toward a Feminist Theology*. Boston: Beacon Press, 1983. Discusses the methodology, sources, and norms for a feminist theology and treats traditional theological topics from a feminist point of view.

———. *Womanguides: Readings Toward a Feminist Theology*. Boston: Beacon Press, 1985. Offers a collection of Christian and extra-Christian women-centered sources that may be useful for feminist theology.

———. *Women-Church: Theology and Practice*. San Francisco: Harper & Row, 1985. Brings together a history and theology of Women-Church, with guidance on how to develop communications and liturgies.

Russell, Letty, ed. *Feminist Interpretation of the Bible*. Philadelphia: Westminster Press, 1985. A collection of essays by biblical scholars and theologians on feminist methods in approaching the Bible.

———. *Household of Freedom: Authority in Feminist Theology* Philadelphia: Westminster Press, 1987. Proposes a theory of authority that deals with the Bible and feminist experience in a patriarchal church.

Schneiders, Sandra. *Beyond Patching: Faith and Feminism in the Catholic Church*. New York: Paulist Press, 1991. Offers a definition of feminism and a theory of interpretation of the Bible and Catholic Church teaching.

———. *The Revelatory Text: Interpreting the New Testament as Sacred Scripture*. San Francisco: Harper San Francisco, 1992. A theory of interpretation that integrates Scripture and spirituality within a feminist perspective.

———. *Women and the Word*. New York: Paulist Press, 1986. A feminist approach to the theological interpretation of androcentric names and categories of biblical language.

Tracy, David. *Plurality and Ambiguity: Hermeneutics, Religion, Hope*. San Francisco: Harper & Row, 1987. Discussion of method in contemporary pluralism that integrates feminist theology and its implications in a hermeneutical perspective.

Weaver, Mary Jo. *New Catholic Women: A Contemporary Challenge to Traditional Religious Authority*. San Francisco: Harper & Row, 1985. Provides historical analysis of the emergence of feminist consciousness among various groups of Catholic women.

Young, Pamela Dickey. *Feminist Theology/Christian Theology: In Search of Method*. Minneapolis: Fortress Press, 1990. The first full-length book to deal with method in Christian feminist theology; analyzes the methods of several feminist theologians and suggests several categories that must be distinguished in an adequate Christian theological method.

THE BIBLE AND FEMINISM

— Biblical Theology —

Sandra M. Schneiders

UNTIL VATICAN COUNCIL II most Catholics encountered the Bible almost exclusively in the Sunday liturgy, which was the only time the liturgical readings were in the vernacular. The Roman Missal did not present even the New Testament completely or in systematic fashion. Furthermore, the biblically based homily was a rarity, the readings serving most often as a convenient point of departure for moral exhortation that often had little to do with the biblical text. Thus the average Catholic had at best a cursory and fragmentary acquaintance with the Bible and practically no real formation in Scripture.[1]

The remote preparation for the postconciliar biblical renaissance among Catholics began with the publication in 1943 of Pius XII's encyclical on biblical studies, *Divino Afflante Spiritu*.[2] This document belatedly permitted Catholic scholars to use the historical-critical methods of biblical study that had long been current in Protestant biblical scholarship. The pope encouraged Catholic biblical scholars to make their new findings available in the church, especially to theologians and pastors.[3] Consequently, by the time the Council opened in 1962 there was a solid body of Catholic biblical scholarship available to the Council participants and a corps of trained biblical scholars ready to aid in their work. Despite the deficiency that the complete absence of women among the scholars or Council participants represented, the Council constituted a watershed in Catholic engagement with the Bible.

Vatican II's Dogmatic Constitution on Divine Revelation, *Dei Verbum,* was published at the very end of the Council, November 18, 1965.[4] Although as a compromise document it contained inconsistencies and even some virtually irreconcilable tensions, it introduced some genuinely new emphases that had a profound effect on the life of Catholics.[5]

First, it laid to rest the two-source theory of divine revelation, which most Catholics since the Council of Trent regarded as doctrine. According to this theory Scripture and tradition constituted two parallel and equal sources of divine revelation. And, since the insistence on tradition was a uniquely Catholic tenet proposed and defended against the Protestant principle of *sola scriptura* or Scripture alone as the source of revelation and the norm of faith, the *de facto* polemically inspired position in Catholicism was the practical if not theoretical superiority of tradition to Scripture. For most Catholics the "teaching of the church," which for all practical purposes meant the current position of the Vatican on any given theological or pastoral question, was equivalent to tradition and constituted all one really needed as a norm of faith and morals. The Bible was viewed as a sourcebook for church authorities who alone had the training and divine guidance necessary to interpret it correctly and who communicated, in the form of official teaching, whatever of its contents the ordinary Catholic needed to know. *Dei Verbum* recognized that there is only one source of divine revelation, Jesus Christ who is "the mediator and the sum total of Revelation" (*DV* 1.2). Therefore, the interplay of the biblical text and ecclesial tradition in witnessing to and mediating this unique revelation in Jesus had to be thoroughly reconceptualized.

Second, in attempting to explain the interaction between Scripture and tradition the Council made it clear that the "Magisterium [that is, the teaching authority of the church] is not superior to the word of God, but is its servant" (*DV* 2.10). Thus Scripture, which during the four centuries since the Protestant Reformation had been reduced to an arsenal of prooftexts in the theological enterprise of the church and to a source of Sunday liturgical fragments for the average Catholic, reemerged as an indispensable and critical factor in theology and pastoral practice.

Third, Scripture was recognized as a rich resource for the spiritual life of Catholics. In the Scriptures, *Dei Verbum* taught, God comes to meet and commune with us. Therefore, "all the preaching of the Church, as indeed the entire Christian religion, should be nourished and ruled by Sacred Scripture" (*DV* 6.21). Scripture, long a *terra incognita* for Catholics, must be "open wide to the Christian faithful" (*DV* 6.22). This requires committed effort on the part of biblical scholars to make the meaning of the text clear so that it might function as the very "soul of sacred theology" and the content and form of all pastoral activity and especially of the celebration of the liturgy (*DV* 6.23–24). The biblical text, translated in a graceful vernacular and supplemented by accessible notes, belongs in the hands of all the faithful. Catholics, in short, were to become "people of the book" in a way they had not been since before the Middle Ages.

The response of Catholics to the Council's teaching on the Bible was astonishingly enthusiastic. Bible study groups in parishes, summer courses in Scripture, lectures by Catholic biblical scholars, and Bible based retreats and workshops proliferated and were habitually oversubscribed. Catholic publishers brought out new translations of the Bible and a wide array of study tools.[6] Liturgical musicians created a repertoire of hymns based on biblical texts, and the biblical homily replaced the Sunday sermon and became a common feature of both daily liturgy and biblical prayer services of all kinds. Catholics discovered the biblical text as a mediator of the encounter with God that was, as the Council had suggested, parallel to the Eucharist (*DV* 6.21).

Women, both lay and religious, were among the most enthusiastic students and promoters of the Bible in the immediate wake of the Council. But the Council closed just as the "second wave" of feminism broke on western shores.[7] It was only a matter of minutes, metaphorically speaking, before feminist consciousness and the renewed love of Scripture clashed. Once women began to read the whole of Scripture rather than listening to a few selected passages and began to hear it in contemporary vernacular rather than in Latin or in an archaic English made innocuous by overfamiliarity, they began to find the beloved text highly problematic.

THE TENSION BETWEEN THE BIBLE AND FEMINISM

The tension between the biblical text and women whose feminist consciousness was rising began with particularities of the text and progressed to theoretical problems about the Bible itself. Two broad areas of difficulty emerged as women studied and prayed the Scriptures.

First, the scriptural presentation of humanity not only privileged the male as the normative human but presented women (insofar as they were featured at all) as inferior in themselves, subjected to males by divine design, marginal to salvation history, and far more marked by and responsible for sin and evil in the world than men. As women biblical scholars, whose numbers increased dramatically after the Council, examined the Bible they were forced to conclude that this text, which was presented by the church as good news of salvation for all people, was actually a book written largely if not exclusively by men, about men, and for men. Women appeared in Scripture in much the way they appear in church and society, as support systems for males, used and abused by men for the latter's purposes, and most often relegated to the margins or total obscurity.

Feminist biblical scholars began to develop a vocabulary and theoretical framework, suggested by feminist theory in other disciplines, for talking about the problematic masculinity of Scripture. The biblical text, like most texts in world history, arose in a patriarchal historical setting, that is, in a society and culture in which ruling males owned and dominated other people and most property and used them with impunity for their purposes.[8] *Patriarchy* is the term that refers to the ideology and social system of "father rule," which was the virtually universal pattern of social organization in the world of the Bible. The biblical text pervasively reflects this domination-subordination pattern in human relations and often legitimates it as divinely ordained. Religiously legitimated or sacralized patriarchy is called *hierarchy*. Not only did the Catholic church not repudiate or condemn patriarchy in general, but it also taught that hierarchy was willed by Jesus as the only appropriate form of organization for the church. The legitimation of patriarchy in family and society follows logically from this theological premise.

Patriarchy, both as ideology and as social system, proceeds from and nourishes a pervasive privileging of males and male reality. The term *androcentrism,* that is, male centeredness, denotes this obsession with the masculine at the expense of the feminine. Feminists regard androcentrism as not only socially pernicious but idolatrous. Affirming the intrinsic superiority of the male assimilates masculinity to divinity and implies a masculinizing of God. When the Vatican Congregation for the Doctrine of the Faith argued that women could not be ordained because they lacked a "natural resemblance" to Christ,[9] it unwittingly made explicit the heretofore unacknowledged, and heretical, presupposition that underlies much antiwoman theory and practice in the church: that God became human in male form because the male human is a more adequate image of God and this likeness is specifically sexual.[10]

The attitudinal and behavioral consequences of androcentrism and patriarchy is called, collectively, *sexism,* that is, the conviction, and its consequences in every sphere of life, that men are superior to women simply because they are male. In its more virulent forms sexism betrays its roots in *misogyny,* fear and hatred of women. The innumerable forms of discrimination, marginalization, exclusion, oppression, and abuse of women and their dependents is sexism in action, often fueled by misogyny.

As women studied Scripture carefully it became increasingly clear that the Bible is an androcentric text that arose in and from a patriarchal culture. The text is frequently explicitly sexist and even misogynist in its depiction of women, and the actual inferior status of women in contemporary Christian family, church, and society is corroborated by the biblical text. In other words, it was not simply painful and repugnant to women's religious sensibility to find themselves so negatively presented in Holy Scripture; it was evident that Scripture stood squarely in the path of the feminist agenda of full personhood and equality for all persons, including and especially women. What many Christians believe to be in some sense "the word of God" is, in some important respects, very bad news for women because it legitimates and promotes male oppression of women.[11]

The second problem concerned the biblical presentation of God in overwhelmingly male terms. The biblical metaphors for God are frequently patriarchal: father, lord, king, landowner, slave master, leader of armies. Even the less dominative metaphors such as shepherd reflect an androcentric social universe. Although there are feminine metaphors for God in Scripture (mother, bakerwoman, female householder, mother bear or hen, midwife),[12] and even more importantly a remarkable and sustained personification of God in feminine gestalt as Holy Wisdom,[13] the masculine presentation of God is so pervasive that the theological and liturgical tradition of the church has virtually excluded the feminine from divinity. The language about and to God in public prayer, preaching, theology, and spirituality has been exclusively masculine, and even the most recent attempts to translate the Bible in more inclusive terms have generally stopped short of modifying exclusively masculine language for God.[14] Although male church authorities maintain that God is Spirit and therefore the category of sex does not apply to God, they continue to insist that only male language is suitable for talking about or to God, at least in public worship.

This problem of a male-gendered God is exacerbated by the fact that God's ultimate self-revelation in human history is a human being, Jesus of Nazareth, who seemed to prefer to address God as "Abba," a caritative form of *father*.[15] The New Testament as it is actualized in the church's ritual and teaching is the story of a father-God who sent his son as a male human being to redeem all "men" and make them "brothers" and "sons of God."

Within a couple decades of the Council, many Catholic women, as their feminist consciousness developed, moved from enthusiasm for the Bible as a privileged locus of encounter with God to vague discomfort, rising anger, deep alienation, and finally rejection of the Bible as a hopelessly oppressive tool of historical and contemporary patriarchy. The problem was no longer simply how to handle individual misogynist narratives (like the rape and murder of the concubine, Jgs 19:22–30) or sexist images (like the comparison of unfaithful Israel to a whore, for example, Hos 2) or patriarchal injunctions (like the banning of women from liturgical leadership, for example, 1 Cor 14:34–35) or even pervasive masculine language for God and humans. The nature of the text itself as revelatory had become a burning question. How can a text that contains so much that is damaging to women function authoritatively in the Christian community as normative of faith and life?

Not all Catholic women have followed this path, nor have all who walked it ended in alienation and rejection. But the theology of the Bible is under enormous pressure from feminist interrogation, and the outcome of the struggle is not a foregone conclusion. A major step forward, however, is the increasing recognition that the problem is not superficial or trivial but theologically substantive and that it must be engaged honestly and rigorously by the best scholarship available. The oppressive character of the text is neither the figment of a paranoid imagination nor the unhappy accident of maladroit translators or exegetes nor an understandable cultural peculiarity like drachmas. The problem is in the text itself, and only a theology of Scripture that takes the problem completely seriously can hope to reclaim this text for women as the "pure and lasting fount of spiritual life" as Vatican II claimed it is (*DV* 6.21).

REFORMULATING THEOLOGICAL QUESTIONS ABOUT THE BIBLE

A christological analogy has often been invoked to talk theologically about Scripture: as Jesus is the Word of God made flesh, truly divine and truly human without diminishment or confusion of either nature, so Scripture is God's self-communication in human language, truly divine revelation and truly a human text without diminishment or confusion. The shorthand for this faith affirmation is the confession that the Bible is the "word of God." If this expression is taken literally and reductively the result is biblical docetism, the reduction of the human text to a linguistic disguise for divine speech, absolutely inerrant and authoritative in every detail.

Although Catholics in general do not tend to embrace the theories of verbal inspiration or divine dictation and resultant inerrancy associated with Protestant fundamentalism, they often enough arrive at the same practical conclusions about biblical authority on the basis of a naive literalism in regard to the text. Where such a theory of the inerrancy and infallibility of the biblical text reigns, those who find themselves denigrated by the text, for example, women, have little choice but to accept their inferiority as divinely revealed or to take their religious quest elsewhere.

Three theological questions are raised by this impasse. First, what exactly is meant by calling Scripture the word of God? Second, what are the implications of the answer to the first question for the status of the Bible in the church? Third, is the Bible materially normative for postbiblical Christians?

1. *What Does It Mean to Call Scripture the Word of God?*

Language, as contemporary linguistic and philosophical studies attest, is a much more complex phenomenon than is often thought. Words, which might be naively assumed to be a system of labels designating in relatively unambiguous fashion the concrete realities of everyday experience, are in fact often used in nonunivocal and nonliteral ways. This means that in order to understand language one must recognize the kind of language being used and understand how such language functions.

The linguistic character of "word of God": Metaphor. The term *word of God* is not univocal or literal when it is used to speak of the Bible. First, *word of God* designates not only, or even primarily, Scripture. It denotes first of all the second "person" of the Trinity[16] and that person made flesh in Jesus of Nazareth. From this it is immediately apparent that *word of God* is not a literal designation, for Jesus is obviously not a unit of language in bodily form but a human being. Second, theological reflection supports the observation that *word of God* is not a literal designation for the Bible. God is spirit and therefore does not have the physical apparatus of speech, does not think discursively, and is not limited in self-communication by the vocabulary, grammar, and syntax of language. In short, nothing about language, which is a human phenomenon, is literally pertinent to divine self-disclosure.

The foregoing leads to the realization that the term *word of God*, whether applied to Jesus or to the Bible, is linguistically a metaphor. Sallie McFague, with other modern theorists of language, insists that genuine metaphor is not primarily a rhetorical decoration or an abbreviated comparison.[17] It is a proposition (explicit or implied) constituted by an irresolvable tension between what it affirms (which is somehow true) and what it necessarily denies (namely, the literal truth of the assertion). For example, the proposition "Individualism is a cancer of American society" creates a tension between the true affirmation that individualism is a pernicious, even ultimately destructive, characteristic of American culture, and the necessary denial that individualism is a physical pathology. The metaphor is, at the literal level, absurd, but obviously it intends serious meaning. It forces the mind to reach toward meaning that exceeds or escapes effective literal expression.

Effectively used, metaphor is one of the most powerful forms of human language. It carries more meaning and generates deeper and more holistic response than literal language because it appeals not only to the mind but also to the imagination. Because true metaphor is not a stand-in for literal language but the only way to express some complexes of meaning that defy adequate literal expression, effective metaphors cannot be translated into univocal, literal language.

The linguistic tension that constitutes metaphor destabilizes the literalistic mind. This is its purpose and power. But because that destabilization is uncomfortable, keeping the mind "in motion" when it would like to "land" in literalistic concreteness, there is an inveterate temptation when confronted with metaphor to literalize it. A powerful example of how the literalization of a metaphor can wreak intellectual and affective havoc in the religious imagination is the metaphorical proposition "God is our Father." Obviously, God is not literally a father because God is not a male sexual being who copulates with a female sexual being to beget offspring. God does not literally beget, generate, or father. But so imaginatively entrenched is the literalization of *father*, a necessarily masculine metaphor for God, that most Christians are genuinely shocked by the use of feminine metaphors, such as *mother*, for God. The idolatrous result of this literalization can be traced through church history in the patriarchalization of Christian faith.

The temptation to literalize the metaphor *word of God* is particularly strong in relation to the biblical text precisely because, unlike the second person of the Trinity or Jesus Christ, the Bible is actually composed of human words. It is literally a linguistic reality. Consequently, the mind is not immediately arrested in the process of literalization the way it is when we call Jesus the Word of God incarnate. The literalization, however, results not only in fundamentalistic conclusions about the inerrancy and authority of the biblical text falsely imagined as God's actual speech, but also in the kinds of complicated and unsatisfactory theological theories of inspiration that both Catholic and Protestant Christianity have generated to explain how God speaks through human words and what the theological implications for faith might be. We will return to this issue shortly.

The referent of "word of God": Revelation. Obviously, God does not literally speak, but the metaphor *word of God* certainly intends meaning. Its referent, what it points to, is the entire domain of reality that we call divine revelation, that is, the self-disclosure of God as it is perceived and received by human beings.[18] The ultimate and definitive received self-communication of God, according to Christian faith, is Jesus himself. In Jesus the divine self-gift and human receptivity perfectly coincide in a person who therefore can be called, in truth (though not literally), the Word of God incarnate.

Nature, history (especially that of Israel and the church), and Scripture are also called "word of God" because of their revelatory character. In the wonders of nature, the saving events of history, the words of Scripture, and especially in Jesus, God's self-gift is offered to and received by human beings. But none of these realities is literally God's word because, as we have seen, God does not literally speak. One implication of this is that they are not carriers of propositionally formulated (or formulatable) divine information. Revelation is not the communication of otherwise unavailable facts about God or creation but the loving encounter of God and humans in which the self-disclosure of God invites the responding self-gift of the believer resulting in a shared life, a participation of the human being in the divine life of God as God has shared our life in Jesus. The correlate of this realization, in regard to Scripture, is that the only sense in which the term *word* literally applies to the Bible is the human sense. The Bible is literally a human linguistic artifact. This statement must be taken with absolute seriousness, just as the affirmation that Jesus is a human being must be taken as literally and fully true. Just as Jesus' humanity is not a disguise laid over his divinity, so the human language of the Bible is not a veneer, a semantic shell for divine meaning. Nor is it the alienated discourse of a human secretary taking divine dictation. Scripture is really, truly, and insofar as it is language, only human discourse.

The human discourse that constitutes the Bible can (but does not necessarily) mediate the encounter with God that we call revelation. But when it does so it is not in spite of the human discourse that constitutes the text but in and through that discourse. Recognition of the truly human character of the text opens up the theological possibility of acknowledging the limitations and mistakes, even the untruths and the oppressiveness in the text, without attributing these shortcomings to God or investing them with divine authority. Inadequacy, distortion, error, and even perversion are intrinsic possibilities of human language that cannot escape the weight of the historical situation in which it occurs or the incapacity of the human agents who use it. We will return shortly to the implications of this realization, namely, the absolute necessity of interpretation, including ideological criticism, if the biblical text as human discourse is to mediate the revelatory encounter.

2. *The Special Status of the Bible in the Church*

Inspiration and canonicity. The theological question about the special status of the biblical text in the church, that is, its role as sacred Scripture, is usually framed in terms of *inspiration,* the divine influence in the production of the book, on the resulting text, and in the process of its interpretation, and *canonicity,* the church's recognition of this text and no other as its sacred Scripture. Many people are under the erroneous impression that these two categories are related as cause and effect: The church accepted the biblical text as canonical because it recognized this text, and only this text, as divinely inspired. In fact, the situation is virtually the reverse. The church holds that the biblical text is inspired because it has accepted this text as canonical.

The process of canonization (official ecclesiastical acceptance) of the seventy-two books that make up the Bible took several centuries.[19] The earliest Christians regarded the Jewish Bible, which Christians now call the Old Testament, as sacred Scripture inspired by God (cf. 2 Tm 3:15–17). But within twenty years of the death of Jesus the community of his disciples had begun to produce and circulate writings of its own, first letters and then narratives of the life and death of Jesus as well as apocalyptic literature and theological tracts, some of which eventually came to be regarded as Scripture equal in status to the Jewish Bible, which the church continued to regard as Scripture. The path to canonization of the various Epistles, Gospels, and apocalyptic writings composed in the early churches was complicated, but by the fourth century the church had arrived at relative unanimity about which Christian writings, along with the Old Testament, constituted the church's Bible. However, only at the Council of Trent in 1546, under pressure from the Reformation's questioning of the canonical status of certain books (notably, in the New Testament, the Epistle of James), did the Catholic church dogmatically define its biblical canon, the list of seventy-two books that alone can and must be considered by all Catholics to compose the Holy Scriptures or the Bible.

The long and complicated history of the acceptance of some books of the Bible and the eventual exclusion of other books, some of which for many years had been regarded as canonical, makes it obvious that there was no litmus test, such as inspiration, by which to establish the canonicity of a text. If such had existed it surely would have been used. Rather, the canonicity of the Scriptures was established by the believing community as it tested the fit between certain ancient texts and its faith. Those texts that were virtually universally accepted by the authorities in the churches as expressive of the faith, often signified by a widespread belief in the apostolic authorship of the book, found their way into the canon. The church expressed its faith in the divine influence on and through these texts by claiming that they were divinely inspired. Consequently, the issues of canonicity and inspiration, although related, are quite distinct.

The Bible's special status for feminists. Feminist scholars have begun to raise questions about the process and product of biblical canonization. Like the canon of literary classics that has governed education in the Western world since the Renaissance, the biblical canon was established by men who selected writings by men that men found valuable since they reflected male experience, interests, and theological positions, because these male authorities obviously thought that male experience was equivalent to human experience.

There is little doubt that early church leaders were suspicious of the initiative and authority of women and tended to regard as heretical any literature created by women or that exalted the position of women in the church. Some feminist scholars have suggested that the biblical canon needs to be expanded and/or supplemented by some of the apocryphal literature (early Christian writings not included in the canon), such as the Gospel of Mary, Pistis Sophia, and the Acts of Paul and Thecla, which present women such as Mary Magdalene and Thecla as confidantes of Jesus or Paul and as apostles.

While an actual expansion of the canon is not likely, if indeed it is even possible, scholars in general are tending to pay increasing attention to the noncanonical literature of earliest Christianity, such as the Gospel of Thomas, as indispensable supplemental data for interpreting the canonical literature.[20] Even literature emanating from nonorthodox circles such as Gnosticism can help in the work of reconstructing the largely obliterated history of women in early Christianity.

Furthermore, "heresy" as a condemnatory and delegitimating category is beginning to be examined and criticized for its ideological agenda rather than being simply accepted as a straightforward and objective theological judgment.[21] Sometimes heresy is whatever challenges the position of those currently in power. In other words, heresy might be simply the definition of the "historical losers" by the "historical winners." Consequently, feminist scholarship calls for a reexamination of literature excluded or condemned as incompatible with divine revelation but that contains provocative material about women in early Christianity.

The notion of inspiration, although distinct from that of canonicity, is related to the latter in that inspiration is predicated of canonical texts and is a way of talking about their authoritative and normative character. Inspiration has been variously understood in the course of the church's theological development.[22] The earliest theological understanding of inspiration was based on the Old Testament model of prophetic oracle in which "the word of the Lord came" to the prophet to be delivered to the people (for example, Jer 30:1–2). This ecstatic model of inspiration virtually equated it with revelation. God (quasi-miraculously) communicated the content that the biblical author, for example, Moses or Jeremiah, committed to writing.

It is precisely this virtual equation of inspiration with revelation that, although not theologically defensible, raises the feminist question about inspiration. If all and only the canonical books are inspired, are these the final and sole sources of divine revelation? If these sources are injurious to women, can women continue to regard these texts as authoritative and normative for their religious experience? Women have an interest in maintaining the distinction between biblical inspiration and revelation because the fact that the biblical canon is regarded as inspired does not necessarily entail that all and everything in these texts is revealed by God as authoritative and normative or that no extrabiblical texts can be regarded as revelatory.

In the Middle Ages, Thomas Aquinas refined the prophetic model of inspiration by using the categories of primary efficient causality and secondary instrumental causality from Aristotelian metaphysics. He explained how God could be the true author of the biblical text by using the human author according to the latter's own nature (including finitude and fallibility) to effect God's design. For example, God, through the human instrument Jeremiah, authored (in the primary and ultimate sense) the book of Jeremiah, which was written (in a secondary but real sense) by the prophet. The Reformers were reluctant to tie the notion of inspiration and/or revelation so closely to a philosophical system, but Catholic theologians continued to use this explanation of inspiration until the second half of this century.[23] In fact, although the scholastic metaphysics underlying this medieval explanation of inspiration is not generally accepted today, it did help to emphasize the reality of the human dimension of the biblical text with which we are still struggling.

A new period of speculation on the topic of biblical inspiration was precipitated by the discoveries resulting from the so-called higher criticism or historical-critical exegesis. As it became clear that most of the biblical books, especially in the Old Testament, were composed over fairly long periods of time during which multiform traditions were used by successive redactors, it became more and more difficult to envision inspiration according to the prophetic model of personal divine communication to a particular individual author or even divine primary causality acting through a particular secondary cause, the author. Furthermore, as the discrepancies between the findings of science and history, on the one hand,

and some of the data in the biblical text, on the other hand, became apparent and indisputable, the virtual equation of inspiration with revelation
created serious problems. How and why would God have communicated
erroneous information to the biblical authors and/or permitted them to
misrepresent the divine mind? Obviously, a more refined theology of the
biblical phenomenon was necessary.

Essentially there were two possible responses to the conundrum
raised by the findings of historical criticism. Fundamentalists invested
enormous energy in the effort to use the tools of historical criticism to
establish the congruence of the biblical material with the findings of contemporary science, an effort that has not proven convincing to most of the
academy or to the mainline churches.[24] The second response was to
rethink the theological category of inspiration, attempting to explain in
more philosophically nuanced and historically realistic ways the interaction of divine and human agency in the production of the biblical texts.

In the period immediately before and after the Council there was
considerable ferment among Catholic systematic theologians[25] and biblical scholars[26] around the question of inspiration. None of the resultant
theories of inspiration has gained general acceptance. Scholarly attention
gradually has turned away from the subject of how biblical inspiration
occurred or is to be explained. While no one denied the notion of biblical
inspiration, there seemed no generally convincing way to establish its location (the text, the author, the reader, the interaction among them?) or its
mode of occurrence (individual prophetic or social historical?), although
Catholic teaching has tended to favor assigning inspiration primarily to
the text and to favor a more historical and/or social explanation of its
mode.

As theological interest in the question of inspiration waned, attention turned to the more important question of revelation, increasingly
seen to be much more inclusive and less propositional than was previously
thought. While fundamentalists, mainly in Protestant circles, continued
to insist on the plenary verbal inspiration and consequent inerrancy of the
biblical text, Catholic scholars began to reframe their questions. The really
important issues were how God communicates with us and how we participate in that communicative encounter. The Bible is neither the sum
total of that communication nor its only mode. Therefore, it is important
to understand how the Bible functions in the encounter between God
and humanity. As we will see, interpretation mediates this encounter.

The normativity of biblical subject matter. A final question basic to feminist questions about the Bible concerns the relation of biblical material to subsequent church life and thought. Early feminist biblical scholars shared with current church officials the conviction that the New Testament testimony to women's roles was materially normative for later church practice. Thus, for example, if women did not preside at Eucharist in the early church they cannot be ordained today, whereas, if it could be established that women did preside, their ordination would be legitimate and even mandatory.[27] Consequently, great efforts have been made to prove either that women did or did not exercise certain roles in early Christianity. Despite the 1976 finding of the Pontifical Biblical Commission that the New Testament by itself does not provide an answer to the question of what roles women may or may not play in the contemporary church,[28] the magisterium has argued that because Jesus included no women among the Twelve (who are erroneously considered to have been ordained by Jesus and to be the actual predecessors in office of later bishops) the church is not free to ordain women.[29] Some feminist biblical scholars, implicitly granting the premise that early church practice is materially normative for later church discipline, have attempted to counter this argument by establishing that women did, in fact, exercise the roles of apostle, community leader, liturgist, prophet, evangelist, and so on, which would adequately ground their exercise of the contemporary roles, such as ordained ministry, that are the successors of these early positions.[30]

This type of argument seems ultimately futile. The church cannot hold itself to material imitation of early Christian practice or even of the practice of the earthly Jesus, without getting itself into untenable positions. Are we, for example, to continue to defend the legitimacy of slavery because Paul accepted it (cf. Eph 6:5–8)? Obviously, the church has and must continue to modify its teaching and practice in terms of its developing insights into what is good, true, and just, what is in accord with the good news of salvation, even if the early church had not yet arrived at such realizations or Jesus did not explicitly teach them. Consequently, establishing that women did or did not play certain roles in the early church does not settle the question of what roles they may play today.

Elisabeth Schüssler Fiorenza has offered a much more important argument for the careful investigation of early materials about women, especially the New Testament material.[31] It is crucial to the religious identity of contemporary Christian women, she argues, that they be able to find themselves in the history of Christianity from the beginning. Furthermore, it is crucial to Christianity that it realize and value the important role of women, largely obscured and suppressed, in its development. The feminist reconstruction of Christian origins has as its purpose, not the legitimation of current inclusion of women in church life, but the restoration of their Christian history to women and of women to Christian history. This project, Schüssler Fiorenza maintains, is important even for women who are not believers, because Western society is thoroughly impregnated with biblical history and tradition. Furthermore, much of the sexism that marginalizes and oppresses women in family and society as well as in the church is based on the interpretation of the Bible that legitimates patriarchy.

In the next section of this chapter I will suggest how a contemporary theory of interpretation can supplement ideologically sophisticated historical criticism in subverting the appeal to the biblical text for the legitimation of patriarchy. However, it is also necessary to develop a more adequate understanding of the relationship between the biblical text and its subject matter and between the biblical text and its readers. In other words, feminist biblical studies must develop a position on the question of the normativity of the Bible for contemporary church teaching and practice if it is to be able to make nonoppressive use of Scripture as normative for contemporary church life.

In brief, two presuppositions underlie a more adequate theory of this relationship. First, the biblical text is an authoritative testimony to the Christ event in Jesus of Nazareth. As human testimony to revelatory experience it is subject, as all testimony is, to the limitations of the human witness and process of testifying. Acceptance of the testimony entails both an acceptance of its substantial authority in regard to the proclamation of salvation in Jesus and a recognition of its fallibility in the offering of that testimony.[32] Second, accepting the authority of the Bible does not entail material imitation or replication of the arrangements of first-century Christianity any more than the imitation of Christ entails being a carpenter, a Jew, a male, or an itinerant preacher. The normativity of the Bible cannot be reduced to materialistic replication. Consequently, the discovery, insofar as it is possible, of the roles of women in early Christianity, important as this is for the feminist agenda, cannot be used positively or negatively to establish the roles of women in the current church community.

INTERPRETATION

If, as I have tried to show, the biblical text is not a straightforward communication of divinely guaranteed propositions that are materially normative for later generations, then the text, if it is to function salvifically within the believing community, must be interpreted. Interpretation is the process of coming to understand any phenomenon, including a text. Interpretation is especially necessary when the phenomenon, for some reason, resists understanding. The biblical text resists understanding because it was written in an ancient culture, in languages most moderns do not command, according to literary genres that differ among themselves and often from modern genres, about events that sometimes do not correlate with contemporary happenings, and because it makes claims that require adjudication. Anyone who claims that the biblical text can be read "at face value," without interpretation, does not understand the nature of texts in general or of this text in particular. The question is not *whether* to interpret the text, for this is the only way it can be understood, but only *how* to interpret it.

Contemporary scholarship regarding textual interpretation, known as the field of hermeneutics, is vast in scope and immensely complex.[33] It is possible here to invoke only those conclusions from this field of theory that are immediately useful for the question of feminist interpretation of the Bible. Essentially, interpretation is a dialectical process that takes place between a reader and a text and culminates in an event of meaning.[34] This definition has several important implications.

First, it implies that a text does not have one right meaning, which was put into it by its author and is to be extracted by the reader. Rather, the text is a linguistic structure that is susceptible of a number of valid readings by different readers or the same reader at different times. The truth of this statement is clear to anyone who has ever seen a film with a group of friends, each of whom interprets it in a recognizably valid but somewhat different way, or who has read a novel a second time and found a great deal more (or less!) in it in the second reading.

Second, and correlative, meaning is not "in" the text but occurs in the interaction between text and reader, just as music is not "in" the score but occurs as an event when the score is performed. This implies that the reader makes a genuine contribution to the meaning rather than being simply a passive consumer of prefabricated meaning.

Third, the meaning is not finally under the control of the author. Although the author obviously meant something when he or she wrote the text and intended to convey that meaning, once the text is completed it means whatever it means, regardless of what the author intended.[35] It is common experience that we often say more (or less) than we intend and that our words can mean very different things in different contexts or to different people. This is even more true of texts that are separated by thousands of years from their authors.

The process of interpretation, then, is not merely a matter of extracting the meaning intended by the author from an inert text, but a matter of interacting with the text in the effort to achieve meaning. In this process both the text and the reader are affected, that is, both change. It is more obvious to most people that the reader is affected by what he or she reads. A powerful text expands our horizons, deepens our humanity, challenges our assumptions, raises questions about reality, enhances our perception, and so on. But the reading of a text by successive generations of readers also affects the text. For example, the text "all men are created equal" in the American Declaration of Independence means much more in the late twentieth century than it did in the eighteenth century when it was written. The founding fathers clearly meant by *men* only adult, white, property-owning, free males. Today *men* in this text includes children, people of color, the poor, and women, while the category of slave has been banished from the national vocabulary altogether precisely because of the ongoing interpretation of this foundational text. Such an understanding of the way meaning occurs in the interaction between reader and text opens up the possibility that the biblical text, in interaction with feminist readers, might be susceptible of a liberating interpretation, even of its patently patriarchal and sexist texts. The fact is that the believing community, like the American people in relation to the nation's founding documents, has grown and developed on the basis of its founding documents beyond the narrow perspectives of the original articulators of the Christian vision. From the gospel of Jesus, Christians learned to repudiate the slavery Paul accepted. From the gospel, Christians have learned that women for whom Jesus died are not inferior to men for whom he died, and that when Jesus condemned the attempt of his followers to lord it over one another he was also condemning the patriarchalism that is the foundation of sexism, clericalism, colonialism, classism, and all the other forms of domination that have marred the Christian tradition. In other words, the biblical text has equipped us to call into question some of the material content of the Bible itself.

The major problem facing feminist interpreters is how to engage the biblical text in such a way that the oppressive potential of the Bible is neutralized, while its liberating power is invoked on behalf of the victims of church and society. One approach has been either to excise from the Bible those texts that are oppressive or to deny revelatory status to them.[36] Neither of these strategies is satisfactory. The Bible is so permeated with patriarchalism that excising texts that are actually or potentially damaging to women would leave such massive lacunae that the kerygma would be difficult to discern in what remained. Denying the revelatory status of oppressive texts is equally problematic. First, what is oppressive to one group or at one time or from one point of view might be an important resource in other circumstances. But more importantly, the revelatory character of Scripture cannot be attached to individual texts in virtue of their semantic content without implicitly reintroducing a propositional understanding of revelation. It is Scripture itself, as a whole, that either is or is not the medium of divine self-disclosure. Just as we cannot regard nature as divinely revelatory only when the sun shines and reject it when it erupts in earthquakes or fires, we cannot confer revelatory status on certain biblical passages while rejecting others.

To claim that the biblical text is revelatory is not, as has been argued above, to claim that the text delivers true propositional information that must be accepted as the divine will for the community. Rather, the text is a linguistic structure with which successive generations of Christians interact within the ever-widening horizon of understanding of the Church. Because the text is human language giving voice to human experience of God in Christ, as well as to the experience of the early community in all its weakness and sinfulness, the text, even though it is inspired (written and read under the influence of the Holy Spirit) is as capable of error, distortion, and even sinfulness as the church itself.

Interpretation is the process of discerning what the text means in relation to the issues that exercise the contemporary community by interacting—from within the contemporary context—with what the text says in its own compositional context. This means that the community might experience a particular text as an object lesson in and warning against evil, rather than as a formulation of the divine will. For example, we might derive from Paul's restrictions on women in the liturgical assembly not a warrant for oppressing women today but a warning of how deleterious it is to sacrifice the good of some members of the community to a fear of offending the powerful.

Biblical interpretation, especially of problematic texts, is always a process of wrestling with the text. Just as nineteenth-century interpreters realized that they had to struggle with strange literary genres, ancient customs that seemed bizarre and even uncivilized, a nonscientific cosmology, and forms of social organization for which they had no contemporary analogues if they were to understand the meaning of these ancient texts, so the contemporary interpreter who has become conscious of the ideological obstacles in the text must struggle with androcentric, patriarchal, sexist, and misogynist material if she or he is to liberate the message of salvation for today's readers.

Feminist biblical scholars have developed an impressive program for wrestling with the text, although none would be ready to claim that the problem is solved or even that it is clear that, in the long run, it can be solved.[37] Among the hermeneutical approaches that have been developed are the following: scrupulous translation that helps to defeat the gratuitous linguistic masculinizing of biblical material that is actually inclusive;[38] using the liberating traditions in the Bible, such as the prophetic tradition[39] or the original plan of creation of male and female in the image of God,[40] to criticize the oppressive material; retelling misogynist biblical stories such as that of Jephthah's daughter or the rape of the concubine "in memoriam," as "texts of terror" rather than as an acceptable part of the history of salvation;[41] pressing the silences of the text for the hidden story of women;[42] using rhetorical analysis of oppressive texts such as Paul's disciplinary injunctions against women to establish women's actual roles and practice in early Christianity;[43] reinterpreting with feminist sensibilities texts dealing with women, such as the story of the Samaritan woman in John 4, which have been distorted or trivialized in the male-dominated exegetical and homiletic tradition;[44] discerning the liberating trajectories opened up within texts, such as Paul's injunction that husbands are to love their wives, even though those texts are, in their current form, still oppressive.

The practice of liberating interpretation by scholars must be supplemented by a pastoral practice that avoids, first, the public proclamation—without counter commentary—of oppressive texts and, second, the development of inclusive-language liturgical texts that take proper account of the difference between the intention of a text read as history of an ancient community and the same text proclaimed as kerygma to the present community.

CONCLUSION

Although it is not by any means clear or certain that the Bible can or will continue to function as revelatory for women whose feminist consciousness has been raised, there are at least three motives for making every possible effort to develop a theology of the Bible and a hermeneutical theory that will enable it to do so. The first is theological. The Bible, especially the New Testament, is the normative witness in the Christian community to the Christ event in Jesus of Nazareth. It is also the linguistic mooring of the present community of believers to its foundational past. To surrender the Scriptures as irremediably patriarchal and sexist and therefore destructive of women is to relinquish our history and therefore, to an important degree, our identity as Christians.

The second motive is ecumenical. The primary common faith resource of the still-divided Christian communities is Scripture. If we are finally forced, by our integrity as self-respecting human beings, to abandon our relationship to this foundational text, we will have surrendered the major shared inheritance around which we might someday regather in unity.

The final motive is perhaps the most important: spirituality. If Scripture is the sacrament of the word of God, the pure and perennial source of the spiritual life that Vatican II called it, and the one sacramental medium of revelatory encounter that men do not control, it will be tragic indeed if women must renounce it as hopelessly oppressive.

As long as the biblical text is regarded as a semantic container of propositional revelation, its clearly oppressive material cannot function salvifically for women. But if the text is understood as a text, that is, as human witness in human language to the human experience of divine event, then all the flexibility and power of the process of interpretation can be mobilized to liberate the text from its own limitations and women from the oppressiveness of the text. If it is true that the word of God is not bound (cf. 2 Tim 2:9) and that all Scripture is written for our instruction and edification (cf. 2 Tim 3:16), then there is still hope that Christian women will be able to affirm both themselves and this text as revelatory.

NOTES

1. This situation was implicitly recognized in "Sacrosanctum Concilium," the Constitution on the Sacred Liturgy of Vatican II 2:51–52, which decreed that the "treasures of the Bible are to be opened up more lavishly . . . for the faithful" (51) and that the homily should consist in expounding the faith "from the sacred text" (52). The documents of the Council are available in *Documents of Vatican II,* ed. Austin P. Flannery (Grand Rapids: Eerdmans, 1988), 2 vols. "Sacrosanctum Concilium" is found in 1:1–40.

2. "Divino Afflante Spiritu" is available in English translation in James J. Megivern, *Bible Interpretation,* Official Catholic Teachings (Wilmington, NC: McGrath Publishing, 1978), 316–42.

3. For a concise history and evaluation of official church documents concerning biblical studies and interpretation, see Raymond E. Brown and Thomas Aquinas Collins, "Church Pronouncements," in *The New Jerome Biblical Commentary,* ed. Raymond E. Brown, Joseph A. Fitzmyer, and Roland E. Murphy (Englewood Cliffs, NJ: Prentice-Hall, 1990), 1166–74. Henceforth the volume will be cited as *NJBC* with appropriate article reference.

4. The text of the conciliar document, in English translation, is available in *Documents of Vatican II,* ed. Flannery 1:750–65.

5. See John R. Donahue, "Scripture: A Roman Catholic Perspective," *Review and Expositor* 79 (Spring 1982): 231–44, for an analysis of the document and the relation of its contents to Protestant developments in the theology of the Bible.

6. The most recent and complete Catholic Bible study resource is Donald Senior, ed., *The Catholic Study Bible* (New York: Oxford Univ. Press, 1990). This one-volume study resource contains general introductory articles, reading guides to every section of both testaments, and brief introductions and notes to each book as well as material on the use of the Bible in the lectionary, and on biblical archaeology and geography. It includes the full text of both testaments.

   The *NJBC* is a more detailed resource supplying a commentary on every book of the Bible as well as lengthy topical articles on such topics as canonicity, inspiration, and hermeneutics.

7. For a succinct history of the feminist movement, see Maria Riley, *Transforming Feminism* (Kansas City, MO: Sheed and Ward, 1989), esp. 14–42.

8. For a brief explanation of feminist terminology, see Sandra M. Schneiders, *Beyond Patching: Faith and Feminism in the Catholic Church* (New York: Paulist Press, 1991), 5–36.

9. The document *Inter Insigniores,* published by the Sacred Congregation for the Doctrine of the Faith on October 15, 1976, is available in English as "Declaration on the Question of the Admission of Women to the Ministerial Priesthood," in *Women Priests: A Catholic Commentary on the Vatican Declaration,* ed. Leonard Swidler and Arlene Swidler (New York: Paulist Press, 1977), 37–49. The now-infamous "fifth argument" against the admission of women to orders, namely, their lack of natural resemblance to Christ, is in paragraphs 25–46.

10. Several articles in the Swidler and Swidler volume, *Women Priests,* address the issue of women as image of God and Christ. See, for example, Pauline Turner and Bernard Cooke, "Women Can Have a Natural Resemblance to Christ"; Sonya A. Quitslund,

"In the Image of Christ"; Carroll Stuhlmueller, "Bridegroom: A Biblical Symbol of Union, Not Separation"; and Robert W. Hovda, "Recognizing Christ in Women Priests." The last cites the important article by R. A. Norris, "The Ordination of Women and the 'Maleness' of Christ," *Anglican Theological Review,* suppl. ser. no. 6 (June 1976): 69–80, which shows the argument from Jesus' maleness to be not only a theological novelty, but a doctrinally dangerous one.

11. This point has been made most clearly and convincingly by Elisabeth Schüssler Fiorenza in numerous writings such as *In Memory of Her: A Feminist Theological Reconstruction of Christian Origins* (New York: Crossroad, 1983), esp. xiii–40. See also her collection of essays, *Bread Not Stone: The Challenge of Feminist Biblical Interpretation* (Boston: Beacon Press, 1984).

12. For a brief summary on biblical metaphors for God, see Sandra M. Schneiders, *Women and the Word: The Gender of God in the New Testament and the Spirituality of Women,* 1986 Madeleva Lecture in Spirituality (New York: Paulist Press, 1986), 28–37. For a more detailed presentation, see also Virginia R. Mollenkott, *The Divine Feminine: The Biblical Imagery of God as Female* (New York: Crossroad, 1983).

13. Roland E. Murphy, *The Tree of Life: An Exploration of Biblical Wisdom Literature,* Anchor Bible Reference Library (New York: Doubleday, 1990), offers a succinct and synthetic presentation of the figure of Wisdom in the Old Testament in the chapter "Lady Wisdom," 133–49. A more detailed theological presentation is Elizabeth A. Johnson, "Jesus, the Wisdom of God: A Biblical Basis for Non-Androcentric Christology," *Ephemerides Theologicae Lovanienses* 61 (December 1985): 261–94.

14. This hesitation is evident in the *New Revised Standard Version* (1989), *The Catholic Study Bible* (1990), *The New International Version* (1978).

15. Rosemary Radford Ruether is a major contributor on this issue. See her *Sexism and God-Talk: Toward a Feminist Theology* (Boston: Beacon Press, 1983), 116–38.

16. Person language for the Trinity is both important and problematic. On this issue, see Catherine M. LaCugna, *God for Us: The Trinity and Christian Life* (San Francisco: Harper San Francisco, 1991), esp. 244–305. See also her shorter treatment, "The Trinitarian Mystery of God," in *Systematic Theology: Roman Catholic Perspectives,* vol. 1, ed. Francis Schüssler Fiorenza and John P. Galvin (Minneapolis: Fortress Press, 1991), 151–92, esp. 178–80.

17. Sallie McFague, *Metaphorical Theology: Models of God in Religious Language* (Philadelphia: Fortress Press, 1982), esp. 31–42. See also Paul Ricoeur, "Creativity in Language: Word, Polysemy, Metaphor," in *The Philosophy of Paul Ricoeur: An Anthology of His Work,* ed. Charles E. Reagan and David Stewart (Boston: Beacon Press, 1978), 120–33.

18. See Mary Catherine Hilkert, "Can the Center Hold?" in this volume.

19. On the notion and history of the formation of the biblical canon, see Raymond E. Brown and Raymond F. Collins, "Canonicity," *NJBC,* 1034–54. An accessible book-length treatment is Lee Martin McDonal, *The Formation of the Christian Biblical Canon* (Nashville: Abingdon Press, 1988).

20. A good example of this trend is the best-selling volume by John Dominic Crossan, *The Historical Jesus: The Life of a Mediterranean Jewish Peasant* (San Francisco: Harper San Francisco, 1991), which reconstructs the gospel tradition from all the canonical and noncanonical sources supplying records of Jesus' life and work.

2 1. See Schüssler Fiorenza, *In Memory of Her,* 53–56.

2 2. See Raymond F. Collins, "Inspiration," *NJBC,* 1023–33. An excellent theory of the interrelation of the theological affirmations about the Bible is Thomas A. Hoffman, "Inspiration, Normativeness, Canonicity, and the Unique Sacred Character of the Bible," *Catholic Biblical Quarterly* 44 (July 1982): 447–69.

2 3. The standard definition of inspiration up to Vatican II was that of Leo XIII in "Providentissimus Deus," the encyclical on the Study of Holy Scripture of Nov. 18, 1893 (available in English in Megivern, *Bible Interpretation,* 191–220): "For, by supernatural power, He [God] so moved and impelled them to write—He so assisted them when writing—that the things which He ordered, and those only, they, first, rightly understood, then willed faithfully to write down, and finally expressed in apt words and with infallible truth" (216). Vatican II follows this theology, although it is less explicit about the mode of inspiration and more insistent on the effect: "To compose the sacred books, God chose certain men who, all the while he employed them in this task, made full use of their powers and faculties so that, though he acted in them and by them, it was as true authors that they consigned to writing whatever he wanted written, and no more. [Therefore] the books of Scripture firmly, faithfully and without error, teach that truth which God, for the sake of our salvation, wished to see confided to the sacred Scriptures" (*DV* 3:11). *Dei Verbum* here refers in a footnote to "Providentissimus Deus."

2 4. For a Catholic critique of fundamentalism, see Dianne Bergant, "Fundamentalists and the Bible," *New Theology Review* 1 (May 1988): 36–50; for a Protestant critique, see James Barr, *Fundamentalism* (Philadelphia: Westminster Press, 1978). His *Beyond Fundamentalism* (Philadelphia: Westminster Press, 1984) offers an evangelical alternative to fundamentalism.

2 5. See, for example, Karl Rahner, *Inspiration in the Bible,* 2d ed., trans. C. Henkey, Questiones Disputatae 1 (New York: Herder and Herder, 1964).

2 6. See, for example, Pierre Benoit, *Inspiration and the Bible,* trans. J. Murphy-O'Connor and M. Keverne (New York: Sheed and Ward, 1965).

2 7. The Vatican Declaration against the ordination of women gives, as its second argument, the attitude of Jesus in excluding women from apostolic roles (see Swidler and Swidler, *Women Priests,* 39–40). The position paper "Women and Priestly Ministry: The New Testament Evidence," of the Task Force of the Catholic Biblical Association, which had been appointed to study the issue of biblical data pertinent to women's roles in the early Church, adopted essentially the same premise in concluding "that women did in fact exercise roles and functions later associated with priestly ministry. [Therefore] the NT evidence, while not decisive by itself, points toward the admission of women to priestly ministry" (published in *The Catholic Biblical Quarterly* 41 [October 1979]: 608–13).

2 8. The Pontifical Biblical Commission did a two-year study, requested by the Vatican, of whether the biblical data permitted the presbyteral ordination of women. The results of the study, completed in April 1976, were never officially published, but the final votes were leaked to the press in July. The members of the PBC voted 17–0 that the New Testament does not settle in a clear way the question of whether women can be ordained and 12–5 that Christ's plan would not be transgressed by such ordination. For a copy of the unofficial report see "Appendix II, Biblical Commission Report. Can

Women Be Priests?" in Swidler and Swidler, *Women Priests,* 338–46. Serving on the commission at that time were conciliar era luminaries such as Albert Deschamps, Jean Dominique Barthélemy, Pierre Benoit, Raymond Brown, Henri Cazelles, Stanislas Lyonnet, Carlo Martini, and David Stanley. Stanley resigned from the commission in protest of the congregation's ignoring of this study in its declaration.

29. This line of argumentation is clear in the section of the declaration on the "The Attitude of Christ." I dealt with this argument in some detail in "Did Jesus Exclude Women from Priesthood?" in Swidler and Swidler, *Women Priests,* 227–33.

30. See, for example, Elisabeth M. Tetlow, *Women and Ministry in the New Testament* (New York: Paulist Press, 1980).

31. Schüssler Fiorenza, *In Memory of Her,* xiii–xxv.

32. I have dealt with this issue in detail in *The Revelatory Text: Interpreting the New Testament as Sacred Scripture* (San Francisco: Harper San Francisco, 1991), 133–38.

33. A reference book treating most of the topics in hermeneutics a reader would need to understand is R. J. Coggins and J. L. Houlden, eds., *A Dictionary of Biblical Interpretation* (London: SCM; Philadelphia: Trinity Press International, 1990). An accessible theory of hermeneutics applied to the interpretation of Scripture is James M. Reese, *Experiencing the Good News: The New Testament as Communication,* Good News Studies 10 (Wilmington, DE: Michael Glazier, 1984).

34. The best short explanation of this process, in my opinion, is Paul Ricoeur's lectures, *Interpretation Theory: Discourse and the Surplus of Meaning* (Fort Worth: Texas Christian Univ. Press, 1976), esp. chap. 4.

35. See Ricoeur, *Interpretation Theory,* 29–37.

36. Elisabeth Schüssler Fiorenza, in many places, espouses the latter position. See, for example, *In Memory of Her,* 33, or the more nuanced expression in *Bread Not Stone,* 60.

37. Some typologies of feminist interpretive positions are the following: Carolyn Osiek, "The Feminist and the Bible: Hermeneutical Alternatives," in *Feminist Perspectives on Biblical Scholarship,* ed. Adela Yarbo Collins (Chico, CA: Scholars Press, 1985), 93–105; Katherine Doob Sakenfeld, "Feminist Uses of Biblical Material," in *Feminist Interpretation of the Bible,* ed. Letty M. Russell (Philadelphia: Westminster Press, 1985), 55–64; Elisabeth Schüssler Fiorenza, *In Memory of Her,* chap. 1; Mary Ann Tolbert, "Defining the Problem: The Bible and Feminist Hermeneutics," in *The Bible and Feminist Hermeneutics,* ed. Mary Ann Tolbert, Semeia 28 (Chico, CA: Scholars Press, 1983), 113–26.

38. See Letty M. Russell, "Changing Language and the Church," in *The Liberating Word: A Guide to Nonsexist Interpretation of the Bible,* ed. Letty M. Russell (Philadelphia: Westminster Press, 1976), 82–98; Katherine Doob Sakenfeld, "Feminist Perspectives on Bible and Theology: An Introduction to Selected Issues and Literature," *Interpretation* 42 (January 1988): 5–18, esp. 16–18.

39. Rosemary Radford Ruether, "Feminist Interpretation: A Method of Correlation," in *Feminist Interpretation of the Bible,* ed. Russell, 111–24.

40. Letty M. Russell, "Authority and the Challenge of Feminist Interpretation," in *Feminist Interpretation of the Bible,* ed. Russell, 137–46.

41. Phyllis Trible, *Texts of Terror* (Philadelphia: Fortress Press, 1984).

42. Schüssler Fiorenza, *In Memory of Her,* chap. 2.

43. Cf. Antoinette C. Wire, *The Corinthian Women Prophets: A Reconstruction Through Paul's Rhetoric* (Minneapolis: Fortress Press, 1991).

44. I attempted such an interpretation as chap. 7 of *The Revelatory Text.*

FOR FURTHER READING

"Dei Verbum." In *Documents of Vatican II,* edited by Austin P. Flannery, 1:750–65. Grand Rapids: Eerdmans, 1988. The Dogmatic Constitution on Divine Revelation of Vatican II, published in 1965.

"Divino Afflante Spiritu." In *Bible Interpretation,* edited by James J. Megivern, 316–42. Wilmington, NC: McGrath, 1978. The 1943 encyclical letter of Pius XII that launched contemporary Catholic biblical scholarship.

"Sacrosanctum Concilium." In *Documents of Vatican II,* 1:1–40. The Constitution on the Sacred Liturgy of Vatican II, published in 1963. Contains considerable material on the use of Scripture in worship.

Brown, Raymond E., and Raymond F. Collins. "Canonicity." In *The New Jerome Biblical Commentary,* edited by Raymond E. Brown, Joseph A. Fitzmyer, and Roland E. Murphy, 1034–54. Englewood Cliffs, NJ: Prentice-Hall, 1990.

Brown, Raymond E., and Thomas Aquinas Collins. "Church Pronouncements." In *The New Jerome Biblical Commentary,* 1166–74. Provides the history of Catholic theology in relation to the use of Scripture.

Coggins, R. J., and J. L. Hulden, eds. *A Dictionary of Biblical Interpretation.* London: SCM Press; Philadelphia: Trinity Press International, 1990. Encyclopedic dictionary that contains excellent articles on most facets of biblical hermeneutics, each prepared by a major scholar; reliable, readable, and up-to-date.

Collins, Raymond F. "Inspiration." In *The New Jerome Biblical Commentary,* 1123–33.

Collins, Adela Yarbro, ed. *Feminist Perspectives on Biblical Scholarship.* Biblical Scholarship in North America, no. 10. Chico, CA: Scholars Press, 1985. Presents a variety of feminist approaches to Scripture.

Donahue, John R. "Scripture: A Roman Catholic Perspective." *Review and Expositor* 79 (1982): 231–44. Explains *Dei Verbum* with particular attention to the way Catholic thought on the nature and interpretation of Scripture has changed since the Council of Trent and the implications for ecumenical dialogue.

Fiorenza, Elisabeth Schüssler. *In Memory of Her: A Feminist Theological Reconstruction of Christian Origins.* New York: Crossroad, 1983. The first full-scale interpretation of the whole New Testament from the standpoint of feminist hermeneutics; established the academic seriousness of feminist criticism.

———. *Bread Not Stone: The Challenge of Feminist Biblical Interpretation.* Boston: Beacon Press, 1984. A collection of essays by the foremost New Testament scholar engaged in feminist interpretation.

———. *But She Said: Feminist Practices of Biblical Interpretation.* Boston: Beacon Press, 1992. Illustrates the theory of feminist interpretation in actual practice.

Grant, Robert, and David Tracy. *A Short History of the Interpretation of the Bible.* 2d ed., rev. and enl. Philadelphia: Fortress Press, 1984. A brief, readable history of biblical interpretation in the church from the beginning of Christianity to the first half of the twentieth century, followed by three essays on the role of contemporary hermeneutical theory in current biblical interpretation, especially as this influences theological interpretation.

Hoffman, Thomas A. "Inspiration, Normativeness, Canonicity, and the Unique Sacred Character of the Bible." *The Catholic Biblical Quarterly* 44 (1982): 447–69. Offers a contemporary theological understanding of the way the theological claims about Scripture interact to produce the Catholic understanding of the biblical text as sacred Scripture.

Reese, James M. *Experiencing the Good News: The New Testament as Communication.* Good News Studies 10. Wilmington, DE: Michael Glazier, 1984. A readable introduction to the influence of modern language study on biblical interpretation.

Ricoeur, Paul. *Interpretation Theory: Discourse and the Surplus of Meaning.* Fort Worth: Texas Christian Univ. Press, 1976. Difficult reading but presents in brief form the foundational thought of Ricoeur on texts and interpretation.

Riley, Maria. *Transforming Feminism.* Kansas City, MO: Sheed and Ward, 1989. A brief history of the feminist movement in relation to Catholic social teaching.

Russell, Letty M., ed. *Feminist Interpretation of the Bible.* Philadelphia: Westminster Press, 1985. Gives examples of how feminist interpretation is done.

Schneiders, Sandra M. *Beyond Patching: Faith and Feminism in the Catholic Church.* The Anthony Jordan Lectures, 1990. New York: Paulist Press, 1991. An introduction to feminism, its vocabulary, history, and various forms; includes a chapter on feminist biblical interpretation.

———. *The Revelatory Text: Interpreting the New Testament as Sacred Scripture.* San Francisco: Harper San Francisco, 1991. A theory of biblical hermeneutics that integrates theology with other disciplines relevant to interpretation.

———. *Women and the Word: The Gender of God in the New Testament and the Spirituality of Women.* 1986 Madaleva Lecture in Spirituality. New York: Paulist Press, 1986. Deals with the most serious problem that the content of the Bible presents to women, namely, the masculinity of the biblical God-image and the maleness of the historical Jesus.

Tolbert, Mary Ann, ed. *The Bible and Feminist Hermeneutics.* Semeia 28. Chico, CA: Scholars Press, 1983. Shows the relationship between the Bible and feminism.

Trible, Phyllis. *Texts of Terror.* Philadelphia: Fortress Press, 1984. A feminist interpretation from the foremost feminist Old Testament scholar of four Old Testament passages that denigrate or violate women, showing how such interpretation can be liberating.

EXPERIENCE AND TRADITION—

CAN THE CENTER HOLD?

— Revelation —

MARY CATHERINE HILKERT

Here's the thing, say Shug. The thing I believe. God is inside you and inside everybody else. You come into the world with God. But only them that search for it inside find it. And sometimes it just manifest itself even if you not looking, or don't know what you looking for. Trouble do it for most folks, I think.[1]

ALICE WALKER'S WOMANIST classic, *The Color Purple,* highlights a perspective central to any feminist understanding of a theology of revelation:

God is to be discovered in human experience. Many women's writings in spirituality, literature, and theology proclaim that for those who search, God can be discovered in the depths of the human heart—"God inside you and inside everybody else." As in any claim to have discovered the divine within human experience, there is always an element of surprise: "Sometimes it just manifest itself even if you not looking, or don't know what you looking for." Human friendship, such as that between Celie and Shug, is often used as the key metaphor for the experience of divine-human relationship.[2] For feminists who do theology as a specific form of liberation theology, the experience of suffering often initiates a deeper, and unexpected, experience of God: "Trouble do it for most folks, I think."[3]

The experiences in which feminists locate the disclosure of the passionate mystery of love at the heart of the universe are rich and diverse: women's friendships with one another as well as with men and children; gatherings of Women-Church; women's solidarity with the suffering and the marginalized; women's political efforts to change social, ecclesial, and global structures of injustice; women's connection with nature, the body, and the earth; and women's mystical experience even in the mode of the dark night. What remains a common thread, however, is the firm conviction that women's experience can be, and is, revelatory of the divine.[4] Beneath that claim is the belief that human experience, history, and indeed all of creation have the potential to disclose the divine. Feminists who identify themselves as Christians recognize in Jesus of Nazareth a privileged and central disclosure (or revelation) of the God who nonetheless remains hidden. Jesus embodied the God whose true name is compassion as he gathered women and men into an inclusive community of friends, as he lived and died in solidarity with the poor and rejected, as he interpreted his own religious tradition radically in light of what would truly serve human well-being, as he invited sinners and those excluded by social or religious boundaries to join at a table of thanksgiving and joy.

While women do write and speak of the mystery of divine love as disclosed or embodied within human history and human experience, the traditional language and categories of revelation are largely absent from, or heavily critiqued in, feminist theology. At the core of the conflict is the consistent marginalization, if not complete exclusion, of women's experience from what has been named by the Christian churches as God's revelation. Other areas of theological dispute are closely related: Who constitutes the church? Who recognizes and names the Spirit of God at work in human life and the Christian community? Who has the authority to interpret events, persons, symbols, writings, or teachings as revelatory of the divine and therefore normative in the community? Appeals to "divine revelation" have served all too often as the closing argument in the final court of appeal officially representing the Roman Catholic community, the hierarchical magisterium. Assertions of "divine revelation" or "God's will" have functioned to limit, critique, or deny women's attempts to empower the full human dignity and baptismal equality of women as well as men.

The reasoning of the Congregation for the Doctrine of the Faith in its 1976 Declaration on the Admission of Women to the Ministerial Priesthood (*Inter Insigniores*)[5] illustrates the fundamental issues raised in the Roman Catholic tradition. According to that document, the church "through the voice of her magisterium" decides what can change and what must remain immutable. The Catholic church's practice of restricting ordained ministry only to men is said to have "a normative character" based on "unbroken tradition throughout the history of the church." This norm, traced to Christ's example, is "considered to conform to God's plan for his church." The declaration maintains that the incarnation of the Word according to the male sex "while not implying an alleged natural superiority of man over woman, cannot be disassociated from the economy of salvation: it is, indeed, in harmony with the entirety of God's plan as God himself has revealed it." Claiming biblical revelation as a foundation, the dual anthropology of the document emphasizes sexual differences as "the effect of God's will from the beginning." The problems of sacramental theology related to the ministerial priesthood cannot be solved, according to the declaration, except "in the light of revelation." Further, the contribution of the human sciences to this discussion is limited, "for they cannot grasp the realities of faith: the properly supernatural content of these realities is beyond their competence."

Feminist theologians resist such dogmatic appeals to the example or teaching of Jesus Christ, the inspired Word of God, or the unbroken tradition of the church when there is no acknowledgment of the patriarchal lens through which the life and ministry of Jesus, the interpretation of biblical sources, and the constitution and interpretation of the church's tradition have been filtered. The very language of "supernatural truths," "immutable teaching," "the unchanging inspired Word of God," being "bound" not only to Christ's example but also to "the church's unbroken tradition," and submission to the authority of the (all-male and clerical) magisterium, is alien to a feminist theological framework. Instead, Christian feminists emphasize historical consciousness and social location, relationality, mutuality, equal and responsible discipleship rooted in baptism, participation in decision making for the common good, a dialogical model of learning/teaching, and fidelity based on discernment, integrity, and creativity. Even more basic are feminist questions about the fundamental symbol system at the center of the Christian tradition. Mary Hunt speaks for many when she says, "Women are now quite sure that God the Father, Jesus his only Son (no daughters), and a male-dominated church are not adequate to pass on to children."[6]

Both feminists and those who are alarmed by feminist claims are raising similar questions: Is a feminist perspective compatible with Roman Catholic tradition? Official Roman Catholic theology of revelation changed significantly between the first and final drafts of *Dei Verbum,* the Second Vatican Council's Dogmatic Constitution on Revelation, but the challenge of feminism extends to the very roots of the tradition. How radically can the tradition be expanded and still remain faithful to the gospel of Jesus Christ? Is the Bible the revealed Word of God? Are the boundaries of the canon fixed? Are the canonical scriptures the *norma non normata* in the Christian tradition? What role do dogma, liturgy, and the magisterium play in the church of Jesus Christ? Is human experience a source of revelation? If so, whose experience counts, and who is doing the counting? What, if anything, critiques the claims and operation of the Roman Catholic magisterium as well as those of feminists who claim to stand within the Catholic tradition? It soon becomes obvious why questions in this area are considered fundamental or foundational to the entire field of theology.

VATICAN II AND FEMINISM: POINTS OF CONVERGENCE AND CONFLICT

The Nature and Locus of Revelation

Dei Verbum is the most recent and most important official statement issued by the Catholic church on the subject of revelation.[7] Key topics from that document can serve as a helpful structure from which to highlight recent important shifts in Roman Catholic theology of revelation that converge remarkably with feminist theology as well as issues that remain disputed from a feminist perspective.

The first two chapters of the final text of *Dei Verbum* reflect significant shifts in Roman Catholic understanding of both the nature of revelation and the process of tradition. From the Council of Trent until Vatican II Catholics had identified revelation with a body of supernatural truths that had been handed down through the twofold sources of Scripture and tradition. The latter was generally identified with official church teaching. This propositional view of revelation was reinforced by the First Vatican Council's 1871 declaration on faith and revelation, *Dei Filius,* which asserts: "All those things are to be believed with divine and Catholic faith which are contained in the word of God, written or handed down, and which by the Church, either in solemn judgment or through her ordinary and universal teaching office, are proposed for belief as having been divinely revealed."[8]

Two significant moments occurred in the development of *Dei Verbum* with the rejection of the original schema on the twofold sources of revelation and the inclusion of a new opening chapter clarifying the nature of revelation as most fundamentally God's self-disclosure and offer of friendship to humankind. Faith, in turn, is described as "entrusting one's whole self to God" (*DV* 5). As a compromise document, the constitution on revelation still includes an earlier propositional understanding referring to revelation at points as "religious truths" and faith as "full submission of intellect and will" (*DV* 5.6). The basic shift, however, is to a relational and dialogical model of revelation as divine-human friendship in which God invites and human beings respond with their whole being. The offer of revelation transcends human experience, but that offer can be perceived and responded to only in and through human categories. Because human beings are constituted as body-spirit, relationship with God who is pure spirit requires mediation in concrete, tangible, social, embodied, historical experience. The Vatican document locates God's "speaking" primarily in the events of salvation history and the words that proclaim and clarify the mystery contained in those events.

An increasing number of theologians, however, would argue that in this dialogical model one cannot separate the revelation of God from the faith that perceives, receives, and responds to that offer. God's action in history had to be interpreted in faith by a believing community in order to be recognized, and responded to, as an action of the divine. God's Word expressed in and through the prophets, Jesus, or the Christian community, was always a human word that claimed to have its source in God's presence, power, or activity. The exodus event, for example, was a social-political event, but the Jewish people interpreted that very human event in light of their faith in a God who promised to liberate them. This is not to claim, however, that revelation is totally subjective. Rather, the revelation of the mystery of love that lies at the heart of reality occurs as a disclosure experience within ordinary human events as human beings become aware of the religious ground or depth dimension of reality. This symbolic model of revelation[9] presumes that faith (human response) and revelation (divine offer) may be distinguished but never separated and that while the dialogue or disclosure experience has a divine origin, it necessarily occurs within human experience. *Dei Verbum* never asserts that revelation occurs within human experience, a claim that has been problematic within Roman Catholicism since the Modernist crisis at the beginning of the twentieth century. Nonetheless, many theologians, most notably Karl Rahner, have pointed out that a dialogical and relational understanding of revelation does implicitly locate the revelatory dynamic of call and response within human consciousness.

Feminist theologians, while rejecting earlier understandings of revelation as supernatural truths that are authoritatively defined by an official (all-male) magisterium to which one is bound to offer "full submission of intellect and will," can find a much richer point of dialogue with a theology of revelation that is relational, dialogical, and experiential. Rosemary Radford Ruether, for example, describes revelatory experiences as "breakthrough experiences beyond ordinary fragmented consciousness that provide interpretive symbols illuminating the means of the *whole* of life."[10]

Feminist depictions of the experience of revelation can be discovered in accounts of various sorts of conversions (radical changes in awareness and/or lifestyle) as well as in descriptions of the experience of growing in friendship or other love relationships. For feminists, not only is friendship a paradigm for the divine-human encounter, but human friendships are profoundly revelatory in themselves. As Hunt maintains, "Friendship, at least as women's friendships prove, reveals a good deal about ourselves, one another, the natural community in the world, and our relationship with the divine."[11] Human friendship, befriending the earth, and friendship with God are closely related dimensions of an ongoing process of self-transcendence.

Feminists who emphasize the interconnections of human life with the rest of the cosmos can find a surprising affinity with the traditional Catholic insistence on the possibility of "natural revelation," which presumes that divine wisdom can be discovered throughout creation and all of human history (*DV* 6). Avery Dulles has noted that Vatican II's Pastoral Constitution on the Church in the Modern World, *Gaudium et Spes,* offers "hints of a wider view of revelation" with greater stress on its secular and cosmic dimensions.[12] Not content with hints, feminists explicitly locate the mystery of divine love within the mystery of human life and the cosmos. While the possibility that every human person, even the sincere atheist, can be drawn into relationship with God is clearly affirmed by the conciliar documents (*GS* 22), nowhere in the documents are the religions of the world or human experience named as revelatory. Feminist theologians, on the other hand, rely on multiple sources of revelation drawn from the religious experience of traditions beyond Christianity and from human experience.

Another undeveloped implication in the Vatican documents is that if revelation constitutes a relationship of communion with God as mediated through creation and human history, then it is necessarily an ongoing process that must be expressed and symbolized anew in every age and culture. Feminists note that not only time and culture, but also race, gender, and class, among other factors, affect the symbolic imagination through which experience of God is filtered. The process of revelation is necessarily ongoing because neither the divine nor the human mystery can ever be defined, and the relationship between the two remains ongoing and surprising. This perspective appears to contrast with the traditional Christian claim that revelation closed with the end of the apostolic age. The central point of that claim, however, was not to identify a fixed body of truths that constituted the "deposit of faith," but rather to secure the finality and uniqueness of Jesus Christ as the definitive revelation of God-among-us.[13]

The church's official teaching about the decisive climax of revelation in Jesus Christ is quite clear: "By this revelation then, the deepest truth about God and human salvation is made clear to us in Christ, who is the Mediator and at the same time the fullness of all revelation" (*DV* 2). Christian feminists, on the other hand, espouse a variety of related, but distinct, positions on whether Jesus Christ is the definitive mediator and fullness of all revelation. Some maintain (or at least imply) that Jesus is the unique and definitive revelation of God but at the same time clearly emphasize the liberating and inclusive love of God that Jesus embodied and preached.[14] Further, they sometimes cast their incarnational Christology in the female metaphor of Wisdom (Sophia) rather than the more traditional metaphor of the incarnate Word (Logos).[15] While not denying that Jesus is unique revelation of God, a number of feminist theologians call attention to the limits of *any* historical revelation of the mystery of the unknown God. Retrieving an apophatic spirituality and theology, they remind us that the incomprehensible and radically free God remains ultimately a *hidden* God and that the revelation of God even in Jesus of Nazareth remains necessarily limited.[16]

Others would concur that Jesus was a liberating prophetic figure in whose life and ministry God's all-inclusive love was experienced but would question as exclusive or arrogant any emphasis on the uniqueness or normativity of Jesus Christ.[17] Still others identify with the far more radical christological vision expressed by the Episcopalian theologian Carter Heyward:

> For here is no "male God," nor an individual able to be reified and glorified as the unique and only Son of God. . . . The focus then and now is *on us*, as participants who are empowered by the same Spirit which moved Jesus and his earlier disciples. This is, in my opinion, the christological basis of our Christian feminist movement into solidarity. . . .[18]

In this spectrum of theological positions on the central question of whether Jesus Christ is the definitive revelation of God, one can begin to see how radically the notion of the Christian tradition is being challenged. The questions keep arising: Is the Christian tradition compatible with feminist experience? Can a feminist remain a Christian and a Catholic?

Fidelity to a Living Tradition

An answer to either of those questions depends on one's understanding both of the term *tradition* and of how one remains faithful to a tradition in a radically new situation. Anthropologist Mary Catherine Bateson has suggested that the "art of improvisation" is a particular strength women have learned to cultivate whether in cooking, the arts, or making sense of their own lives when unforeseen circumstances or decisions have radically disrupted familiar patterns. The feminist attempt to reenvision a living tradition in spite of the absence of women's stories and the exclusion or faulty naming of women's experience finds a parallel in Bateson's chapter on "the vicissitudes of commitment." Using examples from the arts of painting and music as well as human relationships, she suggests that "when there is a rent in the canvas, a discord in the harmony, a betrayal, it is important not only to recover but to discover a new and inclusive pattern of meaning."[19]

Another helpful image for a feminist approach to tradition can be found in the art of quilting. While the quilting process is clearly creative, the pieces come from the earlier fabric of one's life. The art involves collaboration. Women gather (sometimes with men) to tell stories of the past as they weave together a new creation. The pieces they work with come from that past, but the inspiration and art come in designing something new. Some of the pieces come from treasured garments: baptismal gowns, wedding dresses, vestments fashioned by mothers or grandmothers but now outgrown; other pieces come from scraps that others have discarded.

The image of the quilt already suggests some of the crucial questions that arise in relation to a feminist theology of tradition. Who designs the quilt and decides what pieces will be included? From what "scrap bags" can pieces of the Christian quilt be drawn? What constitutes "usable tradition"? Are there privileged pieces that must be included in—or are even central to—the quilt of the Christian tradition? Matthew's Gospel compares the scribe who is learned in the reign of God with "the head of a household who brings forth from the treasure house things that are both new and old" (Mt 13:52). But who are the heads of the household who decide what is to be treasured and what discarded?

Specifically, when a Catholic Christian woman defines her project as "feminist theology," to what community and to whose tradition is she accountable? Rosemary Ruether, for example, identifies Women-Church[20] as a community base for her theological reflection. She states clearly that she necessarily operates within a particular historical tradition—Christianity—but from a feminist perspective consciously seeking out minority as well as majority traditions within that community, its repressed pre-Christian side as well as its dominant tradition.[21] She explicitly rejects any form of Christian exclusivism and affirms an equal value to different feminist theologies drawn from different cultural syntheses.

One of the few Catholic feminists to state explicitly her view of tradition, Ruether would expand the boundaries of "usable tradition" to include five sources: (1) Scripture, both Hebrew and Christian (Old and New Testaments); (2) marginalized or "heretical" Christian traditions such as Gnosticism, Montanism, Quakerism, Shakerism; (3) the primary theological themes of the dominant stream of classical Christian theology—Orthodox, Catholic, and Protestant; (4) non-Christian Near Eastern and Greco-Roman religion and philosophy; and (5) critical post-Christian worldviews such as liberalism, romanticism, and Marxism.

Yet because all of these traditions remain sexist, she is explicit about her norm for inclusion, exclusion, or "correction" of a tradition: the feminist critical principle of the promotion of the full humanity of women. Specifically, "Whatever denies, diminishes, or distorts the full humanity of women is, therefore, appraised as not redemptive. . . . What does promote the full humanity of women is of the Holy, it does reflect true relation to the divine, it is the true nature of things, the authentic message of redemption and the mission of redemptive community."[22]

Ruether speaks of appropriating "the best insights" of Christianity and Judaism into "a new option" and remaining "open to authentic spirit wherever it is found."[23] Obviously the notion of tradition and ecclesial identity has been expanded radically here. Can this changing, dynamic, creative, and inclusive feminist approach to tradition find points of dialogue and compatibility within a tradition that calls itself "catholic," or are the two "beyond speaking terms"?

Previous to Vatican II, the term *tradition* was often used interchangeably with the term *revelation,* and both were identified with a body of unchanging church teachings defined authoritatively by the official magisterium. While tradition was never defined by the Council, the title of chapter 2 of *Dei Verbum* gives the best clue to its fundamental approach to tradition: "The Transmission of Divine Revelation." Tradition is first and foremost a process—the transmission or handing on of the mystery of God's self-communication in creation and history that culminates in salvation history and reaches its fullness in Christ. As Joseph Ratzinger has noted, "Tradition is ultimately based on the fact that the Christ event cannot be limited to the age of the historical Jesus, but continues in the presence of the Spirit."[24]

The content of tradition—the *traditum* or that which is handed on—is as broad as the authentic life of the church. As *Dei Verbum* states: "Now what was handed on by the apostles includes everything which contributes to the holiness of life, and the increase in faith of the People of God; and so the Church, in her teaching, life, and worship, perpetuates and hands on to all generations all that she herself is, all that she believes" (*DV* 8).

While that last sentence initially appears to incorporate historical distortions into the church's authentic tradition, a careful hermeneutic of this church document reveals that its intent was quite the opposite. The original draft of *Dei Verbum* proposed the wording "the Church perpetuates and generates all that she herself is, *all that she has,* and all that she believes" (emphasis added). The Council speeches reveal that the underlined phrase was omitted precisely because of the danger of distortions creeping into the living tradition of faith. As Ratzinger noted, however, in commenting on this passage soon after the Council, even this deletion was an inadequate adjustment to make the point; Vatican II "more or less ignored the whole question of the criticism of tradition."[25]

For Catholics, tradition is located not in specific texts, but in a people, the community of faith. If tradition is ultimately the process through which the Church, in the power of the Spirit, hands on its authentic identity, where is that identity to be found? In a privileged and primary way, the Christian churches have insisted that the mystery of Jesus Christ—the Word of God that has been entrusted to the church—is to be found in the Scriptures. Thus, to the great delight of observers from the Reformation tradition, *Dei Verbum* asserts, "[The Church] has always regarded the Scriptures together with sacred tradition as the supreme rule of faith, and will ever do so" (par. 21).[26]

Another primary form of tradition is the liturgy or public worship of the church. Recent theological work by liturgical theologians has demonstrated that the liturgical praxis of the early church was a primary source of both biblical kerygma and later church doctrine (for example, divinity of Christ, Trinity). The "fathers of the church" are cited specifically as classic witnesses to the presence of the Spirit in the practice and life of the believing and praying church.

While the Scriptures and the liturgy are the richest expressions of the religious experience of the Christian community and are foundational for the formation of the faith of the community, multiple interpretations of their meaning are possible precisely because of their richly symbolic and evocative mode of expression. Some interpretations of faith, however, threaten the core beliefs and identity of the Christian community. Thus official church teaching or doctrine (called dogma when it is proclaimed with solemn authority) has been called by Karl Rahner "theology for which the church is responsible."[27] Based on the judgment of the official teachers in the community (magisterium), doctrine defines the limits or boundaries of the formulation of the beliefs of the church. Most frequently official doctrines have been concerned with specific issues disputed in polemical contexts (for example, the divinity of Christ during the fourth-century Arian controversy). While Ratzinger and others oppose terminology that speaks of Catholic teaching as changing and prefer to speak of the "development of doctrine and the continuity of the tradition," the historical evidence is indisputable: slavery, forbidding usury, anti-Semitism, even the torture of prisoners in the papal states were all acceptable practices and teachings at one point in the history of the church, yet no one would claim any one of them as part of the authentic tradition.[28]

The broadest and most elusive category *Dei Verbum* uses in speaking of how tradition is interpreted and handed on is the reference to "the life of the church." Noting that the Holy Spirit is the primary active subject of tradition, the document speaks of tradition "growing" or "making progress" through the religious experience of believers and of the community of faith:

> The tradition that comes from the apostles makes progress in the Church, with the help of the Holy Spirit. There is a growth in insight into the realities and words that are being passed on. This comes about in various ways. It comes through the contemplation and study of believers who ponder these things in their hearts (cf. Lk 2:19 and 51). It comes from the intimate sense of spiritual realities which they experience. And it comes from the preaching of those who have received, along with their right of succession in the episcopate, the sure charism of truth. (*DV* 8)

The most recent Roman Catholic teaching on tradition has some remarkable points of convergence with feminist theology. Both approach tradition as a process of handing on the mystery of revelation that includes the wisdom of ancestors in the tradition as well as "the intimate sense of spiritual realities" of present communities of believers. Both call for handing on the community's wisdom through words, rituals, and "the entire life of the community." Both recognize the possibility of distortion within a living tradition of faith.

But there are significant differences—troubling especially to those who claim a place in both traditions. At the core of the differences are questions of boundaries and authority, of dogmatic teaching and official teachers, of normative Scriptures and classic liturgical symbols. Behind it all, the refrain recurs: "Whose experience counts?"[29] Attention to disputes over how the primary Christian symbols of liturgy and Scripture function within the Catholic Christian tradition will underscore the basic issues in conflict as those who would call themselves both feminist and Catholic wrestle with their deepest fidelities.

LEX ORANDI, LEX CREDENDI:
LITURGY AND THE LIVING TRADITION

The questions surrounding the tradition and "whose experience counts" are brought into focus nowhere more painfully than in liturgy. With the liturgical renewal in the Catholic church, the profound truth of the ancient claim *lex orandi, lex credendi* (the rule of prayer forms the rule of belief) has been highlighted. Yet precisely because communal ritual celebration is recognized as central to the formation of a community of faith by feminists as well as other Christians, liturgy has become arguably the most divisive and painful reminder of the pervasive patriarchy within the Roman Catholic tradition. The church does indeed perpetuate itself in worship (*DV* 8). At the deepest level this means that the mystery of the Body of Christ is formed and handed on in worship and in a central way through the Eucharist. At the same time, an androcentric worldview and patriarchal control are also perpetuated in a male-dominated sacramental system that is legitimated in the name of Jesus and by the authority of "God's will." A symbolic analysis of the eucharistic assembly makes it painfully clear "whose experience counts." If the Eucharist is indeed the center of Catholic spirituality, then for an increasing number of feminists "the center can no longer hold."

A growing number of women (and men) are voting with their feet by forming alternative communities of worship more inclusive of women's experience. As Ruether explains:

> Women in contemporary churches are suffering from linguistic deprivation and eucharistic famine. They can no longer nurture their souls in alienating words that ignore or systematically deny their existence. . . . We must begin to incarnate the community of faith in the liberation of humanity from patriarchy in words and deed, in new words, new prayers, new symbols, and new praxis.[30]

Not all feminists are agreed, however, that separation from the traditional Roman Catholic eucharistic table is wise or necessary. Liturgical theologian Mary Collins admits that a "clash of eucharistic horizons" is at the very heart of contemporary conflict over the authentic Catholic and Christian tradition. Yet it is precisely for that reason that she argues for the importance of women reclaiming the Eucharist. No matter how clerical and patriarchal the actual celebration, the Eucharist is the action of the whole church according to the documents of Vatican II.[31] She grants that the institutional church has in many ways failed to implement this profound reform and perpetuated instead "neoclerical liturgy and church order." Yet she insists that while "power relations in the church are a facet of the eucharist's meaning," to reduce eucharistic symbolism to that accurate but limited, political analysis is to miss the central meaning of Eucharist: "The strong sign of the assembly of outcasts and strangers—

people so unlike that they would never choose one another's company—being invited to welcome and to forgive one another in Jesus' name, to be at peace, to sin no more—is suppressed when we reject ambiguity and demand clarity and coherence in our ecclesial relationships before we can celebrate eucharist."[32]

Calling on the tradition of "ordinary women and the poor [who] have often worn the clerical construction of reality lightly," Collins argues for a prophetic and contemplative fidelity to the church's "living tradition of eucharistic spirituality" rather than the turn to rites of empowerment for women recreated from "an undocumented past."[33]

For feminists the critical norm for praxis and theology is: What will foster the full humanity of all women, men, and children as well as the well-being of all of creation? For Christians, fidelity to the apostolic tradition remains a touchstone of authenticity. Christian feminists argue that fidelity to both norms is possible; in fact, the two are deeply intertwined. Even more basic than the question of how one remains faithful to the apostolic tradition in our age, culture, and social location, however, is the thorny question of what constitutes the authentic apostolic tradition.

APOSTOLIC TRADITION AND THE CANONICAL SCRIPTURES

Elisabeth Schüssler Fiorenza's *In Memory of Her,* a ground-breaking feminist theological reconstruction of Christian origins, argues that the assumption that women were marginal in early Christian history is not the result of authentic fidelity to the life and ministry of Jesus and early Christian beginnings, but rather of an androcentric process of selecting, interpreting, editing, and handing on the apostolic tradition.[34] Schüssler Fiorenza contends that women did have power and the authority of the gospel in the earliest Christian discipleship of equals. They were central in the early Christian movement and assumed important roles of leadership. Her fundamental claim is that the authentic apostolic tradition cannot be identified with the canonical Scriptures, nor can the entire biblical text be considered revelatory.

Again the questions become ones of boundaries and authority to interpret the tradition. Feminist critique of the process of the formation of the canon and the identification of the canonical Scriptures with the inspired and authoritative Word of God are crucial disputes about revelation that find parallels in later controversies over heresy and official church doctrines. However, because the Christian community proclaims that sacred Scripture not only witnesses to God's Word (revelation), but in some sense *is* God's Word and remains the normative expression of the apostolic tradition for all later generations, that claim must be addressed first.

Here feminists underline a position they share with other critical biblical scholars: the expression *Word of God* is a metaphor that refers to the entire mystery of revelation—God's self-communication and offer of friendship—especially as that revelation has taken place in Jesus Christ. The Scriptures witness to the mystery of revelation, but the biblical Word of God is available only in limited human words. Feminist biblical scholars and theologians remind us that the limits of the human expression of Scripture include a patriarchal bias and an androcentric traditioning process that can fundamentally distort the revelatory good news of salvation.

While the androcentric bias of the text is widely agreed upon, what remains disputed among feminists who continue to claim their Jewish or Christian heritage is whether the entire Bible can still be considered revelatory and whether the canonical Scriptures hold authority or have a privileged place in the community. Those questions, discussed in detail in Sandra Schneiders's chapter, remain crucial to a systematic theology of revelation. Schüssler Fiorenza, for example, asserts that "the locus or place of divine revelation and grace is therefore not the Bible or the tradition of a patriarchal church but the *ekklesia* of women and the lives of women who live the 'option for our women selves.'"[35]

While some feminists dispute whether selected biblical texts can be considered revelatory, Schneiders argues that the entire discussion needs to be reframed. She describes the biblical text as a whole as revelatory but wrestles with questions of how problematic texts function within the scriptural canon. Does every text function salvifically? May not other non-biblical texts hold equal or even greater revelatory power, and therefore authority, for women? Similar issues were raised throughout the process of the development of the canon. The need for a canon of classic texts to safeguard the authentic apostolic tradition is usually defended as a necessary step in limiting and shaping the faith of the Christian community in the face of heresy.

Feminist theologians exercise a hermeneutic of suspicion, however, about the patriarchal bias operating in the process of developing the canon. That process cannot be separated from the disputes and struggles regarding women's leadership in the church. Schüssler Fiorenza reminds us that the canon is the record of the "historical winners" and remarks that "feminist studies in religion must question the patristic interpretive model that identifies heresy with women's leadership and orthodoxy with patri-archal church structures."[36] If both the content of the Scriptures and the process through which texts were selected for inclusion in the canon reflect the patriarchal control of that period of early Christianity, once again the broader issue reemerges. How does a community discern fidelity to the apostolic tradition rooted in the life and ministry of Jesus?

Here Schüssler Fiorenza proposes a broader ecumenical perspective: "Early Christian history and theology must become 'ecumenical,' that is, inclusive of all Christian groups. *All* early Christian groups and texts must be tested *as to how much* they preserve and transmit the apostolic inclusivity and equality of early Christian beginnings and revelation."[37]

This ecumenical approach with its emphasis on apostolic inclusivity and equality does not mean a rejection of the canon but rather a critical reading of both canonical and noncanonical texts. Feminists note that the canon has preserved plural visions and that the canon serves not only to perpetuate and legitimate women's inferior status but to critique it. Schüssler Fiorenza also cautions against an idealization of what have been traditionally considered "heretical texts" since they too are the products of patriarchal cultures and can be equally (or more) oppressive of women.[38]

The feminist challenge regarding the interpretation and unques-tioned normativity of the Scriptures in judging all later developments in the Christian community (including feminism) is at least theoretically compatible with a Roman Catholic perspective on the relationship be-tween Scripture and tradition. The Bible remains the church's book; it developed from the experience of early Christian communities; it has been interpreted and handed on by the church throughout the ages; and it remains the task of the church to interpret the Word of God in every time and culture.

DOGMA, *SENSUS FIDELIUM*, AND THE MAGISTERIUM: WHOSE EXPERIENCE COUNTS?

Essentially the process of the development of doctrine or official church teaching raises issues similar to those surrounding the canon of Scripture. In the face of polemical disputes that seemed to threaten the very identity of the authentic Christian tradition, some official boundaries for belief were judged to be necessary. Thus the Christian church, while never attempting to define the mystery of Christ, for example, made classic statements about what was beyond the scope of Christian belief (for exam-ple, denial of the full humanity or full divinity of Christ).

Feminists critically appropriate church teaching only after analyzing the political dynamics at work in the process, the dominant "interests" that were being protected, the doctrine's "effective history" or impact on the ongoing life of the Christian community, and the ideologies that may have been operating in the development or transmission of the doctrine. This hermeneutic of suspicion is used regardless of the "level of authority" with which a doctrine is taught because Christian feminists take seriously the claim that divine revelation, the Word of God, is entrusted to "the entire church" and assume that baptismal charism and responsibility include a role in the prophetic mission of the church.

This claiming of voice and responsibility within the life of "the entire church" can be viewed as an active exercise of the role of the *sensus fidelium*[39] in the development and preservation of the authentic tradition of the church. Both the Arian crisis of the fourth century and the emergence of the Marian dogmas in the nineteenth and twentieth centuries give evidence of the importance of listening to the experience and insights of "the entire church" before speaking on behalf of the whole community. Yet feminists protest that women's voices have been systematically filtered out of the decision making of the church when those voices are in conflict with the dominant voice of the magisterium.[40] While *Dei Verbum* rejected an earlier distinction between "the teaching church" (*ecclesia docens*) and the "learning church" (*ecclesia discens*) and clearly moved beyond Pius XII's assertion that the Word of God is entrusted "solely to the magisterium,"[41] no structures were established to promote and protect the kind of dialogue necessary for discerning what are authentic developments of the tradition in our day if the Word of God truly is entrusted to "the entire church."

Vatican II, while highlighting the role of all the baptized in handing on the authentic Word of God, nonetheless emphasizes that the ultimate judgment of the authenticity of an interpretation of the Word of God "has been entrusted to the living teaching office of the Church alone" (*DV* 10). The magisterium (bishops throughout the world in union with the pope) is seen to exercise a divinely authorized role of leadership, governance, and judgment that can be traced back to the apostles. Still that authority is itself subject to a higher authority: "Yet this Magisterium is not superior to the Word of God, but is its servant. It teaches only what has been handed on to it" (*DV* 10).

If the Word of God has been entrusted to the entire church, feminists question how that Word can be heard and proclaimed if the people of God are not listened to or even consulted. How a feminist ecclesiology might structure the role of "discernment of spirits" and judgment on behalf of the community is a question beyond the scope of this chapter.[42] In terms of the handing on of the authentic tradition, however, feminist objections to the role of the magisterium center around the all-male and clerical control of the magisterium, legitimated by claims about Jesus' selection of twelve male apostles, as well as the authoritarian and hierarchical operation of the magisterium at the present time. In the end, the crisis of tradition is an ecclesiological crisis. Who constitutes the community of the church? Who speaks in the name of the community? Whose experience is considered revelatory or congruent with earlier privileged revelation? By whom and by what process are those judgments made?

CAN THE CENTER HOLD? THE CRITICAL QUESTIONS

Feminism challenges profoundly the understanding of revelation in the Roman Catholic tradition. It raises fundamental questions about the relationship of revelation and human experience, the centrality of Jesus Christ, the identity and structure of the church, the public worship of the church, the normativity and authentic interpretation of Scripture and the apostolic tradition. On the one hand, in what sense can the Catholic church (or even the larger Christian Church) claim to be faithful to the life and mission of Jesus when it is so fundamentally distorted by patriarchal structures and sexist attitudes and practices? On the other hand, at what point are Christian feminists no longer identifiably Christian in belief, ritual, or practice?

Whether there is room in the Roman Catholic tradition for the growing number of committed feminists and whether feminists can continue to find life and truth in the Roman Catholic tradition remain to be seen. At the present time many feminists consider themselves "the loyal opposition." Other see themselves in exile. Still others have begun the "exodus from patriarchy" and are looking for, or have found, homes elsewhere—in other Christian communites, in a wide variety of gatherings of Women-Church, or even beyond the boundaries of Christianity. The question remains: Can the center hold?

To date, most feminist theological work in this area has focused on critique of the dominant patriarchal bias throughout the tradition, retrieval of forgotten persons, memories, and moments that were excluded from the dominant androcentric naming of the tradition, and creative reconstruction of the tradition. As feminist theological scholarship continues to develop, diversity begins to unfold at the center—at the level of fundamental theology.

While feminists, for example, claim that revelation is located in experience, the meaning of that assertion is notoriously difficult to clarify. Does experience refer to an individual interior awareness or feeling, something like Shug's claim that "God is inside you and inside everybody else"? Is revelation mediated through human experience, or are the two identical? Is revelation located in the "transcendental depths" of the human person and mediated through her historical and social existence? If the experiences of suffering and oppression of women (and others) is the starting point for a liberationist approach to feminist theology, can we speak more fruitfully of revelation as located in "contrast experience"? Is revelation located only or primarily or in any privileged way in women's experience? If so, which women's experiences and on what basis is that claim made? Further, what experience is considered revelatory: women's historical experience of marginalization; women's experience as rooted in the body, imagination, and sexuality; women's friendships; women's mystical experience; women's bonding in circles of celebration, support, and activity for justice in Women-Church and/or beyond?

Claims that women's experience is revelatory or that revelation is located within the *ekklesia* of women or the process of women opting for "women selves" all reflect the feminist reminder that we can speak only from our own experience, not make universal claims. Such statements do not necessarily limit revelation to women's experience but rather highlight what has been overlooked or intentionally excluded in the history of the tradition. Nonetheless, for feminists who also identify their stance as Christian, that statement needs to be balanced by the radical inclusivity of the gospel and other feminist claims regarding apostolic inclusivity and equality.

Feminists are not alone in raising questions that go to the very heart of the Christian tradition. The question of the uniqueness of Jesus Christ as revelation of God faces many other Christian theologians who are attempting to rethink traditional Christian claims in the context of the religions of the world. The questions of normative Christian liturgical symbols and appropriate leadership at liturgy are being raised in diverse situations of enculturation around the globe. More fundamental are the issues of fidelity and identity. As Christians claiming our baptism we commit ourselves to the God revealed in Jesus Christ in and through the power of the Spirit, to a life of discipleship, to fidelity to the gospel and the apostolic tradition, to the central symbols of Scripture and liturgy, to the authentic tradition of the church, to communion with the universal Church. As feminists we also make explicit our basic commitment to the full life and dignity of every woman, man, and child and to the flourishing of creation. Feminist Catholics continue to hope that the revelation of God among us may be discovered in the intersection of those commitments.

NOTES

1. Alice Walker, *The Color Purple* (New York: Washington Square Press, 1982), 202.

2. See Elisabeth Schüssler Fiorenza, "Why Not the Category Friend/Friendship?" *Horizons* 2, no. 1 (Spring 1975): 117–18; Anne Carr, *Transforming Grace: Christian Tradition and Women's Experience* (San Francisco: Harper & Row, 1988), 150, 213; Mary Hunt, *Fierce Tenderness: A Feminist Theology of Friendship* (New York: Crossroad, 1991), esp. 80–84; Elizabeth A. Johnson, *She Who Is: The Mystery of God in Feminist Theological Discourse* (New York: Crossroad, 1992); Sallie McFague, *Models of God: Theology for an Ecological, Nuclear Age* (Philadelphia: Fortress Press, 1987).

3. See Luz Beatriz Arellano, "Women's Experience of God in Emerging Spirituality," in *With Passion and Compassion,* ed. Virginia Fabella and Mercy Amba Oduyoye (Maryknoll, NY: Orbis Books, 1988), 135–50; Dorothee Sölle, *Suffering* (Philadelphia: Fortress Press, 1975). For systematic analysis, note Johnson's use of the category of "contrast experience" as revelatory in *She Who Is,* 58–60.

4. For a fundamental rejection of the category *divine revelation* and critique of the universal term *women's experience* see Sheila Greeve Davaney, "The Limits of the Appeal to Women's Experience," in *Shaping New Vision: Gender and Values in American Culture,* ed. Clarissa W. Atkinson, Constance H. Buchanan, and Margaret Miles (Ann Arbor: UMI Research Press, 1987), 31–49.

5. "Women in the Ministerial Priesthood," *Origins* 6 (Feb. 3, 1977): 518–24. The quotations that follow are taken from 522–23.

6. Hunt, *Fierce Tenderness,* 79.

7. Cf. Avery Dulles, *Revelation Theology: A History* (New York: Herder & Herder, 1969), 156.

8. *DS* (Denzinger Schoenmetzer) 3011. The issues at Vatican I actually centered around the relationship of faith and reason, rather than the nature of revelation and faith. See Dermot Lane, *The Experience of God: An Invitation to Do Theology* (New York: Paulist Press, 1981), 45–49.

9. See Avery Dulles, "The Symbolic Structure of Revelation," *Theological Studies* 41 (1980): 51–73; Lane, *The Experience of God,* 28–49; Thomas F. O'Meara, "Toward a Subjective Theology of Revelation," *Theological Studies* 36 (1975): 401–27; and Edward Schillebeeckx, *Christ: The Experience of Jesus as Lord,* trans. John Bowden (New York: Seabury Press, 1980), 29–79.

10. Rosemary Radford Ruether, *Sexism and God-Talk* (Boston: Beacon Press, 1983), 13. Cf. Avery Dulles's description of the dynamics of religious conversion as a process of discovery in "Revelation and Discovery," in *Theology and Discovery,* ed. William J. Kelly (Milwaukee: Marquette Univ. Press, 1980), 10.

11. Hunt, *Fierce Tenderness,* 80.

12. Dulles, *Revelation Theology,* 158.

13. See Avery Dulles, "The Meaning of Revelation," in *The Dynamic in Christian Thought,* ed. Joseph Papin (Villanova, PA: Villanova Univ. Press, 1970), 76–79.

14. See, for example, Sandra M. Schneiders, *The Revelatory Text* (San Francisco: Harper San Francisco, 1991), 53: "[Jesus] is the Word made flesh, God incarnate, symbolic revelation fully achieved." Cf. Sandra M. Schneiders, *Beyond Patching* (New York: Paulist Press, 1991), 50. In *Transforming Grace* Anne Carr refers to "the divine presence this historical figure [Jesus] bears as 'God with us'" (161). See also Therese Souga, "The Christ-Event from the Viewpoint of an African Woman," in *With Passion and Compassion,* ed. Virgina Fabella and Mercy Amba Oduyoye (Maryknoll, NY: Orbis Press, 1988), 22–29.

15. See Elisabeth Johnson, "Jesus, the Wisdom of God: A Biblical Basis for a Non-Androcentric Christology," *Ephemerides Theologicae Lovanienses* 60 : 4 (December 1985). 261–94.

16. See Johnson, *She Who Is,* 106–7; Carr, *Transforming Grace,* 156. Cf. David Tracy, "The Hermeneutics of Naming God," *Irish Theological Quarterly* 57 (1991): 253–64; Roger Haight, *Dynamics of Theology* (New York: Paulist Press, 1990), 67; and Edward Schillebeeckx, *Church: The Human Story of God,* trans. John Bowden (New York: Crossroad, 1990), 165–66.

17. See Rosemary Radford Ruether, *To Change the World: Christology and Cultural Criticism* (New York: Crossroad, 1981), 38–39, and *Sexism and God-Talk,* 121–22.

18. Carter Heyward, "An Unfinished Symphony of Liberation: The Radicalization of Christian Feminism Among White U.S. Women," *Journal of Feminist Studies in Religion* 1, no. 1 (1985): 115.

19. Mary Catherine Bateson, *Composing a Life* (New York: Penguin, 1989), 211.

20. Rosemary Radford Ruether, *Women-Church: Theology and Practice* (San Francisco: Harper & Row, 1985), 59–61. For alternative descriptions of Women-Church (or Womanchurch) see Carr, *Transforming Grace,* 200; Elisabeth Schüssler Fiorenza, *In Memory of Her: A Feminist Theological Reconstruction of Christian Origins* (New York: Crossroad, 1983), 343–51; Schneiders, *Beyond Patching,* 105–6.

21. Ruether, *Sexism and God-Talk,* 21. See also *Women-Church,* 38. Cf. Schüssler Fiorenza's "critical commitment to Christian community and its traditions," *In Memory of Her,* xxii.

22. Ruether, *Sexism and God-Talk,* 18–19. For the discussion of "usable tradition," see 20–22.

23. Ruether, *Women-Church,* 40.

24. Joseph Ratzinger, "The Transmission of Divine Revelation," chap. 2, *Dogmatic Constitution on Divine Revelation,* in *Commentary on the Documents of Vatican II,* vol. 3, ed. Herbert Vorgrimler (New York: Herder & Herder, 1969), 189.

25. Ratzinger, "The Transmission of Divine Revelation," 185.

26. Any explicit statement that Scripture judges the church still remains lacking, but Ratzinger does note that Scripture is used factually as a yardstick of tradition in Article 21; see "The Transmission of Divine Revelation," 193.

27. Karl Rahner, "What Is a Dogmatic Statement?" in *Theological Investigations,* vol. 5, trans. Karl-H. Kruger (Baltimore: Helicon Press, 1966), 42–66.

28. See Walter Principe, "When Authentic Teachings Change," *The Ecumenist* (July–Aug., 1987), 70–73. The best example in recent times of a major change in Catholic teaching is Vatican II's "Decree on Religious Liberty."

29. See Monika Hellwig, *Whose Experience Counts in Theological Reflection?* The Pere Marquette Lecture, 1982 (Milwaukee: Marquette Univ. Press, 1982).

30. Ruether, *Women-Church,* 5. Note Schüssler Fiorenza's comment in response to the charge that the church of women does not share in the fullness of church: "This is correct, but neither do exclusive male hierarchical assemblies"; *In Memory of Her,* 346.

31. General Instruction on the Roman Missal, 1–7; *Sacrosanctum Concilium,* 14.

32. Mary Collins, "Is the Eucharist Still a Source of Meaning for Women?" *Origins* 21 (Sept. 12, 1991): 228.

33. Collins, "Eucharist," 229. See also, however, Collins's *Women at Prayer* (New York: Paulist Press, 1987), where she argues for the importance of feminist contemplative and liturgical prayer and encourages women to listen for "the inner word of divine mystery trying to find its voice through them" (43–44).

34. Schüssler Fiorenza, *In Memory of Her,* 56. Note that this patriarchal traditioning process continues with the privileged status accorded the "fathers of the church" and even the naming of that period of early Christianity as the "patristic period."

35. Elisabeth Schüssler Fiorenza, "The Will to Choose or to Reject: Continuing our Critical Work," in *Feminist Interpretation of the Bible,* ed. Letty M. Russell (Philadelphia: Westminster Press, 1985), 128. Elsewhere she describes this locus more broadly to include "the discipleship of equals in the past and present." "The locus of revelation is not the androcentric text but the life and ministry of Jesus and the movement of women and men called forth by him"; *In Memory of Her,* 41.

36. Schüssler Fiorenza, *In Memory of Her,* 53, 55.

37. Schüssler Fiorenza, *In Memory of Her,* 56.

38. Schüssler Fiorenza, *In Memory of Her,* 56; 66 n. 37.

39. See J. M. R. Tillard, "Sensus Fidelium," *One in Christ* 11 (1975): 2–29; Avery Dulles, "Sensus Fidelium," *America* (Nov. 1, 1986): 240–42, 263; J. B. Metz and E. Schillebeeckx, eds., *The Teaching Authority of All Believers,* Concilium 180 (Edinburgh: T. & T. Clark, 1985).

40. Note Bishop P. Francis Murphy's observation that "the most serious concern raised by Vatican officials [regarding the proposed U.S. Bishops' Pastoral on Women's Concerns] was the consultation process. . . . They asserted that bishops are teachers, not learners; truth cannot emerge through consultation"; "Let's Start Over: A Bishop Appraises the Pastoral on Women," *Commonweal* (Sept. 25, 1992), 12.

41. Ratzinger, "The Transmission of Divine Revelation," 196.

42. Note Ruether's comment that "the agents of tradition have a valid task of 'testing the spirits' for not everything that claims to be of God is so" (*Women-Church,* 35).

FOR FURTHER READING

Carr, Anne. *Transforming Grace: Christian Tradition and Women's Experience*. San Francisco: Harper & Row, 1988. Overview of how women's experience can transform the Christian tradition. Particularly helpful for issues of fundamental theology are the sections on "women's experience"; feminist spirituality; the underlying issues in debates on women's ordination.

Chopp, Rebecca S. *The Power to Speak: Feminism, Language, God*. New York: Crossroad, 1989. From a Protestant perspective, reconstruction of proclamation as discourse of emancipatory transformation and the Word as perfectly open sign. Envisions feminist theology as proclamation of the Word in women's words that envision new ways of human flourishing.

Fiorenza, Elisabeth Schüssler. *In Memory of Her: A Feminist Theological Reconstruction of Christian Origins*. New York: Crossroad, 1983. A feminist reconstruction of the earliest Christian movement that emphasizes women's leadership and agency. Addresses fundamental issues of the locus of revelation, the authority of the Bible, the development of the canon, the androcentric selection and transmission of early Christian traditions and texts, and critical biblical hermeneutics.

Hellwig, Monika. *Whose Experience Counts in Theological Reflection?* Milwaukee: Marquette Univ. Press, 1982. Highlights the revelatory role of experience in contemporary theology; argues for the importance of listening to the voices that have traditionally been excluded or marginalized in theological discourse if we are to discern God's self-revelation in history.

Hunt, Mary E. *Fierce Tenderness: A Feminist Theology of Friendship*. New York: Crossroad, 1991. Suggests that the mystery of divine love is most fully disclosed in women's friendships characterized by justice. Dismisses traditional categories of revelation and inspiration and proposes that women's friendships reveal something about one another, the natural order, and the divine.

Isasi-Díaz, Ada María, and Yolanda Tarango. *Hispanic Women: Prophetic Voice in the Church*. Philadelphia: Fortress Press, 1988. Presents the experience of Hispanic women as revelatory and authoritative through the use of first-person narratives. Emphasizes the importance of locating the experience of revelation in community, culture, and popular religiosity and argues that biblical revelation has not been central to Hispanic women's experience.

Johnson, Elizabeth. *She Who Is: The Mystery of God in Feminist Theological Discourse*. New York: Crossroad, 1992. Rethinks the Trinity from a feminist perspective and analyzes women's experience; gives brief lines of a hermeneutic of revelation with a strong accent on the hiddenness and incomprehensibility of God.

Ruether, Rosemary Radford. *Sexism and God-Talk*. Boston: Beacon Press, 1983. Discusses explicitly the meaning of the claim that women's experience is revelatory, critiques the sociological process by which the authoritative canon of Scripture and orthodox tradition is defined, and offers a proposal for what might constitute "usable tradition" for feminists.

Schneiders, Sandra M. *The Revelatory Text: Interpreting the New Testament as Sacred Scripture*. San Francisco: Harper San Francisco, 1991. Presents a clear and nuanced discussion of a number of issues in fundamental theology, including a theology of revelation as symbolic, the meaning of the term *Word of God* as applied the Scriptures, the relation-ship of Scripture and tradition, and the development of the canon.

———. *Beyond Patching: Faith and Feminism in the Catholic Church*. Mahwah, NJ: Paulist Press, 1991. Overview of questions related to biblical revelation and women's experi-ence as revelatory.

CHAPTER FOUR

GOD IN COMMUNION WITH US

— The Trinity —

CATHERINE MOWRY LACUGNA

THE MOST FAMOUS artistic portrayal of the Trinity is the icon painted by Andrei Rublev early in the fifteenth century in Russia. It depicts three angels seated around a table on which there is a eucharistic cup. In the background are a house and tree. The icon was inspired, as the greatest works of trinitarian art have been, by the story in Genesis 18 of the visit of three men to the home of Abraham and Sarah. Abraham met the strangers outside, and despite not knowing their identity he called upon Sarah, and together they showed the visitors extraordinary hospitality. While the visitors reclined under the oaks of Mamre, Sarah baked bread and Abraham prepared the meal. In the process of sharing the resources of their household, the identity of the visitors was revealed to be Yahweh and two angels. Yahweh then promised that the elderly Sarah and Abraham would have a child, Isaac.

How fitting indeed that hospitality, and the quite ordinary setting of a household, should have emerged as the inspiration for this icon and so many other artistic interpretations of the Trinity. In Rublev's icon, the temple in the background is the transformation of Abraham's and Sarah's house. The oak tree stands for the Tree of Life. And the position of the three figures is suggestive. Although they are arranged in a circle, the circle is not closed. One has the distinct sensation when meditating on the icon that one is not only invited into this communion but, indeed, one already is part of it. A self-contained God, a closed divine society, would hardly be a fitting archetype of hospitality. We should also not miss the significance of the eucharistic cup in the center, which is, of course, the sacramental sign of our communion with God and with one another.

This icon expresses the fundamental insight of the doctrine of the Trinity, namely, that God is not far from us but lives among us in a communion of persons. And yet, ironically, the doctrine of the Trinity has been seen as a stumbling block to the concerns of Christian feminism on at least two fronts. First, trinitarian theology has been seen to compromise the feminist concern for the equality of women and men, primarily because the relationship among the divine persons has been seen as hierarchical. This arrangement has been used to reinforce a "complementarity" theory of the true nature of male and female. According to this theology, femaleness and maleness are radically different ways of being human. Man is the head over woman; man fully images God while woman images God by virtue of her relationship to man. Woman's being is derived from man's. Further, sexual differentiation between women and men is interpreted to mean that it is God's will that men serve in public leadership roles, while women are created for domestic roles. These roles are not interchangeable. Although women and men are equal with respect to their God-given dignity, it belongs to natural law and to the order of creation that women be subordinate to men. Although the theology of complementarity belongs properly to theological anthropology, it emerges in the present chapter because appeal is often made to the doctrine of the Trinity to support the subordination of women to men.

Second, because God is named Father, Son, and Spirit, the doctrine of the Trinity has been seen to reinforce solely masculine images for God. The exclusive use of masculine images in worship or in theology contributes to an overwhelming sense of God as male. This constitutes religious legitimization of patriarchy in the sense that not only is the human male normative for all human experience, God is imaged and addressed and conceptualized in terms that are thoroughly masculine.

The problem seems to be that we have forgotten the essential truths expressed in the doctrine of the Trinity. In this chapter I will first give an account of how the doctrine of the Trinity emerged and retrieve and reformulate its essential affirmations about the nature of God for us and the nature of human personhood. The doctrine of the Trinity is the specifically Christian way of speaking of God, and therefore it frames the discussion of the common ground of Christian theism and feminist concerns. Second, I will examine from the perspective of trinitarian theology the theology of complementarity and third explore various approaches to God-language that have been offered, ending with theological reflection on the common ground between the Christian theology of God and feminist concerns.

THE DOCTRINE OF THE TRINITY:
THE PREEMINENTLY PERSONAL GOD

The doctrine of the Trinity emerged in the protracted and awkward process of sorting out competing christological claims being advanced early in the fourth century.[1] In the early 300s Arius taught that Jesus Christ was subordinate to God and therefore of a different "substance" (*ousia*) than God. The Council of Nicaea (325) countered that Jesus Christ was *of the same substance* (*homoousios*) with God the Father, begotten from the substance of the Father. The Council's teaching hardly settled the matter. The next fifty years were a time of great ferment and controversy, with outstanding theologians such as Athanasius taking the lead and eventually setting the standard for doctrinal orthodoxy.

Arianism, however, was not eliminated but mutated into new forms. One particularly strong strain was Eunomianism. Eunomius believed the basic Arian premise that God was so utterly transcendent that God could not traffic with any element of the created order except through intermediaries. Jesus Christ was just such an intermediary, less than God. Further, Eunomius believed that he could name the essence of God: Unbegottenness. To be God is to be Unbegotten; since Jesus Christ is Begotten, he cannot be of the same essence as God.

The Cappadocians—Basil, Gregory of Nyssa, and Gregory of Nazianzus—brought to bear their considerable theological acumen against Eunomius. They began with the assumption that the essence of God is, strictly speaking, unknowable and unnameable. It is important to keep in mind that up to this point there was not yet a doctrine of the Trinity per se, not yet a sense of "intradivine" Fatherhood, at least as this eventually was understood. Second, *God* and *Father* were synonyms. Thus when Nicaea proclaimed that the Son was begotten from the substance of the Father, this was tantamount to saying the Son was begotten from the substance of God. Third, there was no clear distinction between *ousia* (substance) and *hypostasis* (person). Accordingly, the two Gregories argued against Eunomius that unbegottenness is not the property of the un-knowable divine essence. Rather, unbegottenness is the property of a divine *person*, namely, the person of the Father. Begottenness is the prop-erty of another divine person, namely, the Son. Therefore Father and Son *can share* the same substance, even though they are altogether different hypostatically (in personhood).

This brilliant move against Eunomius, which gave birth to the first complete trinitarian doctrine of God, produced three important distinc-tions: first, between *hypostasis* and *ousia*. It was now proper to distin-guish between *hypostasis* and *ousia* and to speak of the one God as existing in three hypostases. Second, a new distinction emerged between Father-hood and Godhood; they were no longer synonyms. It was now possible to think of "God" as self-differentiated: the Father is God, and the Son is God. Third—and this is most important of all—the Cappadocians made *person rather than substance* the primary ontological category. The theoretical and practical significance of this should not be overlooked, as if it were only a fine point within speculative theology. As a matter of fact, this principle not only made a doctrine of the Trinity possible in the first place, it is also the very principle that stands in direct contradiction to the patriarchal idea of God as essentially unrelated. Eunomius, like Arius, made God's nonrelationality primary. This was the significance of calling God Unbegotten. For Eunomius, in other words, the personal property of God—that which makes God to be God—is to be altogether unrelated to another. The Cappadocians rejected Eunomius's definition of God as Unbegotten and argued instead that the unoriginate God is always the Unoriginate *origin:* origin of the Son, of the Holy Spirit, and of the world.

In other words, the radical move of the Cappadocians was to assert that divinity or Godhood originates with personhood (someone toward another), not with substance (something in and of itself). Love for and relationship with another is primary over autonomy, ecstasis over stasis, fecundity over self-sufficiency. Thus personhood, being-in-relation-to-another, was secured as the ultimate originating principle of all reality. The metaphysical implication of the Cappadocian argument is that the divine essence derives from divine personhood. As the contemporary Greek theologian John Zizioulas puts it, "God exists on account of a person, the Father, and not on account of a substance."[2] If God were not personal, God would not exist at all.

According to Greek theology, persons are defined by their "relation of origin," from whence they come. For example, the Son is defined by origin from the Father: the Son is begotten from the Father. The Holy Spirit likewise originates from the Father: the Spirit proceeds from the Father. The identity and unique reality of a person emerges entirely in relation to another person. Persons, whether divine or human, are not first who or what they are and then have relationships to another. Although God the Father's personhood is defined as "to be from no one" (Unoriginate), it is precisely the economy of Christ and the Spirit that introduces the all-important qualification: the unoriginate God is by nature originating and related. God by nature is outgoing love and self-donation.

This new way of conceiving God greatly affected many previously held assumptions about God. One in particular is important for our purposes here. For the Bible, the liturgy, early creeds, and for all the theologians stretching from the Apologists through Irenaeus, Origen, Athanasius, and the Cappadocians, God the Father was seen as the monarch (*monē archē,* sole rule or origin), the origin and cause of everything, including origin and cause of Son and Spirit. The idea of the divine monarchy worked well enough as long as God and Father were synonyms and as long as the Son was seen as subordinate to the Father. However, neither is tenable if Father, Son, and Spirit are equally God.[3] The theoretical apparatus had been put in place to rule out any subordination of Christ to God. Gregory of Nazianzus resolved the tension over the monarchy with a radical proposal. He wrote, "The three most ancient opinions concerning God are Anarchia, Polyarchia, and Monarchia. Monarchy is that which we honor: not a monarchy limited to a single person but a monarchy constituted by equal dignity of nature, accord of will, identity of movement, and the return to unity of those who come from it."[4]

In effect, Gregory's idea of a shared divine *archē* entirely eliminated any remaining traces of an Arian subordination of the Son to the Father-monarch. Further, this unprecedented reconception of the divine monarchy contained the seeds of a radical social order. The divine unity was no longer located in the Father-God who was prior to or greater than everyone and everything else. Instead, the divine unity and divine life were located in the communion among equal though unique persons, not in the primacy of one person over another. *Trinitarian* monotheism was in this way vastly different from the unitarian monotheism of Arius and Eunomius. Trinitarian monotheism preserved the principle of shared rule and banished once and for all—at least theoretically—the idea that any person can be subordinate to another. This is the kernel of the radical theological and political proposal of the Cappadocians that is relevant to the program of feminism today.

Thus far the focus has been on the Greek theology of the Trinity. Since many readers have been shaped not by this tradition but by the Latin theology of God, it is essential to present it briefly, by way of contrast. Augustine was the most influential Latin theologian of the Trinity from this period. Unlike the Greeks, who emphasized the unique but equal roles of God, Christ, and the Spirit in the economy of salvation, Augustine began with the unity of Father, Son, and Spirit according to the divine substance. For Augustine, God is first one, then threefold; personhood is derived from essence. The three divine persons are coequal because they share a common essence.

Because of the text of Genesis that we have been created in the image and likeness of God, Augustine thought that vestiges of the Trinity have been imprinted in the human soul. Thus one should be able to discern within oneself a pattern of threefoldness that is the image of the Trinity. Augustine saw the Christian life as a kind of contemplation of the image of God within us, a means of ascent to and eventual union with God. In the effort to characterize the shape of the trinitarian image of God within us, Augustine formulated several different analogies, including lover-beloved-love, but his favorite was memory-intellect-will. These three faculties of the soul are in some sense a mirror image of God's own act of being; just as God knows and loves Godself, so we know and love ourselves. Interiority is the key to knowledge of God: know thyself, and you will discover God therein.

Augustine's theopsychology is a profound meditation on the *imago Dei,* and it had enormous influence on subsequent Latin theologies, especially the monastic spiritual tradition and the Scholastic theologies of Thomas Aquinas and Bonaventure. Even so, the emphasis on interiority as the place to discover the Trinity had the effect of locating God's economy not in the history of salvation but within each human person. While he was surely correct that because we are created in the image of God we should be able to discover that image in some aspect of our humanity,

Augustine's theology, at least as it was received by his interpreters and passed down through the Christian tradition, led to the idea of a self-enclosed Trinity of persons who reach out to the creature in one undifferentiated act. There is a certain abstractness to Augustine's formulation, even though his clear intent was to defend the intelligibility of the doctrine of the Trinity and provide a means of access to its existential truth. Moreover, Augustine's theology contributed to the idea of the self as an "individual" rather than, as with the Greeks, someone who comes to self through another. The individual Christian is called to be a mirror image of the solitary, though self-differentiated, divine self.

Thomas Aquinas's famous treatment of the Trinity in the *Summa theologiae* attempted to combine the Greek idea of the Father's monarchy with Augustine's schema of interiority. Thomas achieved this synthesis using Aristotle's metaphysics of being-in-act. For Thomas, God's essence and existence are indistinguishable; God is the pure act of being. It is well known that Thomas denied that God has a "real" relation to creation. What he meant is that while the creature is entirely contingent on God for its act of being (and so does have a real relation to God), God's act of being is not contingent on the creature's act of being. Thomas did not mean by this that God is "aloof" or "coldhearted" toward creation. His point was metaphysical: God alone is the self-sufficient act of being; to be a creature is to be dependent on God. This same metaphysical perspective led Thomas to conceive of perfection as self-sufficiency, as not being determined by any other being. Divine perfection means not being determined in any way by the creature's act of existing. While these metaphysical claims must not be psychologized, it is easy to see some of the reasons why Thomas's theological system has been perceived by many contemporary persons to represent an unsatisfactory theism.

In any case, questions 2 to 26 of Thomas's *De Deo Uno* are devoted to an analysis of the attributes of God's being, such as simplicity and goodness. Questions 27 to 43 treat the Trinity (*De Deo Trino*). Thomas begins with the biblical idea of procession: the Son proceeds from, is begotten by, the Father. From there he explores the notions of relation and person and then the unique characteristics of Son and Spirit. Thomas understands divine relations as "relations of opposition": the Father begets the Son, the Son is begotten by the Father, the Father and Son together spirate the Spirit, the Spirit is spirated by Father and Son. He defines a divine person as a "subsistent relation," that is, a relation (such as begetting) that is constitutive of the person (the begetter). His is a sophisticated metaphysics of the intratrinitarian relations. Even so, the history of redemption does not figure prominently in his discussion of the Trinity. Only in the final question of this section does Thomas take up the question of the divine missions, the sending of Son and Spirit into the economy of salvation. The structure of the *Summa* shows that Thomas conceives of God first in intradivine terms (God's "inner" life) and then God's relationship to the creature. This deductive approach, "seeing all things from the perspective of God," fit the Scholastic paradigm of theology and fit neatly with Aristotle's metaphysics. But as I have argued elsewhere, the net effect of Thomas's theology is to separate God-Trinity and creature by an ontological chasm that not very easily can be overcome.[5] By the medieval period, the combined effect of both Greek and Latin speculative theologies of the Trinity was to depict the Trinity as an intradivine reality, largely cut off from the creature, and self-sufficient. It is true that the Cappadocians had succeeded in overcoming the unitarianism of Arius and Eunomius by confuting the idea of God as a monad. They did this by predicating relationality at the heart of divine being. And it is true that Augustine succeeded in overcoming all traces of subordination by stressing the perfect equality of Father, Son, and Holy Spirit. However, in both traditions, by the medieval period the Trinity itself became a kind of monad, internally self-differentiated perhaps, but relating to the creature much the same way that Arius's God had. The Trinity was thought of as a self-sufficient divine community. Christianity found itself in the strange position of having a trinitarian doctrine of God on the books, but in practice its theology had become unitarian.

Despite this history, a sense of God's triune personhood was kept alive in the liturgy and in spirituality. In the effort to reunite doctrine and practice and restore the doctrine of the Trinity to its rightful place at the center of Christian faith and practice, great potential, I believe, lies in revitalizing the Cappadocian (rather than Augustinian) doctrine of the Trinity. Although the Augustinian-Thomistic doctrine, with its emphasis on the total equality among the divine persons, has appealed to some feminist and liberation theologians as a way to ground a vision of equality among human persons in society,[6] I believe that an even stronger foundation for the same vision is provided by adapting and modifying the principles of the Cappadocian doctrine of the Trinity. The Augustinian-Thomistic framework postulates *substance* (something in itself) as the primary ontological category, whereas Greek theology posits *person* (relation or *hypostasis;* toward another) as the primary principle. In the Latin metaphysics, being underlies communion, whereas in Greek ontology, communion underlies being. The priority of communion among persons over being-in-itself is on the same trajectory as the feminist concern for the equality of women and men.

METAPHYSICS AND POLITICS

Metaphysical positions should not be thought of as solely the provenance of speculative theologians, because every metaphysics has a direct and profound bearing on how we envision the nature of the human person and the shape of human society. Furthermore, one of the lessons learned from the history of trinitarian theology is that metaphysical positions must be rooted in and derived from what we know of God as revealed in the economy of salvation. Otherwise, metaphysical claims about God will appear to be nothing more than projections of human values onto the divine being. These projections can take the form of a hierarchically ordered *or* an egalitarian social arrangement. In both cases, what is usually missing is a firm basis in salvation history—in the person of Jesus Christ—for a particular vision of human society.

To take one example, a substance ontology is never entirely able to overcome the bedrock values of patriarchy: autonomy, nondetermination by another, self-possession as prior to self-donation. The subordination of woman to man is but a symptom of the conceptualization of personhood deep at work in patriarchy: a perfect person is self-sufficient; does not need another except out of weakness; is related to another only after first being what it is in itself and by itself.[7] The idea of personhood as self-sufficiency is perhaps the ultimate male fantasy and substance metaphysics perhaps its ultimate projection.[8] In Eunomius, the Cappadocians directly encountered and rejected the idea of unrelated personhood. Their trinitarian theology postulated *relatedness* as the supreme characteristic of God. But in the Latin doctrine of the Trinity, because it is rooted in a substance ontology, the divine persons are always in some sense secondary to what the divine being is first "in and of itself." Thomas Aquinas tried to overcome the split between nature and person through the concept of "subsistent relation." However, the strong impression remains that being is prior to personhood; being what one is in oneself is prior to being who one is in relation to another. The Cappadocian emanation scheme, by which everything comes from the Father through the Son in the Holy Spirit, looks, on first view, to be a pattern of subordination: the one coming forth is less than the source. This is why it has been rejected by some feminist and liberation theologians. However, the whole point of the doctrine of the Trinity was to renounce Arian subordinationism yet affirm the total equality and complete uniqueness and diversity of the divine persons. The shared life of all persons, whether human or divine, consists in the communion that arises out of genuine diversity among equals.

Jesus Christ remains the sole criterion of human personhood, and God's Holy Spirit remains the sole means by which authentic personhood is achieved. Thus every trinitarian theology is ineluctably both christological and pneumatological.[9] This ties the doctrine of the Trinity to the actual economy of salvation and curtails its tendency toward ungrounded speculation about God's "inner life." Christian feminism is Spirit inspired inasmuch as it is a movement toward authentic communion among persons. Yet the Christian feminist concern for nonhierarchical relationships based on the mutuality and reciprocity of persons equal in dignity must, from a theological standpoint, remain rooted in the stories of salvation through Jesus Christ. Any metaphysical claim, for example, that God exists in a communion of equal yet unique persons, if it is to avoid being discredited as just one more ideology, must show how its political conclusions are rooted firmly in the life of Jesus Christ. Here, feminist biblical hermeneutics is of special significance.[10] Jesus Christ preached the reign of God in which male and female will dwell together in the new household of God. God's household is not the patriarchal arrangement of ancient Roman or Jewish society. Patri-archy is not God's *archē;* the rule of the *pater familias* is not the rule of God. God rules by love, in solidarity with the slave, the poor, the woman, the outcast, the uncircumcised.[11] In this new household of God the slave and the master, female and male, live together in their new unity in Christ in whom there is no longer either the Gentile female slave nor the free Jewish male (Gal 3:28).

A total revision of the theoretical underpinnings of the doctrine of the Trinity, in fidelity to its historical origins yet modified in light of contemporary thought patterns and pastoral problems, provides a strong theological basis for many feminist concerns. The revitalized doctrine of the Trinity, purged of its subordinationist elements and proceeding from the principle that the supreme ontological predicate is personhood, not being-in-itself, understands the destiny of the human person to be that of living in authentic communion with God, with other persons, and with all God's creatures.

The political implications of this principle are far-reaching. First, the social subordination of woman to man is but the logical consequence of the patriarchal idea that the male is the *archē* of woman. Patriarchy means, literally, the rule of the father. According to a literal interpretation of Genesis 2–3, the man is her source and therefore he may rule over her.[12] Feminism, and also a revitalized doctrine of the Trinity, agree on the equality of men and women; neither is the principle or origin of the other, neither is superior to or normative of the other.[13]

Once relatedness rather than autonomy is made primary and all of existence is seen to derive from an absolutely personal principle, we can see that persons are imperfect if self-centered or solitary individuals. Perfection for all persons, divine or human, resides in loving and knowing another, coming to self through another, being who one is in relation to another. God is not a self-sufficient substance with personhood added on. *That* God is, is secondary to *who* God is. Indeed, if God were not personal God would not exist at all.

Second, the doctrine of the Trinity is iconoclastic toward all human political arrangements where one (superordinate) is in power over the many (subordinates). When the doctrine of the Trinity was "defeated" by the return to a concern for God's inner life rather than with God's life with us in salvation history, it was easy to bypass the radical philosophical and theological proposal contained in trinitarian doctrine and instead embrace the idea of a God-monarch who rules over the world that is subordinate to God's will. This pattern was replicated in the church: one God and one bishop, and in society: one God and one emperor. The divine monarchy was used to justify different types of hierarchy: religious, sexual, political.[14] This was clearly the triumph of a patriarchal understanding of God, despite the theoretical possibility to the contrary contained in the doctrine of the Trinity.

Third, through the doctrine of the Trinity the new sense of an "intratrinitarian" Fatherhood (eternal Father of the eternal Son) was developed in order to refute Arius and Eunomius. The doctrine of the Trinity emerged in a patriarchal culture in which the male was assumed to be the active principle in begetting. The Cappadocians flat-out denied any comparisons between divine and human begetting. For example, Gregory of Nazianzus wrote that God is not male because God is called Father, nor is deity feminine because of the gender of the word, nor does God's fatherhood have anything to do with marriage, pregnancy, midwifery, or the danger of miscarriage.[15] In effect the Cappadocians challenged the Christian imagination to renounce biological, cultural, and commonsense notions of fatherhood, including the patriarchal idea of the self-sufficient father. And yet, the Cappadocians were not successful, judging by subsequent history. Indeed, the metaphysical project of subsequent theology to postulate and then dissect God's life *in se,* God's life with God to the exclusion of God's life with us, points to a patriarchal self-projection, an attribution of the qualities of a *pater familias* to God's own being.

COMPLEMENTARITY AND THE TRINITY

Since personhood and communion are the central themes of the Christian doctrine of God, it becomes apparent that the doctrine of the Trinity is intimately tied to theological anthropology. Indeed, the doctrine of the Trinity has been used to argue in favor of the subordination of woman to man.[16] Even though all traces of subordination were eliminated from the orthodox doctrine of the Trinity, the lingering tendency to subordinate Christ to God was transferred to the relationship between male and female, animate and inanimate, rational and emotional, spiritual and carnal, and so forth. This defective trinitarian doctrine has been used, ironically by the self-proclaimed defenders of Christian orthodoxy, to support the subordination of women to men. The hierarchical arrangement between men and women is professed to belong to the so-called natural order of creation and to be confirmed by the doctrine of the Trinity.

The orthodox doctrine of the Trinity, however, makes it plain that subordination is *unnatural,* contrary to the nature and destiny of all personhood, divine and human. In Jesus Christ there is no longer male nor female; all are redeemed in him. And the Spirit of God is at work, bringing about the healing of division and alienation, indeed the inequality between male and female that stemmed from the Fall. Furthermore, God's *archē* is the opposite of hierarchical or patriarchal rule; the rule of God is *absolutely* personal, which means that God has created both men and women with the full capacity to be intimate with God. It means, in short, that God has endowed women and men alike with the sacred image of this personal God.

Despite this, Catholic, Protestant, and Orthodox theologians[17] have argued that God the Father is to God the Son as men are to women. In classical trinitarian theology, God the Father is the source of the Son; by analogy, the man is the source of the woman. God the Son is said to be obedient and even submissive toward God the Father; hence women are to be obedient and submit to men.

This so-called theology of complementarity extrapolates from biology predetermined social and gender roles. One particularly virulent example of this line of argumentation is exemplified by the recent work of German theologian Werner Neuer. He writes that men have a stronger bone structure, which implies that men are designed for contact with the environment in a practical and creative way. The "softer daintier woman's hand is more suited to taking in hand the environment and looking after and caring for it protectively."[18] That women have the physical appearance of motherhood (breasts) even when not pregnant shows they are built for motherhood as the goal and fulfillment of woman's being. The sexual organs of men show that they are active, giving, and life creating, whereas women are passive, receptive, and subject.[19]

From these and similar observations Neuer concludes that God has created men and women to be different because God has different purposes for them. Thus the distinctive character of men and women is not due to anything other than God's intent for creation. Neuer uses Genesis 2–3 to argue that because the woman was created from the man's rib, man is the origin and goal of the woman's life, but not the reverse.[20] The woman was created to be the man's helper, which means she is to be subject to him, even though she possesses fully the image of God.[21] The Fall resulted from the man listening to the woman and submitting to her leadership. The man has been given the responsibility of leadership because the woman is more susceptible to the allurements of the occult.[22] Further, in Genesis 2:23 the man names the woman "Eve," thus expressing his superiority over her. There is a divinely ordained "natural" subordination of woman to man in creation.

Neuer further argues that Jesus called only men into the circle of the twelve; this means that Jesus committed spiritual leadership only to men. Even though women followed Jesus, their activity is characterized as providing support. Neuer favors the teaching of Paul (or deutero-Paul) in 1 Corinthians 11:3, Ephesians 5:12, Colossians 3:18, and Titus 2:5, which describe the analogy that Christ is to God as woman is to man. Neuer imputes to Paul a trinitarian understanding that the subordination of women to men need not lead to their inequality. He cites approvingly Werner Meyer's commentary on Corinthians: "In the loving submission of the woman to the man is reflected the inner trinitarian glory of the relationship of the Son to the Father. Could anything greater be said about women?"[23]

It is a small leap from here to Neuer's judgment about language for God. He notes that through God's revelation in Christ, we learn for the first time that God in his essential nature is a Father. God is the model of fatherhood and does not derive this name from human fatherhood. This title is appropriate to God since fatherhood involves the active procreation of new life, while motherhood involves what he judges to be the passive acts of conceiving, carrying, and bearing life.[24] God's begetting requires no conception, pregnancy, or birth. Thus there is nothing maternal about God's activity of creating. God's fatherhood includes everything possible in the way of motherly tenderness, security, and love. Thus the masculine view of God in Scripture necessarily implies that the man in his maleness is in a special way the reflection and representative of God, whereas the woman in a special way reflects and represents creation and the redeemed church.[25] Just as creation is subordinate to the Creator and was created for God, so the woman is subordinate to the man and was designed for him.[26]

While it may be surprising to read these sentiments, Neuer is by no means the exception. Both women and men theologians can be found making the complementarity argument on the basis of the doctrine of the Trinity. Despite some of the remarks of Pope John Paul II in *Mulieris Dignitatem* on the mutuality of women and men, still the pope argues from a complementarity model.[27] On the Orthodox side, Thomas Hopko describes what he calls a "direct analogical, symbolic and epiphanic" relationship between Adam and the Son of God, and between Eve and the Spirit of God.[28]

> What this means is that as in the Godhead there is and must be union between the Son and the Holy Spirit for the Father to be eternally and divinely expressed, so *on the level of creation* there is and must be male and female so that the same God could be temporally and humanly expressed within the life of his creatures. . . . This means as well that as the mode of being and action of the Son is different from the mode of being and action of the Holy Spirit, both eternally and essentially, as well as in the dispensation of salvation—or, more traditionally put, both according to *theologia* and *oikonomia*—so in a similar manner, the mode of being and action of the male in creation is different from the mode of being and action of the female within the same nature of created being.[29]

Hopko goes on to say that because Son and Spirit are not interchangeable, neither are male and female in their distinctive roles in creation. Women are created and called to be men's "helpers" in their service of self-emptying love (Genesis 2:18). They are to be "submissive" to men's love and service, and as such to "enable and empower it," just as the Holy Spirit empowers Christ's ministry.[30] In Hopko's view this submission does not degrade women but points to their dignity. He argues from the supposed hierarchical order (*taxis*) of the three divine persons to a hierarchy among human persons, even though, he claims, this does not annihilate their equality. Hopko's whole argument is located in an essay on why women cannot be ordained priests, thus confirming the suspicion that the standard arguments against ordaining women are driven by the theology of complementarity and that both stem from a defective trinitarian theology.

Catholic theologian Joyce Little constructs a similar argument.[31] While she rejects the Aristotelian model of complementarity, which sees reality as composed of a superior, active principle associated with masculinity, and an inferior, passive principle associated with femininity, she notes that dependence, receptivity, submission, and obedience should not be assumed to indicate inferiority. Indeed, using the doctrine of the Trinity she argues that the Son is dependent on the Father, receptive, submissive, and obedient to God the Father. Thus these traits indicate not inferiority or passivity but *order.*

Little turns to Thomas Aquinas's distinction between *esse* (that something is) and *essentia* (what something is), noting that Thomas's metaphysics of God as Pure Act means that both *esse* and *essentia* are active principles. She then constructs the analogy that male is to *esse* as female is to *essentia* and appeals to marital imagery to bolster the analogy.[32] The church is eternally female in her relationship to Christ, just as Christ is eternally male in his relationship to the church. According to Little, the incarnational nature of Christianity is linked to the female because she is linked with the carnal, material, and biological. Little concludes that the role of women is chiefly sacramental: "It is in and through the feminine that the immanent presence of God within a materially good creation is realized."[33] Yet woman's sacramental role cannot be identified with the activity of Christ (as priest) because this would reduce female to male. "To deny [the] marital structure of being, which is Trinitarian in origin and sacramental in history, is to return to a pre-Christian mentality which is either demasculinized or defeminized."[34]

Many other examples could be given from Protestant and Catholic theologians. These arguments all have in common the assumption, first, that it belongs to the divinely intended order of creation that women be subordinate (in role and state) although equal (in dignity) to men and that this arrangement decreed by God does not diminish women or impair their ability to be redeemed. Indeed, redemption for the woman means accepting her subordinate state and fulfilling the domestic role assigned her by God. For a woman to assume a leadership role would be "unnatural." Second is the assumption that the doctrine of the Trinity sustains a hierarchical complementarity between male and female.

From the perspective of the revitalized doctrine of the Trinity outlined above, however, creation and redemption are not two separate orders. Indeed, creation entails a salvation history, a redemptive order, which is the movement back toward the authentic communion that the woman and man in the Garden at one time possessed. All of creation groans toward fulfillment, toward something new. The subordination of woman to man is a consequence of the Fall; it does not belong to God's divinely decreed plan. Redemption means bringing to fruition and completion God's providential plan, revealed in Christ, that male and female, Jew and Gentile, free and slave shall dwell together as one in the new household of God. The church is to be the visible sign and witness to this reign of God in which all the false rulers in the world are exposed and overturned—including the false rule of the *pater* over women, slaves, and children.

Second, the proper destiny of every person, divine or human, is to subsist in communion with other persons. This communion, in order to be authentic and "of God," presupposes not just equal dignity but freedom from the biological and social determinants of race, sex, and standing. In the risen Christ, and through baptism, we no longer are identified or determined by these factors but are new persons, newly constituted.[35] Third, theologians who make the complementarity argument do not seem to realize that their argument hinges on the very heresy that the church tried to overcome in its rejection of Arianism, namely, that the Son is in *any* sense subordinate to the Father. Athanasius and the Cappadocians struggled vigorously to eradicate *all* subordination between Father and Son and asserted their full equality as persons. This tradition is at odds with the complementarity argument; indeed, the doctrine of the Trinity not only supports the full equality of male and female, but also there is no intrinsic reason why men should be correlated with God the Father and women with God the Son.

Consider the application of the dominant male/subordinate female argument to Jew and Gentile. In early Christianity one of the gravest crises was precipitated by the question about the proper place of converted

Gentiles in this new religious movement centered around Jesus Christ. What is important to note is that the Jews were not allowed to say to the Gentiles, "You are welcome to join *our* church; there is room for you if you want to adapt to *our* ways, including circumcision." Nor were the Jews allowed to think that theirs was the true following of Christ and that of the Gentile converts a lesser way. Rather, Jews and Gentiles *together* became something new, namely, Christians, no longer distinguished as Jewish or Gentile. The Gentiles were not subordinate to Jews in the new Christian community. Similarly, male and female are *together* to become the full and perfect image of God, the image that was tarnished by the Fall. It violates the best of Christian convictions to suggest today that some members of the Christian community are subordinate because God has eternally willed that some members (women) are intrinsically "lesser."

Christian feminism expresses an eschatological hope for the true communion among men and women. In the reign of God, when all tears have been wiped away, women and men will no longer find themselves in the estrangement of "otherness" but will be *one* in Jesus Christ, living together harmoniously in the household of God. The divine *archē*, the rule of God, is not the enemy of mutuality and equality among persons but its true foundation. But this follows only if God's rule is continually referred to what Jesus Christ reveals about the reign of God. The life of Jesus Christ is at odds with the sexist theology of complementarity, the racist theology of white superiority, the clerical theology of cultic privilege, the political theology of exploitation and economic injustice, and the patriarchal theology of male dominance and control.[36]

TRINITY AND GOD-LANGUAGE

One of the thorniest pastoral and theological problems at the moment is the question of how to address God in public prayer. Many in our churches find it difficult to address God as Father, Son, and Holy Spirit, while others are disturbed by any changes to the name of God or to fixed patterns of prayer. There is far from a consensus on whether God's name as Father, Son, Spirit is revealed and therefore cannot be changed, or whether it can be changed, on what basis, in what contexts, or by whom. Baptism into the triune name of God presents a special problem, because some churches will not recognize the validity of another church's baptism if there is any deviation from the formula given in Matthew 28:19.

Feminist theologians were the first to call attention to the far-reaching negative consequences of exclusively masculine imagery for God.

There is no doubt that the use of only masculine images and metaphors in worship and in theology creates the impression that God is male. The one-sided way of imaging and referring to God contributes to the religious legitimization of patriarchy in the sense that the male and masculinity are at the center, assumed to be normative for all human beings. In 1973 Mary Daly provided the classic feminist critique of patriarchy and patriarchal God language: "If God is male, the male is God."[37] Although in the first stages of feminist theology the doctrine of the Trinity was dismissed outright as hopelessly patriarchal, as we have seen above, the doctrine of the Trinity, properly conceived, not only does not support a patriarchal doctrine of God but directly overturns it. Indeed, the debate over how to name God, and in particular the considerable controversy over the fatherhood of God, is properly a problem in trinitarian theology, not only in feminist theology.

The questions of God's fatherhood and how to name God are deeply perplexing and cause great pain to those on both sides of the issue. While it is doubtful that definitive answers can be given that will satisfy all parties, still we can hope to advance the conversation beyond both recalcitrance and indignation. It may be some consolation to compare our situation to what was at stake in the debates over Arianism and Eunomianism in the fourth century. The monumental problem of whether Jesus Christ was subordinate to God was not merely academic. Nearly everyone realized that what was at issue was the exact nature of our salvation: whether we are saved by Christ and the Spirit as well as by God. The matter was discussed widely, and not only among theologians, because it touched directly on habits of public prayer as well as private piety. Today the issue of God's trinitarian name is discussed widely and with comparable passion. Because we know the outcome of the christological and trinitarian debates, we might be tempted to underestimate the conceptual, religious, and political difficulties theologians in the fourth century faced in resolving those issues. Likewise it may be equally easy to underestimate the conceptual, religious, and political difficulties of our own situation. At times one is tempted to do what Bishop Leontius did in the fourth century to avoid controversy: mumble one's prayers so that no one can hear what one is saying!

DIFFERENT STRATEGIES

The basic problem of language for God may be stated this way: The exclusive use of masculine images in worship or in theology contributes to an overwhelming sense of God as male.[38] Sallie McFague notes that the problem with the Father image is "its expansion, its inclusiveness, its hegemony, its elevation to an idol."[39] Christian feminism is concerned not only to restore the equality of men and women in social patterns, but also to overturn the idolatry of worshiping a male God. Although there is great disagreement among Catholic, Orthodox, and Reformed theologians about the status of the names Father, Son, Spirit, we can distinguish six different strategies for dealing with God's triune name.

God Is Father, Son, Spirit. A number of theologians, across denominations, argue that Father, Son, and Holy Spirit are the *revealed* name of God.[40] Because these names have the status of divine authorship, they cannot be altered. The argument is not that God is male, only that we have no choice except to call God "Father."

A recent collection of essays by several Reformed theologians sees feminism as a great danger to the church, bringing a new threat of gnosticism and compromising the integrity of the Christian faith.[41] The basic argument of the contributors to this volume is that the Bible determines the name of God and that any innovation beyond what is attested in the Bible is a direct departure from Christianity.

Many of the contributors to this volume claim that *Father* indicates the ontological nature of God. Elizabeth Achtemeier takes up this argument and adds that masculine language is used for God because God will not let himself be identified with his creation, whereas feminine language opens the door for a pantheistic identification of God and world.[42] Others argue that because the Christian tradition has denied that masculine pronouns and images used for God have a sexual reference, replacing these references to God with feminine images would emphasize the sexuality of the images.[43]

This familiar Barthian argument is not unique to Reformed theology. Orthodox theologian Deborah Belonick argues similarly. She regards Father, Son, and Spirit as God's self-revealed name. The revealed status of these names makes them immune from conditioning effects of history and culture. Belonick does not believe these names were products of a patriarchal structure, male theology, or a hierarchical church.[44]

Much of this kind of argumentation is directed against the view, enunciated by Thomas Aquinas, and given special prominence by Sallie McFague in *Metaphorical Theology,* that all biblical names and forms of address to God are metaphors. McFague's work has the merit of freeing the Christian imagination from the stranglehold of a deadly literalism;

however, her theology has been criticized for being more unitarian than trinitarian and thus not really addressing the central issues raised by the doctrine of the Trinity.[45] McFague's linguistic strategy has also come under direct attack by those who see the claim that *Father* is a metaphor as the enemy of true religion. Lutheran theologian Robert Jenson regards the inclusive language crisis as a rerun of the Gnostic crisis and the vulgar Enlightenment. He denies that *Father* functions metaphorically because the title of address identifies a particular relationship. Even though God is ineffable, this does not render ineffable the relational reality posited in the use of *Father* as a term of address. Others undermine McFague's argument by saying that *Father* is a metaphor whereas *Mother* is a simile.[46]

Catholic theologian Joseph DiNoia tries to mediate between the proponents and adversaries of metaphor. He argues that *Father* can be applied to God in three senses: metaphorically to the triune God (the Trinity is the Father of creation); by appropriation to the first person; and literally and properly to the first person. On the last point, we call God Father because this is how Jesus addressed God. These names do not originate in our experience of God and God's agency in the world; God names Godself. This, he says, is a decisive case against substituting *Mother* for *Father* when speaking of the first divine person.[47]

Two points are in order. First, the assumption that biblical terms not only cannot be changed but they express "God's naming of Godself," and thus to change them would be idolatry, is at odds with contemporary biblical scholarship, which recognizes the conditioned character of biblical testimony and the patriarchal context of biblical writings.[48] Second, under the guise of protecting and defending God's sovereign freedom from the creature, God is disassociated from us and from human language, however partial and imperfect it may be. This strategy violates the intention of the doctrine of the Trinity to affirm God's real relation to us in creation and exposes the absence of a truly relational ontology that can affirm God's self-determination and sovereign freedom without creating an unbridgeable chasm between God and us.

The Incomprehensible and Unnameable God. A second, typically Catholic approach to the Fatherhood of God is to take refuge in the ineffability and unnameability of God.[49] This is based on the theological principle that God is, strictly speaking, unknowable. The multiplicity of images and metaphors in Scripture is one warrant for this approach. As Thomas Aquinas said, we know that God is, not what God is. Every word, image, concept, or analogy we use to depict God is necessarily limited. Christian theology affirms that the reality of God transcends the limits of human language. We cannot name God in the same way that we name created realities; according to the rule of analogy, we predicate God's similarity to us only by affirming God's greater dissimilarity. As feminist theologians have reminded us, according to the apophatic approach or the *via negativa,* every statement we make about God must be negated; we must say what God is not as well as what God is.

Every human father we know is male. However, the analogy of divine fatherhood works by dissimilarity between divine and human fatherhood. As Sallie McFague points out, the problem is not that God is imaged as Father, but that Fatherhood has become the root-metaphor for God, thereby replacing the proclamation of God's reign with the institution of patriarchy.[50] If we say that God is a Father, we must acknowledge that God is unlike a father because God is not male (or female). God is not like a human father because human fathers copulate with human mothers; human fathers have male bodies. None of these characteristics of human fatherhood are true of God. Similarly, if we say that God is wise, we mean that God is not wise the way that human beings are wise; nor is God good in the sense that we are good. Every analogy contains a dissimilarity.

Underneath this approach is the same concern as that of evangelical theology: to "let God be God," not subject to the vagaries of human language. At the same time, it must be kept in mind that what makes God incomprehensible is God's nearness to us in the person of Jesus Christ and in the Holy Spirit who unites persons, not in the distance of God or the relegation of God to a distant heaven. We *do* name God, in many different ways, on the basis of God's self-revelation and our experience of God. Thus the incomprehensibility of God must not lead to agnosticism in which we never venture to say anything about God. Still, the caveat is well taken: Since God's mystery cannot be fully captured in any single metaphor, we are licensed to use an array of images and metaphors, feminine as well as masculine.

Feminine as Well as Masculine Images. A third approach, which is pastorally sensitive and faithful to the full range of human experience, is to augment masculine images, metaphors and pronouns with feminine ones, for example, *Mother* and *She* in addition to *Father* and *He.* There is ample evidence in the tradition that the three divine persons have been imaged as feminine. And there is no question that Christian liturgy has always adapted to new circumstances. At present the use of feminine as well as masculine images is one of the most widely accepted approaches. A possible distortion would be the implication that God remains fundamentally masculine, with a feminine side.[51] Another would be that feminine traits are stereotyped by motherly or nurturing roles. Still, the multivalence of metaphors and images goes a great distance toward incorporating the concerns of Christian feminism that God not be imaged solely as male.

Jesus the Iconoclast. Some feminist theologians have suggested that we should not try to explain away Jesus' address to God as Father but instead see Jesus as a protofeminist, an iconoclast and prophet who, even though male, broke through cultural stereotypes of what it means to be male. Sandra Schneiders has argued that

> in Jesus' culture the father-son metaphor was the only one capable of carrying the meaning of his integral involvement in the work of salvation originated by God. Second, by his use of "Abba" for God and his presentation of God as the father of the prodigal, Jesus was able to transform totally the patriarchal God-image. He healed the father metaphor which had been patriarchalized in the image of human power structures and restored to it the original meaning of divine origination in and through love. Third, he deligitimized human patriarchy by invalidating its appeal to divine institution.[52]

This approach has the merit, first of all, of not shying away from the biblical facts. Second, it reckons with the historical and cultural conditioning in Jesus' life. Third, it presents an eschatological hope for human fatherhood and masculinity as able to be healed of patriarchy.[53] As Schneiders says, "Jesus' teaching about God as father and his calling together of a new, non-patriarchal faith community of equal disciples constitute a liberating subversion of patriarchy which can no longer claim divine sanction but stands revealed as a sinful human structure."[54] The Father of Jesus is not Father in the biological or patriarchal sense. God is revealed in Jesus Christ to be the essence of caring, merciful advocacy, especially for those on the margins. God is not an aloof authority figure. At least as far as cultural stereotypes go, and in this country in the age of absentee fathers, God the Father of Jesus is more like a Mother than a Father, a Mother who never abandons her children and does everything, including sacrificing her life, for the sake of her children. To understand the Father of Jesus as a male God would be to misrepresent New Testament testimony.

The Holy Spirit as Feminine. At an earlier stage of Christian feminism there was some enthusiasm toward the recovery of Syriac materials that used feminine imagery for the Spirit.[55] Wisdom, often associated with the Holy Spirit, is portrayed as a female personification of God. This continues to be a promising line of thought, in the sense that the Holy Spirit is God's healing, caring, loving presence in creation and history.[56] However, the Spirit's activities should not be stereotyped according to gender-determined roles for women. Further, a Trinity that is predominantly (two-thirds) male with one feminine dimension concedes that Father and Son are, or should be imaged, solely as masculine. Further, since according to a subordinationist trinitarian theology the Spirit is third, the association of feminine imagery solely with the Spirit would reinforce the subordination of women in church and society

Creator, Redeemer, Sustainer. This solution has an immediate appeal in the sense that the images used are neither masculine nor feminine,[57] and this naming of God carries an immediate reference to who God is in the history of redemption. At the same time, this triad strikes many as impersonal, too functional, either tritheistic or unitarian, and too focused on what God does rather than on who God is.[58] Moreover, the functional language of Creator, Redeemer, Sustainer is not exactly in accord with the biblical testimony that God creates and redeems us *through* Jesus Christ *by* the power of the Holy Spirit. Furthermore, the impersonal naming of God does not fit with the strong claim of the doctrine of the Trinity that God is *essentially and necessarily* personal. At the same time, these experimental triads are efforts toward inclusivity and should be evaluated from the perspective of trinitarian theology, biblical theology, and pastoral effectiveness in calling forth a more just and loving Christian community.

TOWARD A SOLUTION

The Fatherhood of God is susceptible to grave misunderstanding, and has been used to support both a sexist theology of complementarity and patriarchal God-language. The self-revelation of God in Christ remains the only sure source for overcoming distortions in theology and church practice, because it is only by living *in Christ* that we meet the living God whom Jesus proclaimed and through Christ are faithful to the true, living God.

Why did the awareness of the patriarchal aspect of Christian God-language emerge only in the last several decades? The answer lies partly in the fact that women especially, but also men, only relatively recently have come to an awareness of the inequity of the social arrangement between the sexes. This arrangement has become unacceptable, especially in its ecclesial form. The church is supposed to be the harbinger of the new order in Christ in whom the distinctions of male and female have passed away. But the church, as much as society, has shored up the sexist arrangement in which men dominate and eclipse women. This suggests that the basic problem goes much deeper than language. While continuing to explore the various options just outlined, we must change the pattern of relationships in the Christian community as well as depatriarchalize the concept of God.[59]

The insights of trinitarian theology should free our imaginations without forcing us to abandon our tradition. The point of trinitarian theology is to convey that it is the essence or heart of God to be in relationship to other persons; that there is no room for division or inequality or hierarchy in God; that the personal reality of God is the highest possible expression of love and freedom; that the mystery of divine life is characterized by self-giving and self-receiving; that divine life is dynamic and fecund, not static or barren. Theologians today are free to explore many different analogies and metaphors for the relational personhood of God. An interesting precedent was established by the Eleventh Council of Toledo (675), which stated that the Son is begotten *de utero Patris* [from the womb of the Father], that is, from the substance of the Father."

Further, the goal of Christian life is to participate in divine life and to become holy, living in conformity to Jesus Christ by the power of the Holy Spirit. The Christian community is supposed to be an icon of God's triune life. In baptism we are incorporated into the name of God. Living "in the name of" someone else, being blessed into another's name, means being incorporated into their personal history. To take on and live in the name of God is bold and radical. Through baptism we open ourselves to transformation by the Spirit of God who restores in us the blemished image of God, male and female. The distortion of God's image is communal as well as personal; just as the person "puts on Christ" and so becomes a new person in baptism, so the church is to acquire a new identity in which "Christ is all, and in all" (Col 3:10).

Becoming a community of inclusiveness ultimately has as much to do with language as with how we see ourselves and relate to other. The ways in which we address God are a gauge not only of how we view God, but of how we view ourselves. If theologies or church practices denigrate the full and sacred humanity of women, then this will impoverish and falsify how we name and address God. It is easy to see God-language as the only obstacle, but we must admit to the ways in which each of us falls away from the risen Christ in whom there is neither male nor female. Because language shapes worlds of meaning and creates social systems, it requires ongoing revision. In the fourth century Gregory of Nazianzus mocked his opponents who construed the names of God literally, who thought that God is male because God is called Father or that deity is feminine because of the gender of the word or that the Spirit is neuter because it does not beget. Today these arguments do not go far enough. Commitment to inclusive language must be matched by commitment to inclusive community and vice versa.[60] It is true that changing language does not always change hearts, even though changing language can raise consciousness about an exclusion implicit in language. For example, changing from *Negro* to *black* hardly alleviated racism. On the other hand, by being forced to change language, whites were reminded of deep-seated racism and the ways that language bears and perpetuates racism.[61]

Amending religious language does not of itself bring about the communion among persons promised by baptism into the name of God. Changing *Father* to *Mother* in liturgy or theology does not immediately overcome all exclusiveness or literalness.[62] The Christian imagination needs to follow its own course, led by the Holy Spirit who is bringing the church into authentic communion. If the Christian community were truly to become that which it is destined to become, namely, the communion of all persons who have realized their common vocation to praise and glorify God and to be united in service to others, then the question whether to call God Mother or Father would take on a different significance. In a true community of stewards, where orthopraxis (the practice of truth) would finally have coincided with orthodoxy (right opinion about the mystery of salvation), the whole range of human experience would be incorporated into our praise of God. This is where the trinitarian and Christian femininst agenda intersect. In the current controversy it is essential to keep in mind that all of us are united in the common desire to praise God. There are many ways to praise God. No one way of praising God can be dictated by the church or by theology or by one person over another person. Further, ways of praising God should not become a source of division among persons, nor should we overinvest a particular way of praising God with more content than it really has. Every doxology is meant to take us beyond ourselves toward God. The debate over God-language invites all of us to examine our own tendency to try to control God by words or gestures or to settle into a rut in our praise of God.

In sum, first, a variety of images for God is appropriate because God is incomprehensible, inexpressible mystery. Second, no one image or name for God may be turned into an idol, and no one image or name expresses the totality of God's sacred mystery. Third, the appropriate response to the mystery of God's nearness in Jesus Christ is praise, thanksgiving, and adoration (doxology). Fourth, every doxological pattern of prayer must allow the worshiper to praise God. Fifth, every doxology must match some aspect of the pattern of salvation history; the most common form of the doxology directs prayer to God through Jesus Christ by the power of the Holy Spirit. There are different ways of naming this pattern of salvation history and different ways of naming the divine persons; this, of course, is where doctrinal and pastoral controversies arise. Finally, prayer and the giving of praise to God should create an inclusive community of persons who in their communal life are the icon of the Trinity. This communal life is part of the ongoing economy of God, and it requires a discriminating eye to perceive God's hands at work in a new circumstance.

The doctrine of the Trinity affirms that the God into whose name we are baptized is neither the patriarchal Father-God nor a God who created women "less" than men. Rather, it affirms, like Rublev's icon, that true communion among persons is the deepest meaning of life. Fidelity to the Christian tradition does not rule out openness to experience, to a new situation or new needs, but rather demands it. The church is not the sole proprieter of truth. The Holy Spirit speaks through many voices, many reformist movements, which teach the church and call it back to its apostolic charisms and to the message of the reign of God.

NOTES

1. For a fuller examination of the theological and historical development of this doctrine, see Catherine Mowry LaCugna, *God for Us: The Trinity and Christian Life* (San Francisco: Harper San Francisco, 1991), and LaCugna, "The Trinitarian Mystery of God," in *Systematic Theology: Roman Catholic Perspectives,* ed. Francis Schüssler Fiorenza and John P. Galvin (Minneapolis: Fortress Press, 1991), 1:149–91.

2. John Zizioulas, *Being as Communion* (Crestwood, NY: St. Vladimir's Seminary Press, 1985), 41–42.

3. It is important to point out here a decisive difference between Greek and Latin theologies of God. Greek theology is always economy centered. That is, Father, Son, and Spirit are said to be equally divine because they are equally responsible for our salvation. The Latins in contrast argued that Father, Son, and Spirit are equally divine because they share the same divine substance; there is no monarchy of the Father. This will be explained further below.

4. Gregory of Nazianzus, *Orat.* 29.2 (*Patrologia Graeca* 36.76).

5. Cf. LaCugna, *God for Us,* 143–80.

6. See, for example, Patricia Wilson-Kastner, *Faith, Feminism and the Christ* (Philadelphia: Fortress Press, 1983); Leonardo Boff, *Trinity and Society* (Maryknoll, NY: Orbis Books, 1988); Margaret Farley, "New Patterns of Relationship: Beginnings of a Moral Revolution," *Theological Studies* 36 (1975): 627–46; Mary Rose D'Angelo, "Beyond Father and Son," in *Justice as Mission: An Agenda for the Church,* ed. Terry Brown and Christopher Lind (Burlington, Ontario: Trinity Press, 1985), 107–18.

   A common approach is to impose democracy upon the three divine persons, using models of partnership, community, or society, in an effort to rework the trinitarian symbol. The argument is made that because the divine persons exist in equal relationships, human communities can mirror this arrangement and likewise be patterned according to relationships of equality. While this approach has many merits, I believe the more fruitful avenue for dialogue between Christian feminists and the Christian tradition lies in the retrieval and adaptation of the Cappadocian model of the Trinity.

   This retrieval yields (1) the priority of person over substance and therefore of personhood over biological givens; (2) a rethinking of relationality in light of the question of subordination and an ontological grounding of relationship that does not depend on a hierarchical chain of being; (3) a critique of the Western tradition that sees the image of God in the solitary self and a revisioning of what it means to be in the image of God, as persons called to authentic communion with others.

7. Contemporary psychologies that see the task of identity as "differentiation" from the mother are largely male oriented. In contrast, object relations psychology understands the personhood of the child to emerge in relation to the mother or caretaker.

8. LaCugna, *God for Us,* 398.

9. LaCugna, *God for Us,* 363–64.

10. Cf. the chapter of Sandra M. Schneiders in this book.

11. Cf. LaCugna, *God for Us,* 382–88, for a fuller portrait of Jesus Christ and of the reign of God that he preached.

12. Cf. the chapter by Mary Aquin O'Neill in this book. .

13. The basic insight of feminism may be correlated with the Greek idea of *perichōrēsis,* interdependence, which suggests the image of a shared life characterized by mutuality, reciprocity, and equal communion among persons. The shared life is a constant interchange, a dynamic, unceasingly active exchange among unique persons. We should not think of this *perichōrēsis* as a solely *intra*divine occurrence; rather, the communion of divine persons encompasses *all* of existence, past, present, future. To exist at all as a creature is to exist within the everlasting communion of the triune God.

14. LaCugna, *God for Us,* 393.

1 5. Gregory of Nazianzus, *Orat.* 31.8 (*Patrologia Graeca* 36.142). Still, this assertion does not go far enough because it does not overcome the distance between the feminine and the divine.

16. One sees this line of argumentation clearly in *Inter Insigniores,* the Vatican declaration against the ordination of women. The text can be found in Arlene Swidler and Leonard Swidler, eds., *Women Priests: A Catholic Commentary on the Vatican Declaration* (New York: Paulist Press, 1977).

17. See, for example, Orthodox theologians Paul Evdokimov, *La Femme et la salut du monde: Étude et anthropologie chrétienne sur les charismes de la femme* (Paris: Cerf, 1958); Stanley Harakas, *Toward Transfigured Life: The* Theoria *of Eastern Orthodox Ethics* (Lewiston, NY: Edwin Mellen, 1983); Christos Yannaras, *The Freedom of Morality* (Crestwood, NY: St. Vladimir's Seminary Press, 1984), and *Person und Eros: Eine Gegenüberstellung der Ontologie der griechischen Kirchenväter und der Existenzphilosophie des Westens* (Göttingen: Vandenhoeck & Ruprecht, 1982); Lutheran theologian Robert Jenson, *The Triune Identity* (Philadelphia: Fortress Press, 1982); Catholic theologians Matthias Scheeben, *The Mysteries of Christianity* (St. Louis: Herder, 1946); Bertrand de Margerie, *The Christian Trinity in History* (Still River, MA: St. Bede's Publications, 1983); Prudence Allen, "Integral Sex Complementarity and the Theology of Communion," *Communio* 17 (1990): 523–44; Robert E. Harahan, *The Vocation of Woman: The Teaching of the Modern Popes from Leo XIII to Paul VI* (Rome: Pontificia Universitatis Lateranensis, 1983); Laura L. Garcia, "Femininity and the Life of Faith," in *The Catholic Woman,* ed. Ralph McInerny (San Francisco: Ignatius, 1990), 125–30; Janet E. Smith, "Feminism, Motherhood and the Church," in *The Catholic Woman,* ed. McInerny, 41–64.

18. Werner Neuer, *Man and Woman in Christian Perspective,* trans. Gordon Wenham (London: Hodder & Stoughton, 1990), 33. Similarly, Neuer states, the striated muscles are more developed in men than in women, thus men are designed by nature to overcome external environmental obstacles, whereas women are designed for "caring and nursing, in sorting, tidying and polishing" (34).

19. Neuer, *Man and Woman,* 36–41. He writes, "While the man has the more leading role and makes the ultimate decision if and when union takes place, the behaviour of the woman is that of loving subjection, which she fulfills through the offering of her body" (36).

20. Neuer, *Man and Woman,* 73. Note the differences in Mary Aquin O'Neill's interpretation of the same text.

21. The doublespeak that subordination does not amount to inequality is counterintuitive, to say the least. The rhetoric of "subordinate but equal" construes biological function and roles in a patently sexist way.

22. "The divinely intended subordination of the woman has nothing to do with the oppression of women by men, but is a beneficial arrangement that protects men and women from the destructive power of evil. The woman runs into great danger when she steps outside this protective ordinance. The story of the fall shows the woman as a creature in special need of protection and particularly open to Satanic seduction" (Neuer, *Man and Woman,* 77).

23. Neuer, *Man and Woman,* 112.

24. Anyone who has given birth to a child will testify that it is hardly a passive experience.

25. Neuer, *Man and Woman,* 158. From there Neuer goes on to show why a female priest-hood is theologically impossible. The basic reason is that only men can be in leadership positions; to think otherwise violates God's divinely intended order for creation.

26. Neuer, *Man and Woman,* 159.

27. Text in *The Pope Speaks* 34 (1989): 10–47. In accord with the pope see Mary Rousseau, "Pope John Paul II's Teaching on Women," in *The Catholic Woman,* ed. McInerny, 11–32.

28. Thomas Hopko, "On the Male Character of Christian Priesthood," *St. Vladimir's Theological Quarterly* 19–20 (1975–76): 155. See also Vigen Guroian, *Incarnate Love: Essays in Orthodox Ethics* (Notre Dame: Univ. of Notre Dame Press, 1987), 132–33. For a critique of the Orthodox view of complementarity see Verna Harrison, "Yannaras on Person and Nature," *St. Vladimir's Theological Quarterly* 3 (1989): 287–98.

29. Hopko, "Christian Priesthood," 156.

30. Hopko, "Christian Priesthood," 159.

31. Joyce Little, "Sexual Equality in the Church: A Theological Resolution to the Anthropological Dilemma," *Heythrop Journal* 28 (1987): 165–78.

32. It is never made clear why the analogy *necessarily* should run: Father is to Son as male is to female. Why is the female never seen as the originating or active principle if not for the prior and dubious assumption that men are active and primary, women passive and secondary?

33. Little, "Sexual Equality," 173.

34. Little, "Sexual Equality," 176.

35. Cf. LaCugna, *God for Us,* chap. 8; Zizioulas, *Being as Communion,* chap. 1.

36. LaCugna, *God for Us,* 399.

37. Mary Daly, *Beyond God the Father* (Boston: Beacon Press, 1973), 18.

38. See Mary Collins, "Naming God in Public Prayer," *Worship* 59 (1985): 291–304; Catherine Mowry LaCugna, "The Baptismal Formula, Feminist Objections, and Trinitarian Theology," *Journal of Ecumenical Studies* 26 (1989): 235–50; Anne E. Carr, *Transforming Grace: Christian Tradition and Women's Experience* (San Francisco: Harper & Row, 1988), 134–57; Rebecca Oxford-Carpenter, "Gender and the Trinity," *Theology Today* 41 (1984): 7–25; Letty Russell, "Inclusive Language and Power," *Religious Education* 80 (1985): 582–602; Gail Ramshaw-Schmidt, "*De Divinis Nominibus:* The Gender of God," *Worship* 56 (1982): 117–31, and "Naming the Trinity: Orthodoxy and Inclusivity," *Worship* 60 (1986): 491–98, Elizabeth Johnson, "The Incomprehensibility of God and the Image of God Male and Female," *Theological Studies* 45 (1984): 441–65; Dale Spender, *Man Made Language* (London: Routledge & Kegan Paul, 1980); Marjorie Suchocki, "The Unmale God: Reconsidering the Trinity," *Quarterly Review* 3 (1983): 34–49; Barbara Brown Zikmund, "The Trinity and Women's Experience," *Christian Century* 104 (April 15, 1987): 354–56; Gracia Grindal, "Reflections on God 'the Father,'" *Word and World* 4 (1984): 78–86; Ted Peters, "The Battle over Trinitarian Language," *Dialog* 39 (1991): 44–49; Ruth Duck, *Gender and the Name of God: The Trinitarian Baptismal Formula* (New York: Pilgrim Press, 1991).

39. Sallie McFague, *Metaphorical Theology* (Philadelphia: Fortress Press, 1982) 190.

40. See, for example, Lutheran theologians Donald Bloesch, *The Battle for the Trinity: The Debate over Inclusive God Language* (Ann Arbor: Servant Publications, 1985), and Robert

Jenson, *The Triune Identity* (Philadelphia: Fortress Press, 1982). See also the eighteen contributors to Alvin Kimel's *Speaking the Christian God* (Grand Rapids: Eerdmans, 1992). On the Orthodox side see, in addition to those cited in note 17 above, Deborah Belonick, "Revelation and Metaphors: The Significance of the Trinitarian Names Father, Son and Holy Spirit," *Union Seminary Quarterly Review* 40 (1985): 31–42.

41. Kimel, ed., *Speaking the Christian God.*

42. Elizabeth Achtemeier, "Exchanging God for 'No Gods,'" in *Speaking the Christian God,* ed. Kimel, 8.

43. Roland Frye, "Language for God and Feminist Language: Problems and Principles," in *Speaking the Christian God,* ed. Kimel, 24–26.

44. Belonick, "Revelation and Metaphors."

45. For example, does her proposal for the metaphor of Friend-Friend apply to God generically understood or to one of the persons or to all three?

46. Frye, "Language for God and Feminist Language," 36. Both metaphors and similes involve comparison; the Greek word for simile is *homoeosis;* Frye argues that to introduce feminine language for God on the basis of simile is to replay the controversy over the Arian conception of the divine similitude of persons based on the heretical *homoiousios* rather than the orthodox *homoousios.*

47. Joseph DiNoia, "Knowing and Naming the Triune God: The Grammar of Trinitarian Confession," in *Speaking the Christian God,* ed. Kimel, 162–87.

48. Cf. the chapter of Sandra M. Schneiders in this book, also *The Revelatory Text: Interpreting the New Testament as Sacred Scripture* (San Francisco: Harper San Francisco, 1991). In *Women and the Word,* 1986 Madaleva Lecture in Spirituality (New York: Paulist Press, 1986), 20, Schneiders distinguishes at least four different types of language about God in the Old Testament: literal designations, names for God, personifications of God, and metaphors for God.

49. For example, Emmanuel Clapsis, "Naming God: An Orthodox View," *The Ecumenical Review* 44 (1992): 100–12; Mary Collins, "Naming God in Public Prayer"; Elizabeth Johnson, "The Incomprehensibility of God." For a different use of the same principle see Orthodox theologian Thomas Hopko, "Apophatic Theology and the Naming of God in Eastern Orthodox Tradition," in *Speaking the Christian God,* ed. Kimel, 144–61.

50. McFague, *Metaphorical Theology,* 45–52.

51. Cf. Francine Cardman, "The Holy Spirit and the Apostolic Faith, a Roman Catholic Response," *Greek Orthodox Theological Review* 31 (1986): 302; also Jürgen Moltmann, "The Motherly Father," in *God as a Father?* ed. Johannes Metz and Edward Schillebeeckx, Concilium 143 (New York: Seabury, 1981), 53; Pamela P. Allen, "Taking the Next Step in Inclusive Language," *Christian Century* 103 (1986): 410–15.

52. Schneiders, *Women and the Word,* 48. See also Bernard Cooke, "Non-Patriarchal Salvation," *Horizons* 10 (1983): 22–31.

53. Cf. Ruether, *Sexism and God-Talk: Toward a Feminist Theology* (Boston: Beacon Press, 1983), 61–71, 137; Elisabeth Schüssler Fiorenza, "You Are Not to Be Called Father," *Cross Currents* 29 (1979): 301–23.

54. Schneiders, *Women and the Word,* 49.

55. Robert Murray, *Symbols of Church and Kingdom: A Study in Early Syriac Tradition* (London: Cambridge Univ. Press, 1975), esp. 312–20; Donald Gelpi, *The Divine Mother* (Lanham, MD: Univ. Press of America, 1984); Joan Schaup, *Woman: Image of the Holy Spirit* (Denville, NJ: Dimension Books, 1975); Jay G. Williams, "Yahweh, Women and the Trinity," *Theology Today* 32 (1975): 240; Yves Congar, "Motherhood in God and the Femininity of the Holy Spirit," *I Believe in the Holy Spirit* (New York: Seabury Press, 1983), 3:155–64; E. Wurz, "Das Mütterliche in Gott," *Una Sancta* 32 (1977): 261–72; Jürgen Moltmann, with Elisabeth Moltmann-Wendel, "Becoming Human in New Community," in *The Community of Women and Men in the Church: The Sheffield Report*, ed. Constance F. Parvey (Geneva: World Council of Churches, 1983), 36; Mary Grey, "Where Does the Wild Goose Fly To? Seeking a New Theology of Spirit for Feminist Theology," *New Blackfriars* (1991), 89–96.

56. See the chapter of Elizabeth A. Johnson in this volume.

57. Other triads have been suggested, from Augustine's Lover-Beloved-Love, to Gail Ramshaw-Schmidt's Abba-Servant-Paraclete, Letty Russell's Creator-Liberator-Advocate, Mary Rose D'Angelo's Wise God-Wisdom of God-Spirit of Wisdom, and God, Source of Being-Christ, Channel of Life-Spirit, Living Water.

58. Cf. LaCugna, "The Baptismal Formula," 243–44.

59. Cf. Elisabeth Schüssler Fiorenza, *In Memory of Her: A Feminist Theological Reconstruction of Christian Origins* (New York: Crossroad, 1983), 150–51; LaCugna, *God for Us*, 390–400; Judith Plaskow, *Standing Again at Sinai: Judaism from a Feminist Perspective* (San Francisco: Harper San Francisco, 1991), 159.

60. LaCugna, "The Baptismal Formula," 250; Fiorenza, *In Memory of Her*, 150–51.

61. "Racist and sexist language that perpetuates [the mythology that women are inferior to men, or that whites are the superior race, gives] the lie to God's providential plan and the radical reordering of our social and personal worlds entailed in redemption though Jesus Christ. Language that eclipses some persons, language that silences, denigrates, or disheartens persons, language that inhibits the praise of God, is unholy. Since every person is unique, each of us has a unique way of praising God; every voice of praise is indispensable"; LaCugna, *God for Us*, 396.

62. As Ruth Duck points out, in a patriarchal culture *Father* is not equivalent to *Mother* because fathers have different roles and greater importance. But if patriarchal relationships were changed, then there would be more interchangeability between *Father* and *Mother; Gender and the Name of God*, 96.

FOR FURTHER READING

Boff, Leonardo. *Trinity and Society*. Maryknoll, NY: Orbis Books, 1988. A liberation theological perspective on the doctrine of the Trinity.

Carr, Anne E. *Transforming Grace: Christian Tradition and Women's Experience*. San Francisco: Harper & Row, 1988. Demonstrates the compatibility of feminism and Christianity by redescribing fundamental themes in Christian theology.

Daly, Mary. *Beyond God the Father*. Boston: Beacon Press, 1973. Critique of Christianity and Christian theology from the perspective of radical feminism.

Duck, Ruth. *Gender and the Name of God: The Trinitarian Baptismal Formula*. New York: Pilgrim Press, 1991. Deals directly with the language of the baptismal formula and suggests alternative formulations.

Fiorenza, Elisabeth Schüssler. *In Memory of Her: A Feminist Theological Reconstruction of Christian Origins*. New York: Crossroad, 1983. Reconstruction of the early feminist and egalitarian dimensions of Christianity.

Kimel, Alvin, ed. *Speaking the Christian God*. Grand Rapids: Eerdmans, 1992. Eighteen essays by Reformed theologians, antipathetic toward feminism and inclusive language for God.

LaCugna, Catherine Mowry. *God for Us: The Trinity and Christian Life*. San Francisco: Harper San Francisco, 1991. Reformulates the doctrine of the Trinity based on the idea of persons in communion, with attention to the doctrine's spiritual, ethical, and ecclesial implications.

McFague, Sallie. *Metaphorical Theology: Models of God in Religious Language*. Philadelphia: Fortress Press, 1982. Develops a theory of metaphor to revitalize and reform religious language.

Ruether, Rosemary Radford. *Sexism and God-Talk: Toward a Feminist Theology*. Boston: Beacon Press, 1983. A foundational work, the first feminist systematic theology.

Schneiders, Sandra M. *Women and the Word*. 1986 Madaleva Lecture in Spirituality. New York: Paulist Press, 1986. Takes up biblical dimensions of the God-problem, especially Jesus' address to God as Father.

Tennis, Diane. *Is God the Only Reliable Father?* Philadelphia: Westminster Press, 1985. Urges retaining the image of God's Fatherhood, but understood as transcending patriarchal models.

Wilson-Kastner, Patricia. *Faith, Feminism and the Christ*. Philadelphia: Fortress Press, 1983. A feminist reconstruction of the essentials of christology.

CHAPTER FIVE

REDEEMING THE NAME OF CHRIST

— Christology —

Elizabeth A. Johnson

AT A SYMPOSIUM entitled "Christology in Women's Voices" held at a midwestern university one spring weekend, women and their crosses were very much in evidence. In an inspired act of decoration local women were invited to display their personal crosses and to describe how this particular religious symbol connected with their lives. Around the walls of the large meeting hall each artifact was mounted on a colorful scarf with an explanatory card attached. There were marriage crosses with the two rings emblazoned at the top; religious profession crosses worn smooth from repeated kissing and handling; Mexican crosses made of straw; multicolored Salvadoran peasant crosses acquired during missions of accompaniment; Jerusalem crosses received on pilgrimage; crosses with the female form of Christa; Celtic crosses and African crosses; a cross belonging to a woman's friend who gave it to her before he died of AIDS; a cross of sticks made during a retreat; ordinary, garden-variety crosses mass-produced in the United States.

Walking the great hall and perusing the meaning of each specific cross in a woman's own life left one with a profound sense of wonder. No woman had gone out and bought herself a cross. Each replica of the central Christian symbol had been given and received in the context of relationship and at the crossroads of the great and small events of life. In this regard the display was revelatory of the life of the Christian community that is not confined to liturgical assemblies and official pronouncements but goes on continuously and interpersonally as part of the web of daily events. But something even more distinctive was expressed by these crosses. Assembled together they were a text that told the story of women's ongoing relationship with Jesus the Christ and their generous quest for true discipleship. They were a stunning witness to the heart of the matter. For women have consistently read themselves into the christological mystery despite the patriarchal barricades that stand in the way.

Feminist theology brings this situation, both the faith experience and the barriers, to conscious and critical reflection. In a threefold task it seeks first to uncover sexist readings of the narratives, symbols, and doctrines of Jesus the Christ that have skewed what should be good news. Why is the criticism made that of all the doctrines of the church, Christology is the one most used to suppress and exclude women? Feminist theology then searches for alternative interpretations in Scripture, tradition, and women's experience. Is the christological tradition hopelessly patriarchal, or are there marginalized impulses that can be released to shape a Christology of healing and liberation? With critical analysis and alternative possibilities in view, theology then speaks anew about Jesus the Christ according to the feminist model of inclusion and reciprocity, to practical and critical effect.

This respeaking is being done by diverse women in different countries, cultures, races, classes, and churches, and they form a mounting chorus of new interpretation arguably more coherent with the original impulse of the Christ event than is the traditional patriarchal construal.

From an African American perspective, Jacqueline Grant analyzes how poor black women are marginalized not only by sex but also by race and class.[1] Drawing upon the life experience of some of these women, she notes how they interpret Jesus as cosufferer, divine friend, and Lord who knows the troubles they've seen. Since he is in solidarity with the "least of the people," he is with black women in their everyday lives, affirming their basic worth and thereby inspiring active hope to resist dehumanization. The resurrected black Christ who can be found as a black woman signifies and empowers this hope of liberation from oppression.

Articulating the experience of women in Korea and the Philippines, who bear the mark of colonized people in addition to sexist discrimination, Virginia Fabella writes of how the focus is not "who" is Jesus Christ but "where" is Jesus Christ for Asian women.[2] In the community of his Spirit women find the seeds of life rather than death, order rather than chaos, friendship rather than isolation. As healer, exorciser, consoler, and friend, Jesus is an empowering source for women's humanity within the broader struggle toward the full humanity of all, liberated from spiritual impoverishment as well as from the suffering of an unjust, nonegalitarian society.

Amid the exploitation of women in Latin America, Nellie Ritchie rereads the text that Jesus is the Christ to unlock Christ's immersion in the life of the poor to bring them life. As once he said to women in the Gospel so says he now: Woman, don't cry; stand up; go in peace. The cross will inevitably come, but a new world is being born in the resurrection. "That is why we, Jesus' sisters, do not fold up our banners, nor are we afraid to join the struggle," giving to the utmost of women's creative, nurturing, and courageous powers.[3]

Noting that Christ was a refugee and a guest of Africa, Elizabeth Amoah and Mercy Amba Oduyoye write of the mutuality between African women and Christ. They seek to extend hospitality to him and order life so that the whole household of the continent may feel at home with him. At the same time they find him a true friend and companion who liberates and honors them. As the midwife and farmer named Afua prays, "Yesu, who has received the poor and made us honorable, our exceedingly wise friend, we depend on you as the tongue depends on the jaw. . . . We hide under you, the great bush with cooling shades, the giant tree who enables climbers to see the heavens."[4]

For all of these writers and the women whose experience they articulate, the ministry, death, and resurrection of Jesus the Christ are not simply stories, symbols, doctrines, or religious feasts but an empowering way of life. As part of this worldwide conversation among Christian women,

I write in the context of white, academic, middle-class, American culture, yet I seek to be aware of the sufferings of all women in this country and around the world. From this perspective I will trace one pattern of the feminist critique, offer one emancipatory reading of the christological tradition, and conclude by showing how this leads persuasively to new forms of Christian praxis.

DISTORTING THE CHRIST

The basic problem identified from the feminist academic perspective is that Jesus Christ has been interpreted within a patriarchal framework, with the result that the good news of the gospel for all has been twisted into the bad news of masculine privilege. Historically as the early church became enculturated in the Greco-Roman world, it gradually shaped its structures according to the model of the patriarchal household and imperial empire. The image of Christ consequently assumed the contours of the male head of household or the absolute ruler. He was seen as the Pantocrator, the absolute king of glory whose heavenly reign sets up and legitimizes the earthly rule of the head of family, empire, and church. Thus coopted into an imperial model, the powerful symbol of the liberating Christ lost its subversive significance.

This development has been vigorously analyzed by male liberation theologians. But feminist theology makes clear that the imperial tradition that assimilated Christology is precisely patriarchal in character. It values male over female reality, arranging both in a hierarchical social order and assigning the highest value and pride of place to men. Within this worldview the historical Jesus, who was indisputably a male human being, is interpreted as the incarnation of the Logos, an ontological symbol connected with rationality and thus, according to Greek philosophy, with maleness. The Word made flesh is then related to human beings defined according to an androcentric anthropology that sees men as normative and women as derivative. What results is a Christology that functions as a sacred justification for the superiority of men over women. Women are inevitably relegated to a marginal role both in theory and practice, given the priority of the male savior figure within a patriarchal framework.

Let me be very clear about what is at issue here. The fact that Jesus of Nazareth was a man is not in question. His maleness is constitutive for his personal identity, part of the perfection and limitation of his historical reality, and as such it is to be respected. His sex is as intrinsic to his historical person as are his race, class, ethnic heritage, culture, his Jewish religious faith, his Galilean village roots, and so forth. The difficulty arises, rather, from the way this one particularity of sex, unlike the other historical particularities, is interpreted in sexist theology and practice. Consciously or unconsciously, Jesus' maleness is lifted up and made essential for his christic function and identity, thus blocking women precisely because of their female sex from participating in the fullness of their Christian identity as images of Christ. This distortion occurs in at least three ways.

First, Jesus' historical maleness is used to reinforce an exclusively male image of God. If Jesus as a man is the revelation of God, so the usually implicit reasoning goes, then this points to maleness as an essential characteristic of divine being itself. At the very least it indicates, if not an identification, then more of an affinity between maleness and divinity than is the case with femaleness. This view is intensified by the almost exclusive use of father-son metaphors to interpret Jesus' relationship with God. Consequently, as Rosemary Radford Ruether points out, "The unwarranted idea develops that there is a necessary ontological connection between the maleness of Jesus' historical person and the maleness of *Logos* as male offspring and disclosure of a male God."[5]

Second, the fact that Jesus was a man is used to legitimize men's superiority over women in the belief that a particular honor, dignity, and normativity accrues to the male sex because it was chosen by the Son of God "himself" in the incarnation. Indeed, thanks to their sex, men are said to be more conformed to the image of Christ than are women. As stated in the official Roman Catholic argument against women's ordination, men precisely as males enjoy a "natural resemblance" to Christ that women do not, and thus men alone may represent him.[6] While women may be recipients of divine grace, they are unsuited to act *in persona Christi* during the eucharistic act due to their sexual difference from his maleness. Women's physical embodiment thus becomes a prison that shuts them off from full identification with Christ, except as mediated through the christic male. For this mentality, the idea that the Word might have become female flesh is not even seriously imaginable.

Third, in addition to casting both God and the human race in an androcentric mold, sexist Christology jeopardizes women's salvation, at least in theory. The Christian story of salvation involves not only God's compassionate will to save but also the method by which this will becomes effective, namely, by God's plunging into sinful human history and transforming it from within. The early Christian axiom "What is not assumed is not redeemed, but what is assumed is saved by union with God" sums up the insight that Christ's solidarity with all of humanity is what is crucial for salvation. "*Et homo factus est,*" "and became a human being": thus does the Nicene creed confess the universal relevance of the incarnation by the use of the inclusive *homo*. But if in fact what is meant is *et vir factus est* (became a man) with stress on sexual manhood, if maleness is essential for the christic role, then women are cut out of the loop of salvation, for female sexuality is not taken on by the Word made flesh. If maleness is constitutive for the incarnation and redemption, female humanity is not assumed and therefore not saved.

Dualistic anthropology solves this problem by understanding man as the head of woman. In his role as microcosm, his eminence includes her reality along with all the other creatures on the lower rungs of the ladder of being. Thus in assuming male humanity, the Savior in fact includes the female, and women are thereby saved. However, when this androcentric Christology meets an egalitarian anthropology claiming that women and men are equally created in the image of God and equally transformed in Christ through the waters of baptism, such a solution is ruled out. If women are not a lower order of creature subsumed in male humanity but equal partners in essential humanity along with men, then, according to the logic of a male-centered Christology, they are not connected to what is most vital for salvation. In this case the logical answer to the searching question "Can a male savior save women?" can only be no.[7]

Given the radical depth of the feminist analysis of sexist Christology, one might wonder if there is any possible retrieval of a tradition that is so hardened against women. And yet, "something more" has always gone on in the existential and religious lives of women in the Christian community. This is attested by the faith of generations of foremothers, by the array of crosses in that midwestern university, and by the voices of Christian women struggling against dehumanizing systems around the world. Impelled by this living source, feminist theology searches the christological tradition for clues that will bring to expression more clearly its subversion of all master-slave relationships and its life-giving impulse that is inclusive of women, indeed of all creatures and the whole cosmos itself.

DISCOVERING WISDOM

Among the many images and titles first-century Christians pressed into service to name Jesus as the Christ, Wisdom (*Sophia* in Greek) has until recently been the most neglected. Found in the Jewish Scriptures and intertestamental literature, Wisdom is a complex female figure who personifies God's presence and creative action in the world. She comes forth from the mouth of the Most High, pervading and connecting all things. In texts of great variety Sophia creates, redeems, sanctifies, establishes justice, and protects the poor. Searching the world for a dwelling place, she pitches her tent in Jerusalem. Themes of light and dark, finding and seeking, bread and wine, life and death are woven into her symbol. Obviously transcendent, this personified figure comes toward human beings, challenges and comforts them, and lures them to life: "Whoever finds me finds life" (Prv 8:35). We are dealing here with the mystery of God in graceful, powerful, and close engagement with the world.[8]

Early Christians tapped deeply into the tradition of personified Wisdom to articulate the saving goodness they experienced in Jesus the Christ.[9] What Judaism said of Sophia, Christian hymn makers and epistle writers now came to say of Jesus: he is the image of the invisible God (Col 1:15); the radiant light of God's glory (Heb 1:3); the firstborn of all creation (Col 1:15); the one through whom all things were made (1 Cor 8:6). From Paul, who calls Jesus the Wisdom of God (1 Cor 1:24), to Matthew, who puts Sophia's words in Jesus' mouth and has him do her compassionate deeds, to John, who presents Jesus as Wisdom incarnate embodying her ways, her truth, and her life, the use of Wisdom to interpret Jesus had profound consequences. It enabled the fledgling Christian communities to attribute cosmic significance to the crucified Jesus, relating him to the creation and governance of the world. It deepened their understanding of his saving deeds by placing them in continuity with Wisdom's saving work throughout history. It was also the vehicle for developing insight into Jesus' ontological relationship with God. None of the other biblical symbols used—Son of Man, Messiah, Son of God—connotes divinity in its original context, nor does the Word, which is barely personified in the Jewish Scriptures. But Wisdom does. The identification of the human being Jesus with divine Sophia, God's gracious nearness and activity in the world, moved thought to reflect that Jesus is not simply a human being inspired by God but must be related in a more personally unique way to God. Jesus came to be seen as God's only begotten Son only after he was identified with Wisdom. Then her relation of intimacy with God was seen to be manifest in his, her work in the world embodied in his, her spirit poured out in his. "Herein we see the origin of the doctrine of incarnation,"[10] with effects on trinitarian doctrine as well. Without the presence and strength of New Testament sapiential Christology, insight into Jesus' identity and significance would have been very different indeed.

The rediscovery of the wisdom tradition is widening the theological playing field for discourse about Christ. For one thing, unlike the historical and prophetic books, the wisdom tradition is interested not only in God's mighty deeds in history but in everyday life with the give and take of its relationships. The narrow track of encounter with God in salvation history is not the only way, indeed for some not even the primary way, that religious experience occurs. People connect with the holy mystery that surrounds their lives as they actually *live* in the world, in the non-heroic moments, in the effort to be decent and just, in anguish over suffering, in appreciating nature, in trying to work out relationships harmoniously, in the gift and struggle of the everyday—in this, every bit as much as in the peak experiences of personal or community life. Since the whole world is God's creation, life cannot be neatly divided into sacred and profane times or places but even in its dailiness mediates connections with the mystery of the Holy One, hidden and present. Moreover, unlike traditions of law and cult, which were preserved and maintained by the priests, wisdom escapes the control of any one group. It does not find its center in the Temple but is given to anyone who searches out the order of creation in order to live in harmony with it.

On both scores the door is open for women, largely excluded from official religious circles, to bring the trajectory of the wisdom tradition further by reflecting on their own experience of the struggle and beauty of everyday life and naming this religiously important—every bit as significant as what occurs in more explicitly sacred times and places. In this manner, new ways of appreciating Christ can be born, less associated with patriarchal control and more in tune with women's daily life and collective wisdom, so often discounted as a source of insight. There is here an agenda yet to be carried out.

More specifically, the figure of personified Wisdom offers an augmented field of female metaphors with which to interpret the saving significance and personal identity of Jesus the Christ, and the choice of metaphors matters. The gender symbolism not only casts Jesus into an inclusive framework with regard to his relationships with human beings and with God, removing the male emphasis that so quickly turns to androcentrism. But, the symbol giving rise to thought, it also evokes Sophia's characteristic gracious goodness, life-giving creativity, and passion for justice as key hermeneutical elements in speaking about the mission and person of Jesus. In what follows we trace one way that Wisdom enables retelling the story of Jesus, transforming the symbol of Christ, and reclaiming christological doctrine, to practical and critical effect.

RETELLING THE STORY OF JESUS

In his brief ministry Jesus appears as the prophet and child of Sophia sent to announce that God is the God of all-inclusive love who wills the wholeness and humanity of everyone, especially the poor and heavy burdened.[11] He is sent to gather all the outcast under the wings of their gracious Sophia-God and bring them to shalom. This envoy of Sophia walks her paths of justice and peace and invites others to do likewise. Like her, he delights in being with people; joy, insight, and a sure way to God are found in his company. Again and again in imaginative parables, compassionate healings, startling exorcisms, and festive meals he spells out the reality of the gracious goodness and renewing power of Sophia-God drawing near. Sometimes in all trust he calls her Abba. He likens her to a shepherd searching for a lost sheep, a woman looking for her lost coin, a father forgiving his wayward child, a bakerwoman kneading yeast into dough, a mother giving birth. Scandalous though it may appear, his inclusive table community widens the circle of the friends of God to include the most disvalued people, even tax collectors, sinners, prostitutes. In all of this, his compassionate, liberating words and deeds are the works of Sophia reestablishing the right order of creation: "Wisdom is justified by her deeds" (Mt 11:19).

Through his ministry Jesus unleashes a hope, a vision, and a present experience of liberating relationships that women, the lowest of the low in any class, as well as men, savor as the antithesis of patriarchy. Women interact with Jesus in mutual respect, support, comfort, and challenge, themselves being empowered to acts of compassion, thanksgiving, and boldness by Spirit-Sophia who draws near in him. Although long neglected by the later tradition, these women emerge in feminist interpretation in significant ways. They befriend, economically support, advise, teach, and challenge Jesus, break bread with him and evangelize in his name. Others receive the gift of his healing, being empowered to stand up straight beyond physical or mental suffering, spiritual alienation, or social ostracism. One woman whose name has been forgotten by patriarchal tradition prophetically anoints his head in an act that commissions him toward his death. New possibilities of relationships patterned according to the mutual services of friendship rather than domination-subordination flower among the women and men who respond and join his circle. They form a community of the discipleship of equals. All of this is too much for those heavily invested in the political and religious status quo. Mortally threatened, they conspire to be rid of him. In the end Jesus' death is a consequence of the hostile response of religious and civil rulers to the style and content of his ministry, to which he was radically faithful with a freedom that would not quit. The friendship and inclusive care of Sophia are rejected as Jesus, preeminent in the long line of Sophia's murdered prophets, is violently executed.

Jesus' death included all that makes death terrifying: state torture, physical anguish, brutal injustice, hatred by enemies, the mockery of their victorious voices, collapse of his life's work in ruins, betrayal by some close friends, the experience of abandonment by God and of powerlessness in which one ceases to be heroic. Indeed, he descended into hell, being "shattered," a term used elsewhere in Mark's Gospel of women at the tomb (14:33, 16:5).[12] *Ecce homo:* Christ crucified, the Wisdom of God.

For the Christian community the story does not end there. Faith in the resurrection witnesses that Sophia's characteristic gift of life is given in a new, unimaginable way, so that the crucified victim of state injustice is not abandoned forever. Her pure, beneficent, people-loving Spirit seals him in unimaginable life with God as pledge of a future for all the violated and the dead. This same Spirit is poured out on the circle of disciples drawn by the attractiveness of Jesus and his gracious God, and they are missioned to make the inclusive goodness and saving power of Sophia-God experientially available to the ends of the earth.

Along with other forms of political and liberation theology, feminist theology repudiates an interpretation of the death of Jesus as required by God in repayment for sin.[13] Today, such a view is virtually inseparable from an underlying image of God as an angry, bloodthirsty, violent, and sadistic father, reflecting the very worst kind of male behavior. Rather, Jesus' death was an act of violence brought about by threatened human men, an act of sin and therefore against the will of a gracious God. It occurred historically in consequence of Jesus' fidelity to the deepest truth and love he knew, expressed in his message and behavior. In a situation framed by the antagonistic norms of dominance and submission, his liberating life bore the signature of his death; in that sense, suffering was most probable. What comes clear in the event, however, is not Jesus' necessary passive victimization divinely decreed as a penalty for sin, but rather a dialectic of disaster and powerful human love through which the gracious

God of Jesus enters into solidarity with all those who suffer and are lost. The cross in all its dimensions, violence, suffering, and love is the parable that enacts Sophia-God's participation in the suffering of the world.

The victory of love, both human and divine, that spins new life out of this disaster is expressed in belief in the risen Christ. The resurrection itself cannot be imagined. What is affirmed as faith, for evidence continues to contradict this, is that overwhelming evil does not have the last word. The crucified one is not, in the end, abandoned. Sophia-God gathers her child and prophet into new transformed life, promise of a future for all the dead and the whole cosmos itself. The feminist vision of wholeness, of the preservation of the bodily integrity of each, even the most violated, and the interconnectedness of the whole, is here inscribed at the very center of the Christian vision.

Christ crucified and risen, the Wisdom of God, manifests the truth that divine justice and renewing power leavens the world in a way different from the techniques of dominating violence. The victory of shalom is won not by the sword of the warrior god but by the awesome power of compassionate love, in and through solidarity with those who suffer. The unfathomable depths of evil and suffering are entered into in friendship with Sophia-God, in trust that this is the path to life. Guided by wisdom categories, the story of the cross, rejected as passive, penal victimization, is reappropriated as heartbreaking empowerment. The suffering accompanying such a life as Jesus led is neither passive nor useless nor divinely ordained but is linked to the ways of Sophia forging justice and peace in an antagonistic world. As such, the cross is part of the larger mystery of pain-to-life, of that struggle for the new creation evocative of the rhythm of pregnancy, delivery, and birth so familiar to women of all times.[14] Let it be noted that at the moment of final crisis Mary Magdalene, Mary the mother of James and Joseph, Salome, and "many other women" disciples (Mk 15:41) appear strongly in the story and in fact are the moving point of continuity between the ministry, death, burial, and resurrection of Jesus. Near or afar off they keep vigil at the cross, standing in a solidarity with this vilified victim that gives powerful witness to women's courage of relationship throughout the ages. Their presence is a sacrament of God's own fidelity to the dying Jesus, their faithful friendship a witness to the hope that he is not totally abandoned. Having assisted at the burial, they know the path to the tomb. They are the first to encounter the risen Christ, to recognize what has happened, to receive the call to tell the good news to those of their circle in hiding. This they do: "Now it was Mary

Magdalene, Joanna, Mary the mother of James, and the women with them who told this to the apostles" (Lk 24:10), persisting despite male ridicule and disbelief.

It is fascinating to see how the church today asks to hear the words that the men disciples originally disparaged. The Sequence for the Mass of Easter Sunday, sung just before the great Alleluia and reading of the Gospel, urges, "Tell us, Mary, what you saw on the way?" To which she replies with ringing witness:

> I saw the tomb of the living Christ
> and the glory of his rising;
> angelic witnesses, the towel and the linen cloths.
> Christ my hope is risen;
> he goes before his own into Galilee.

Mary Magdalene now speaks throughout the whole world wherever Easter is celebrated in the Catholic liturgy.

Women form an intrinsic part of the circle in the upper room when the Spirit energizes the community in wind and fire at Pentecost. They move out as committed and creative co-workers for the gospel throughout the empire, as apostles, prophets, preachers, missionaries, healers, leaders of house churches, carrying on through history the healing, liberating mission of Jesus-Sophia in the power of the Spirit. The story of Jesus-Sophia cannot be rightly told without at the same time weaving in the stories of the circle of "his own," women as well as men.

Feminist hermeneutics has blazed a trail showing how the gospel story of Jesus resists being used to justify patriarchal dominance in any form. His preaching about the reign of God and his inclusive lifestyle lived and breathed the opposite, creating a challenge that brought down on his head the wrath of religious and civil authority. They crucified him, but Sophia-God receives that death and transforms it to life. When the story of Jesus is told in this way, a certain appropriateness accrues to the historical fact that he was a male human being. If in a patriarchal culture a woman had preached compassionate love and enacted a style of authority that serves, she would most certainly have been greeted with a colossal shrug. Is this not what women are supposed to do by nature? But from a social position of male privilege Jesus preached and acted this way, and herein lies the summons.

Above all the cross is raised as a challenge to the natural rightness of male dominating rule. The crucified Jesus embodies the exact opposite of the patriarchal ideal of the powerful man and shows how steep the price to be paid in the struggle for liberation. The cross thus stands as a poignant symbol of the "kenosis of patriarchy," the self-emptying of male dominating power in favor of the new humanity of compassionate service and mutual empowerment.[15] On this reading Jesus' maleness is prophecy announcing from within the end of patriarchy, at least as divinely ordained.

In the light of the original gospel story of Sophia's envoy and prophet it becomes clear that the heart of the problem is not that Jesus was a man but that too many men have not followed his footsteps, insofar as patriarchy has defined their self-identity and relationships. Reading Scripture with feminist hermeneutics makes it possible to affirm that despite subsequent distortion something more than the marginalization of women is possible, for Jesus-Sophia's story of ministry, suffering, final victory, and new community signify love, grace, and shalom for everyone equally and for the outcast, including women, most of all.

TRANSFORMING THE SYMBOL OF CHRIST

Theology speaks not only of the story of the historical Jesus but of his saving significance and rootedness in God, typically summing up its insight in the confession that Jesus is the Christ. What is the theological import of the symbol of Christ? Does it point to an inevitable link between maleness and divine saving function or to the promise of the compassionate, liberating power of God for all? Does it signify the glorification of a solitary man or the promise of a new community in the power of the Spirit?

Using the female figure of personified Wisdom so influential in biblical Christology to speak about Jesus as the Christ facilitates an inclusive rather than exclusive interpretation of this symbol. Jesus, the Wisdom of God. This foundational metaphor relieves the monopoly of the male metaphors of Logos and Son and destabilizes the patriarchal imagination. Whoever espouses a wisdom Christology is asserting that Sophia in all her fullness was in Jesus so that in his historicity he embodies divine mystery in creative and saving involvement with the world. In Augustine's words, "But she was sent in one way that she might be with human beings; and she has been sent in another way that she herself might be a human being."[16] Such a way of speaking breaks through the assumption that there is a "necessary ontological connection" between the male human being Jesus and a male God, leading to the realization instead that even as a human man, Jesus can be thought to be revelatory of the graciousness of God imaged as female.

Likewise, divine Sophia incarnate in Jesus addresses all persons in her call to be friends of God and can be truly represented by any human being called in her Spirit, women as well as men. Not incidentally, the typical stereotypes of masculine and feminine are subverted as female Sophia represents creative transcendence, primordial passion for justice, and knowledge of the truth, while Jesus incarnates these divine characteristics in an immanent way relative to bodiliness and the earth. The creative, redeeming paradox of Jesus-Sophia points the way to a reconciliation of opposites and their transformation from enemies into a liberating, unified diversity. In the end, from the perspective of Jesus' relationship with divine saving function, gender is not constitutive of the symbol of the Christ.

Neither does gender restrict the identity of the Christ within the human community. For one thing, faith in the resurrection affirms that Jesus in all his physical and spiritual historicity enters into new life by the power of the Spirit. What this ringing affirmation precisely means is inconceivable. His life is now hidden in the glory of God, while his presence is known on earth only where two or three gather, bread is broken, the hungry fed. But this indicates a transformation of his humanity, including sex, so profound that it escapes our imagination. The risen Christ sums up and transcends the particularities of earthly existence in life with God, alive with an energy that is extended into the earthly community by the power of the Spirit.

After his death and resurrection the focus of the ongoing story of Jesus-Sophia shifts from his concrete historical life to the community of sisters and brothers imbued with the Spirit. From the beginning this community is marked by the confession that Jesus-Sophia is the Christ, the anointed, the blessed one. Intrinsic to this confession is the insight that the beloved community shares in this Christhood, participates in the living and dying and rising of Christ to such an extent that it too has a christomorphic character. Challenging a naive physicalism that would collapse the totality of the Christ into the human man Jesus, biblical metaphors such as the Pauline body of Christ (1 Cor 12:12–27) and the Johannine branches abiding in the vine (Jn 15:1–11) expand the reality of Christ to include potentially all of redeemed humanity, sisters and brothers, still on the way. Amid the suffering and conflicts of history, members of the community of disciples are *en Christo,* and their own lives assume a christic pattern.

The fundamental nature of Christian identity as life in Christ makes clear that the biblical symbol Christ, the one anointed in the Spirit, cannot be restricted to the historical person Jesus or to certain select members of the community; rather it signifies all those who by drinking of the Spirit participate in the community of disciples. Christ is a pneumatological reality, a creation of the Spirit who is not limited by whether one is Jew or Greek, slave or free, male or female. The body of the risen Christ becomes the body of the community; all are one in Christ Jesus (1 Cor 12; Gal 3:28). Sandra Schneiders explains it well:

> The Christ is not exclusively the glorified Jesus, but the glorified Jesus animating his body which is the Church. Christ said to Paul "Why do you persecute *me?*" (Acts 9:4) because the literal fact is that the Christ is composed of all the baptized. This means that Christ, in contrast to Jesus, is not male, or more exactly not exclusively male. Christ is quite accurately portrayed as black, old, Gentile, female, Asian or Polish. Christ is inclusively all the baptized.[17]

This theological truth undergirds the insight that women participate fully in the life of Christ. The identification is not accomplished by a literal duplication of the historical Jesus' physical characteristics. If that were the case elderly men, black men, and so forth would not bear a "natural resemblance" to Jesus either. Rather, it is accomplished by participating in Christ's life, having the pattern of his love inscribed in the human heart by the power of the Spirit, empowering creative ways of walking the path of discipleship.

The baptismal tradition that configures both women and men to the living Christ and the martyrdom tradition that recognizes the image of Christ in the women and men who shed their blood have always borne this out. Maleness does not constitute the essence of Christ, but, in the Spirit, redeemed and redeeming humanity does. In a word, the story of the prophet and friend of Sophia, Sophia incarnate, anointed as the Christ, goes on in history as the story of the whole Christ, *christa* and *christus* alike, the wisdom community.

RECLAIMING CHRISTOLOGICAL DOCTRINE

Just as the gospel story of Jesus and biblical speech about Christ have an impulse that can subvert the androcentric construction of Christology, so too does the classical language of doctrine. Hammered out through centuries of controversy, this language affirms that in Jesus Christ, human nature and divine nature concur in one hypostasis: Jesus Christ is *vere Deus, vere homo* in *una persona*. Do these words intend an essential connection between maleness and the mystery of God made flesh? The history of the struggle that generated these phrases shows that such is not the case.

Apart from the major Arian position that sought to protect the transcendence of God by relegating the Logos to the status of a superior creature, thereby denying genuine divinity to Logos/Sophia incarnate, most of the other christological conflicts in the first five centuries circle around the authentic character of Jesus' humanity. From Arianism itself to docetism with its denial of real human flesh to the Apollinarian solution of excising a rational soul, to the monophysite tendency to blur the distinction of natures to the monothelite surgery on the human will, virtually every disputed position sought to shortchange the genuine, *bona fide* quality of Jesus' humanity. What was at issue was not his sex, race, class, or any other particularity but the completeness of his concrete humanity precisely as human. And the stakes were very high, for what is not assumed is not redeemed.[18]

Ultimately, Christian faith opted to affirm the genuine humanity of Sophia incarnate and to do so in the strongest possible language. The earlier Nicene confession that "God from God" became a human being (*et homo factus est*) was further specified by the Council of Chalcedon to mean a genuine human being (*vere homo*). This latter Council also pressed into service the controversial Greek word *homoousios,* "one in being," previously used in the Nicene creed to forge Jesus' identity of nature with God, to forge another identification, namely, that Jesus is also "one in being with us as to his humanity." Given the anthropology then current, this signified a body of real flesh that could feel passion, suffer, and die and a soul with its own spiritual and psychological powers. According to this doctrinal language, whatever else it may mean, Incarnation does not involve the mystery of God in merely dressing up like a human being and living a physically and psychologically truncated charade. Rather, one in being with us as to his humanity, Jesus is born to a life of creaturely finitude marked by the pleasures and pains of the body, nescience and growth in wisdom, and freedom with the need to risk.[19] These texts in their historical context make clear that it is not Jesus' maleness that is doctrinally important but his humanity in solidarity with the whole suffering human race. The intent of the christological doctrine was and continues to be inclusive.

In face of this, the trivialization introduced into the doctrine of the Incarnation by the androcentric stress on the maleness of Jesus' humanity fully warrants the charge of heresy and even blasphemy currently being leveled against it.[20] While Jesus was indeed a first-century Galilean Jewish man, and thus irredeemably particular, as we all are, what transpires in the Incarnation is inclusive of the humanity of all human beings of all races and historical conditions and both genders. Jesus' ability to be Savior does not reside in his maleness but in his loving, liberating history lived in the midst of the powers of evil and oppression and set loose in the wisdom community by the power of the Spirit to the ends of the earth.

TO PRACTICAL AND CRITICAL EFFECT

Theology will have come of age when the particularity that is highlighted is not Jesus' historical sex but the scandal of his option for the poor and marginalized, including women, in the Spirit of his compassionate, liberating Sophia-God. That is the scandal of particularity that really matters, aimed as it is toward the creation of a new order of wholeness in justice. Toward that end, feminist theological speech about Jesus the Wisdom of God shifts the focus of reflection off maleness and onto the whole theological significance of what transpires in the Christ event. Jesus in his human, historical specificity is confessed as Sophia incarnate, revelatory of the liberating graciousness of God imaged as female; women, as friends of Jesus-Sophia, share equally with men in his saving mission throughout time and can fully represent Christ, being themselves, in the Spirit, other Christs. This has profound implications for reshaping ecclesial theory and practice in the direction of a community of the discipleship and ministry of equals.

Furthermore, allowing the wisdom tradition to filter and focus the significance of Jesus promotes a whole range of values that are closely allied with women's experience. Friendship, connectedness, delight and passion, compassion, wholistic rather than dualistic patterns of relationship, the value of the everyday in addition to the heroic deed, the value of bodies as well as minds that seek the truth, the elusive presence of God that is coinherent with the world rather than separated from and ruling over, right order that pervades everywhere: all of these enter into the interpretation of Jesus the Christ, setting doctrine off in a fundamentally new direction that coheres with the praxis of women's equal human dignity.

For example, classical theology has long associated women with matter and the flesh in a derogatory manner. But if Wisdom herself became a human being, then the very matter of creation in the flesh of humanity and in women's own bodies belongs to her and is precious to her. There can be no dichotomy between matter and spirit or prizing of one over the other, but matter itself is a treasure related to God. Resurrection announces that this will always be so, for the body itself is glorified in the power of Wisdom's spirit, not discarded. Furthermore, it is the tortured and executed body of Jesus that is raised. This grounds Christian hope for a future for all the dead and explicitly for all those who are raped, tortured, and unjustly destroyed in the continuing torment of history. Wisdom's gift is ultimately life.

In addition to undermining patriarchal thought and practice in favor of right relationships between women and men, wisdom Christology done in the struggle for women's equal human dignity also contributes to right behavior in at least three other major areas of current concern: justice for the poor, respectful encounter with other religious traditions, and ecological care for the earth. First, justice in society is a central concern of the wisdom tradition of ancient Israel; it sees unjust conditions as a violation of the right order of creation. Prosperity must not be bought at the expense of the neighbor. According to Proverbs, "Those who oppress the poor insult their Maker," while those who reach out to the poor honor God (14:31). Accordingly, the wisdom literature is replete with advice on caring for the widow and orphan and the poor man; with warning that those who are greedy for gain will be caught in their own snare; and with instruction to rulers to love righteousness and govern accordingly: "The righteous know the rights of the poor; the wicked have no such understanding" (Prv 29:7). There is potential in the wisdom tradition for political critique of injustice.[21]

Personified Wisdom herself betrays a strong identification with the concerns of justice. "I walk," she says, "in the way of righteousness, along the paths of justice" (Prv 8:20). Her principles affect not only personal interactions but the social-political order as well: "By me kings reign, and rulers decree what is just; by me rulers rule, and nobles, all who govern rightly" (Prv 8:15–16). In an act that has become paradigmatic for all liberation, Wisdom leads her people out from a nation of oppressors, becoming to them a starry flame of guidance until they find a safe home (Wis 10:15–19).

Interpreting the historical ministry and death of Jesus, his own option for the poor and the price he paid for it, in the context of the wisdom tradition shows that the passion of God is clearly directed toward the lifting of social oppression and the establishing of right relations. The table is set for those who will come, the bread and wine ready to nourish the struggle. What is needed is to listen to the loud cries of Jesus-Sophia resounding in the cries of the poor, violated, and desperate and to ally our lives as the wisdom community to the divine creative, redeeming work of establishing right order in the world.

Second, there is a universal, nonexclusive character to the wisdom tradition that coheres with the recognition of value in all of the world's religious traditions. The sages tend to talk not so much about the "God of Israel" or the "God of our fathers" as about the Creator of all, present and moving everywhere. Again, righteousness and insight are not confined to those of the Jewish faith; even Job was not an Israelite.

Personified Wisdom herself symbolizes God's presence and activity throughout the whole world, not just in Israel. In her grand tour of the world she describes how she holds sway over every people and nation; in every one she has gotten a possession (Sir 24:6). Her kindly, people-loving spirit fills the world, pervading everything and holding all things together (Wis 1:6-7). Her light shines against the darkness everywhere, and those whom she makes to be friends of God and prophets are found in every nation.

Interpreting the meaning of Jesus in this context highlights the universalism inherent in his life, ministry, and destiny. Jesus-Sophia personally incarnates Wisdom's gracious care in one particular history, for the benefit of all, while she lays down a multiplicity of paths in diverse cultures by which all people may seek and, seeking, find her. There is then a continuity of divine action and inspiration between the Christian religion and the multitude of world religious traditions. Jesus uniquely focuses Wisdom for Christians, but the same reality is focused differently in other religious traditions. Wisdom discourse thus directs the community toward a global, ecumenical perspective respectful of other religious faiths.

Third, a relation to the whole cosmos is already built into the biblical wisdom tradition. Its interest lies in the right order of creation, and it focuses often and intensely on human life in the context of an interrelated natural world, both ideally forming a harmonious whole. When wisdom is given to Solomon he is enabled not only to judge wisely but to know the structure of the world, the cycles of the seasons, the constellations of the stars, the tempers of wild animals, the powers of the wind, the varieties of plants, and the virtues of roots: "I learned both what is secret and what is manifest, for Wisdom, the fashioner of all things, taught me" (Wis 7:17–22). Personified Wisdom is the mother of all these good things (Wis 7:12), the master craftswoman through whom they were all made (Prv 8:30). Reaching mightily from one end of the earth to the other she orders all things well and delights in them, playing in the world with rejoicing and elusive gaiety (Wis 8:1; Prv 8:31).

Interpreting the ministry, death, and resurrection of Jesus in wisdom categories orients Christology beyond the human world to the ecology of the earth and, indeed, to the universe, a vital move in this era of planetary crisis. Embodying Sophia who is fashioner of all that exists, Jesus' redeeming care extends to the flourishing of all creatures and the whole earth itself. The power of Wisdom's spirit is evident wherever human beings share in this love for the earth, tending its fruitfulness, respecting its limits, restoring what has been damaged, and guarding it from destruction. In this spirit the community of Jesus-Sophia finds its mandate to be in solidarity with the earth and at the forefront of ecological care.

CONCLUSION

The religious history of women's faith and discipleship that has found life-giving power in Jesus the Christ fully warrants the feminist theological effort to redeem the christological tradition from patriarchy. While Jesus the Christ has been interpreted in distorted ways to support male hegemony in the doctrine of God, Christian anthropology, and ecclesial structures, "something more" also flows through the Christian tradition: the dangerous memory of the liberating prophet of Sophia and the power of her Spirit let loose to renew the earth.

At this historical juncture the task is to redeem the name of Christ: to redeem it from the way it has been used for centuries to exclude and oppress; to redeem it for the healing and wholeness that is Wisdom's saving intent in the power of the Spirit. By retelling the story of Jesus in an egalitarian framework, transforming the symbol of Christ in wisdom and friendship categories, and reclaiming the original inclusive intent of the christological dogma, feminist theology calls the whole church to conversion, away from sexism and toward a community of the discipleship of equals, for the sake of its mission in the world.

NOTES

1. Jacqueline Grant, *White Women's Christ and Black Women's Jesus: Feminist Christology and Womanist Response* (Atlanta: Scholars Press, 1989).

2. Virginia Fabella, "A Common Methodology for Diverse Christologies?" in *With Passion and Compassion,* ed. Virginia Fabella and Mercy Amba Oduyoye (Maryknoll, NY: Orbis Books, 1988), 108–17.

3. Nellie Ritchie, "Women and Christology," in *Through Her Eyes,* ed. Elsa Tamez (Maryknoll, NY: Orbis Books, 1989), 95.

4. Elizabeth Amoah and Mercy Amba Oduyoye, "The Christ for African Women," in *With Passion and Compassion,* ed. Fabella and Oduyoye, 42.

5. Rosemary Radford Ruether, *Sexism and God-Talk: Toward a Feminist Theology* (Boston: Beacon Press, 1983), 117.

6. "Inter Insigniores," in *Origins* 6:33 (Feb. 3, 1977), par. 27.

7. Ruether's question in *Sexism and God-Talk,* 116–38, and in her *To Change the World: Christology and Cultural Criticism* (New York: Crossroad, 1981), 45–56.

8. For more thorough overview, see Roland Murphy, *The Tree of Life: An Exploration of Biblical Wisdom Literature,* Anchor Bible Reference Library (New York: Doubleday, 1990).

9. For more detailed exposition of the christological use of the Wisdom figure, see Elizabeth Johnson, *She Who Is: The Mystery of God in Feminist Theological Discourse* (New York: Crossroad, 1992), 86–100.

10. James Dunn, *Christology in the Making* (Philadelphia: Westminster Press, 1980), 212.

11. See extended treatment of this theme by Elisabeth Schüssler Fiorenza, *In Memory of Her: A Feminist Theological Reconstruction of Christian Origins* (New York: Crossroad, 1983), 118–59.

12. Elisabeth Moltmann-Wendel, *A Land Flowing with Milk and Honey: Perspectives on Feminist Theology* (New York: Crossroad, 1986), 127–32.

13. See Rita Nakashima Brock, *Journeys by Heart: A Christology of Erotic Power* (New York: Crossroad, 1988); Joanne Carlson Brown and Rebecca Parker, "For God So Loved the World?" in *Christianity, Patriarchy, and Abuse: A Feminist Critique,* ed. Joanne Carlson Brown and Carole R. Bohn (New York: Pilgrim Press, 1989), 1–30; and Mary Grey, *Feminism, Redemption and the Christian Tradition* (Mystic, CT: Twenty-Third Publications, 1990).

14. "Final Document: Intercontinental Women's Conference," in *With Passion and Compassion,* ed. Fabella and Oduyoye, 188.

15. Ruether, *Sexism and God-Talk,* 137.

16. Regarding *Sapientia:* "Sed aliter mittitur ut sit cum homine; aliter missa est ut ipsa sit homo"; Augustine, *De Trinitate* 4.20, 27; *Nicene and Post-Nicene Fathers,* vol. 3, ed. Philip Schaff (Grand Rapids: Eerdmans, 1956).

17. Sandra M. Schneiders, *Women and the Word* (New York: Paulist Press, 1986), 54.

18. For this interpretation of Arianism, see Robert Gregg and Dennis Groh, *Early Arianism—A View of Salvation* (Philadelphia: Fortress Press, 1981).

19. The line of thought that I am following coheres with Karl Rahner, "On the Theology of the Incarnation," *Theological Investigations* (New York: Seabury Press, 1974), 4:105–20.

20. Patricia Wilson-Kastner, *Faith, Feminism and the Christ* (Philadelphia: Fortress Press, 1983), 90; Schneiders, *Women and the Word,* 55; Anne Carr, *Transforming Grace: Christian Tradition and Women's Experience* (San Francisco: Harper & Row, 1988), 178.

21. See Leo Lefebure, *Toward a Contemporary Wisdom Christology: A Study of Karl Rahner and Norman Pittenger* (Lanham, MD: Univ. Press of America, 1988), 199–222.

FOR FURTHER READING

Brock, Rita Nakashima. *Journeys by Heart: A Christology of Erotic Power.* New York: Crossroad, 1988. A "feminist redemption of Christ" accomplished by emphasis on Christa-Community, to heal the brokenheartedness of patriarchy.

Carr, Anne. *Transforming Grace: Christian Tradition and Women's Experience.* San Francisco: Harper & Row, 1988; especially "Feminism and Christology." Survey of feminist theology in dialogue with the scholarship of gender.

Daly, Mary. *Beyond God the Father: Toward a Philosophy of Women's Liberation.* Boston: Beacon Press, 1973. Original critique of sexist Christology from the perspective of radical feminism.

Fabella, Virginia, and Mercy Amba Oduyoye, eds. *With Passion and Compassion: Third World Women Doing Theology.* Maryknoll, NY: Orbis Books, 1988. Papers from the Women's Commission of the Ecumenical Association of Third World Theologians, representing Africa, Asia, and Latin America.

Fiorenza, Elisabeth Schüssler. *In Memory of Her: A Feminist Theological Reconstruction of Christian Origins.* New York: Crossroad, 1983. A ground-breaking work delineating principles of feminist hermeneutics and their application to interpreting the New Testament.

Grant, Jacqueline. *White Women's Christ and Black Women's Jesus: Feminist Christology and Womanist Response.* Atlanta: Scholars Press, 1989. Critique of white feminism for its neglect of the oppressions of race and class; retrieval of Christology through focus on the experience of African American women.

Grey, Mary. *Feminism, Redemption and the Christian Tradition.* Mystic, CT: Twenty-Third Publications, 1990. Reinterpretation of symbols of redemption through women's experience of relation.

Johnson, Elizabeth. *She Who Is: The Mystery of God in Feminist Theological Discourse.* New York: Crossroad, 1992. Wisdom Christology within a feminist trinitarian theology, in dialogue with classical theology.

McFague, Sallie. *Models of God: Theology for an Ecological, Nuclear Age.* Philadelphia: Fortress Press, 1987. Outstanding thought experiment of God as mother, lover, and friend, and the world as God's body; connects Christology with erotic love, saving activity, and a healing ethic to benefit the whole world, human beings, and the earth.

Moltmann-Wendel, Elisabeth. *A Land Flowing with Milk and Honey.* New York: Crossroad, 1986. New perspectives on biblical stories about Jesus and women, stressing mutuality and self-love.

Ruether, Rosemary Radford. *Sexism and God-Talk: Toward a Feminist Theology.* Boston: Beacon Press, 1983. A fundamental work exploring foundations of feminist theology; offers a prophetic Christology in the context of new interpretations of all the basic "tracts."

Schneiders, Sandra M. *Women and the Word: The Gender of God in the New Testament and the Spirituality of Women.* New York: Paulist Press, 1986. A luminous analysis of New Testament material that undergirds women's equality in Christ.

Tamez, Elsa. *Through Her Eyes: Women's Theology from Latin America*. Maryknoll, NY: Orbis Books, 1989. New readings of Christology and other themes written from the stance that sees women's struggle inextricably linked to the struggle of their poor communities for social, political, and economic liberation.

Thistlethwaite, Susan Brooks. *Metaphors for the Contemporary Church*. New York: Pilgrim Press, 1983. Focuses on the relational Christ; see also her *Sex, Race, and God: Christian Feminism in Black and White,* which deals with the interrelation of sexism and racism.

Wilson-Kastner, Patricia. *Faith, Feminism and the Christ*. Philadelphia: Fortress Press, 1983. A systematic treatment of the possibilities inherent in the Logos doctrine.

CHAPTER SIX

THE MYSTERY OF BEING HUMAN TOGETHER

— Anthropology —

MARY AQUIN O'NEILL

God the Father is not a male deity. . . . When we reflect upon our addressing God as "Our Father" we soon realize that no sexuality is implied in God. . . . To intrude into the biblical portrait of the eternal Father, the incarnate Son and the adopted sons (male and female) the further picture of God as mother or God as parent is to distort the whole fine balance of the content of revelation. It is to introduce sexuality where none was intended.[1]

ONLY A REVISED theological anthropology can deliver Christianity from such mind-bending theological assertions.

Theological anthropology, itself a relatively new member of the family of theological concerns, raises and answers the question "What does our faith teach us about the mystery of being human?"[2] While every faith tradition has an implicit or explicit theological anthropology, what distinguishes Christian anthropology is that it answers the question on the basis of the Christian revelation and on the experience of life in the Christian community of believers.

As soon as the question is framed, however, it becomes problematic, for there are no generic human beings. There are, simply, male and female human beings. In the initial question, then, three issues are embedded: (1) Christian belief and experience about humanity as such; (2) Christian belief and experience about male human being; and (3) Christian belief and experience about female human being. For too long, Christian anthropology constructed by men has resulted in a conflation of the first issue and the second. The result has been a description of "human being" at once more reflective of the male angle on reality and less in touch with the fullness of Christian revelation and experience. In this chapter I hold all three issues in tension, in order to show the benefits to Christian anthropology of an approach informed by another consciousness and thus existential in a new way.

CREATION IN THE IMAGE OF GOD

At the heart of the Christian teaching about being human is the belief that to be human is to be created in the image and likeness of God. Implicit in this belief are the twin realities of being created and being creator. Between these two poles hangs every human life, holding together on the one hand a desire for the infinite—for the totality—and on the other, the all-too-real limitations of bodily, historical, actualized human existence.

The two creation stories of Genesis carry the theological treasure of this teaching. In the first, God creates humankind in God's image, male and female (Gn 1:27). God bids them to "be fruitful and multiply, and fill the earth . . . subdue it . . . and have dominion" (Gn 1:28). If the Christian community had but this story, it would indeed seem that human beings are to be the gods of the earth, endowed with limitless possibility and power. But the sacred text preserves two stories, and one must be read in light of the other.

In the second creation story, God first creates a single human being and presents this being with all the other created realities. Far from being satisfied with this splendid individual mastery of all surveyed, however, the being is reported to be "lonely"—so much so that God creates again, blessing the being with one who is like and unlike; other, yet given for communion. It is only in the presence of this other that the "lonely" being discovers, in fact, certain potentialities of being.[3] Lest the two together think that theirs is limitless power and possibility, however, in this story God gives a command that sets limits to their participation in the life of the garden.

Thus far the text gives reason to believe that being human in the image and likeness of God means: (1) to have one's existence as a gift from God; (2) to be given a charge to rule over all other things created; (3) to enjoy one's existence only in the company of an "other" like oneself; (4) to know one's self as male or female only in the presence of the sexually differentiated other; and (5) to know that one's rule is limited, bound by the command of God. From the beginning, then, the image of God is reflected in a community of persons, in a humankind that is created male and female. It is this community that receives both the empowering mandate and the limiting word. The community is to be creative without losing sight of the reality that it is itself created. Humankind is "image," not very God.

THE EFFECTS OF SIN

Given this reading of Genesis, the story of the first sin (Gn 3) is all the more illuminating. The representative of the power of evil does not approach the community of persons but singles one out for temptation. And the temptation consists, essentially, in being drawn to a very different interpretation of the meaning of God's no and the meaning of being "like" God.[4] Breaking the bond between them, the woman acts without the man, on the basis of an understanding of the act that has come from outside the communion established between God and the human beings God has created. One act is prelude to another as the chain of individual decisions leads, not to being able to look God in the eye as an equal, but to the shame of hiding from God and from each other.

Much has been made in recent years of the clearly androcentric bias to the second creation story. According to the text the man is created first, the woman is taken from the man, and the woman is the one approached by the serpent to be tempted first. It is also true, as some have said, that

creation first or second has a very different meaning if one takes an evolu-
tionary point of view and that the woman at least enters into debate with
the serpent, while the man just takes and eats without reflection.[5] Such
struggles over the text serve as reminders of how profoundly the sacred
text stands within a cultural context, how much the reader brings from
the culture to the reading of a text. It seems to me that one should never
be surprised at the evidence of cultural bias in literature, even in writings
that the community considers inspired. But the discernment of spirits
enjoined on Christians requires that the community not consider as
revealed what can be accounted for by cultural influences. To recognize
revelation it is necessary to identify the "inbreaking," that which con-
founds cultural expectations and raises human sights to possibilities that
are rooted in God's vision and will for humankind.

In this case, then, there are some wonderful surprises. And they are
revealed in an unlikely place, namely, in the punishments meted out by
God. First, each of the parties to the act of eating of the forbidden fruit
(the serpent, the woman, and the man) receives an appropriate punishment. This means, in the thought world of the text, that each is considered a moral agent and bears responsibility for the act that issued from the
self. Inasmuch as later traditions will treat women as children whose
actions reflect not on themselves but on the men whose possessions they
are considered to be, the fact that the woman is punished is remarkable.[6]
Second, buried in the punishment given the woman is a line that makes
all the difference to a correct interpretation of the fact of the historical
subordination of women. God says to the woman, "Your desire shall be
for your husband, and he shall rule over you" (Gn 3:16). The text reveals
that the subordination of women to men is a result of sin and not part
of the created order portrayed prior to what has come to be known as the
Fall. It is difficult to overestimate the significance of this insight for an
anthropology that begins with a vision of human beings called to be the
image of God together. It means that the connection between longing and
lording—so common as to be taken as essential to any relationship of
women to men—is forged in deviation from the will of God; when God's
will for human beings is realized, the longing of one for the other will not
result in the loss of self we understand to be ingredient to being "ruled
over."[7]

Failure to respect the limit set by God, then, results in a fundamental
dislocation at the heart of the relationship between the man and the
woman as well as in changes in the relationship of the man to the earth

and the woman to childbirth. From now on it is possible to hate the very process that continues life, the very earth that sustains life, the very other whose presence made life less lonely.[8] Moreover, it is possible for that hatred to be institutionalized in patterns of attitude and behavior that precede and shape subsequent generations before they come to consciousness, before they are capable of what the Christian community considers to be personal sin.[9]

In this way the sacred text suggests what contemporary feminist thinkers are coming to articulate with increasing clarity and passion: negative attitudes toward the earth, toward the body, and toward women are of a piece. The social sin of sexism cannot be separated from the other social sins that do not yet have such a commonly accepted name but that entail a disregard for the limitations placed on human power by the earth that is our mother and by the human body that is our most intimate connection to her and through her to the whole cosmos.

To say this is not to put the blame on men, however. The sacred text indicates that God holds the woman as well as the man responsible and acknowledges in addition the mystery of evil that was before them in the figure of the serpent who is also punished. Part of the mystery of being human together is that we share a history of listening to the serpent, of testing the limits, of distorted relationships, of passing on as true what are false images of God and the relationship of human beings to God. We are all implicated in the human history that is in exile.

THE MEANING OF REDEMPTION

The Christian way of telling the story of human history encompasses more than exile, however. It is also replete with promise, the promise of a homecoming that will be both a restoration and a being made new. At the heart of the story, then, is a covenant by means of which human beings are invited anew into a relationship with God, at God's gracious invitation. The covenant is the new garden, the realm in which human beings have revealed to them their own created nature and the ways of conducting themselves that are appropriate to a creature who has been made "little lower than God" (Ps 8:5a). This means that, while human beings know themselves capable of sin in light of the abundant testaments to this human experience, they are never permitted to forget that sin misses the mark of who and what they are, that sin is not freedom but a fundamental infidelity to themselves because it represents a betrayal of their own promises freely entered into. This saving truth is driven home, not only by the stories of human sinfulness but also by the stories of human greatness. When men and women are faithful to the covenant and, through it, to the God of the covenant, the people of God are delivered from the enemy and preserved on the way to the final home that is seeing the face of God.

What gives hope to humanity, then, in the face of all that is evil in our history, are the promises of God. To be believed, these promises must be embodied and visible to human eyes. Somewhere, there must be a glimpse, a foretaste of what has been pledged. Understood this way, the story of the chosen people becomes the story of a community committed to living in such a way that the promises of God become believable to others. It is the very meaning of Torah.

The telling of the human story, the unfolding of what is accepted as revealed by God, requires subtlety and variety, in form as well as content. For this reason we find in the Old Testament all the literary forms known to us: narrative and poetry, law and proverb, myth and apocalyptic. The list goes on as gifted members of the community of faith attempt to preserve what has been understood about the nature and destiny of women and men in time.

But Christians believe that in the fullness of time God entered into a new dimension of the covenant with human beings and through them, with all creation. "Long ago God spoke to our ancestors in many and various ways by the prophets, but in these last days he has spoken to us by a Son, whom he appointed heir of all things, through whom he also created the worlds. He is the reflection of God's glory and the exact imprint of God's very being" (Heb 1:1–3a).

In Jesus of Nazareth, God has drawn near: God allows men, women and children to see and hear and touch and know the being of God in their own way, in their own humanity. And so the human story is told over again, this time with the single personage of Jesus at the center, as the revelatory instance of human life under the reign of God, in the way of God, in the image of God, in the Spirit of God. Once more the garden is a place of testing, as is the desert, only this time the human protagonist is not bested by alien images of what it is to be like God, nor does Jesus turn toward the worship of gods alien to his people. (I might note as well that this time there is no woman with the man, or so it seems from the main lines of the Christian Scriptures.) Yet the image of being like God that Jesus appropriates and presents in his body and the God he worships in spirit and in truth are not universally accepted. He does not unify the people but rather divides them along new lines and in new ways. The God who created human beings still respects human freedom, even the freedom to turn away.

Jesus himself tastes this mystery of freedom as he wrestles with his own call and with the consequences of working it out in his own way. He learns how desperate the people are for leadership and how quickly they can turn when their own expectations of that leadership are not fulfilled. He discovers the difficult way of discernment as he tries to distinguish God's law from human distortion and manipulation of religious devotion. He is led, ultimately, to the realization of the prophets and mystics before him, namely, that only suffering love has any chance of changing hearts. He confronts his own fears and perhaps even his own dark night as followers abandon him, the crowd turns on him, religious and civil authorities determine to bring about his death, and it comes home to him that he can say yes or no to what faithfulness will bring upon him.

Jesus' fidelity to his way of being like God leads to the cross and to death as a criminal and loathed outcast of society. And even in death he causes division: His disciples split up. Some run away in fear and hide. Others stay as near as is permitted during his agony and as soon after his death as possible give his body proper preparation for burial. It is to the latter that the first word of his resurrection comes. Their experience of the risen Lord and their testimony to him becomes the cornerstone of the people who know God through the risen Christ: the Church.

Those who came to believe in him and to follow his way told in their turn the story of his life and what it had done to them. In the first century, they called this story Gospel, for it was to them above all good news. In Gospels, letters, historical writing called Acts, and in visionary writing called Apocalypse, they strove to capture and preserve the meaning of this life that had become the model for their own, to testify to the experience of God that was theirs in and through contact with Jesus the Christ, to hold together the community that had formed around him and that knew him to be risen from the dead.

Christians preached that the promises of God to the chosen people had been fulfilled in the coming of Jesus and the establishment of the church. To be "in Christ Jesus" was to be connected to the living God and to live according to the Spirit of God. Having broken the power of sin and death in his own body, this Christ Jesus could communicate a new life to others who would in turn be his embodied presence in the world. Nothing could be more important than to be on his side, to be under his patronage, to be with him, to live and move and have one's being in him.

In this way, the image of God was given distinct lineaments by the image of Christ. The Hebraic tradition of the imitation of God was transformed into the Christian way of the imitation of Christ.

Out of this emerges a dual anthropology and a problem recognized in our day as plaguing Christian faith from the beginning. Continuity with the Old Testament means believing that human beings are created in the image of God and that God's image is embodied in both male and female. It also entails belief that both men and women are responsible for sin and are affected by the history of sin; both stand in need of forgiveness, deliverance, restoration, redemption. Created together, exiled together, it would seem that they would be covenanted and redeemed together. And it would seem as well that each would be given, in the flesh, an image of redeemed humanity. Yet by the time the New Testament is written, it is clear that another way of imagining is at work in the world. The hierarchy that the Genesis text attributes to sin has been read into the created order. For this reason, a whole theology based on sex can be developed, a theology that will speak of the headship of the man and the submission of the woman as rooted and reflected in the relationship between Christ and the church. Thus an anthropology of mutuality reconstructed from a reading of the Genesis creation texts and from Jesus' way of relating to women and men comes into direct conflict with an anthropology of male superiority and headship. The latter derives in some measure from the way of telling the story of redemption: humankind is redeemed by a male redeemer, and the new being who is the perfect image of God is a man. The conflict is nowhere seen more clearly than in the vision of life for men and women in the church that appears in the writings of the apostle Paul.[10] Compare the following texts:

> There is neither Jew or Greek, there is no longer slave or free, there is no longer male and female: for all of you are one in Christ Jesus. (Gal 3:28)

> But I want you to understand that Christ is the head of every man, and the husband is the head of his wife, and God is the head of Christ. . . . For a man . . . is the image and reflection of God; but woman is the reflection of man. Indeed, man was not made from woman, but woman from man. Neither was man created for the sake of woman, but woman for the sake of man. (I Cor 11:3, 7–9)

> Wives, be subject to your husbands as you are to the
> Lord. For the husband is the head of the wife just as Christ is
> the head of the church, the body of which he is the Savior. Just
> as the church is subject to Christ, so also wives ought to be, in
> everything, to their husbands. (Eph 5:22–24)

Perhaps the androcentrism of the New Testament should surprise us no
more than that of the Old. Perhaps, moreover, we ought to apply the same
criterion for revelation here that I suggested above, looking for the inbreaking, the new possibilities for human being that cannot be accounted
for by culture. Great strides in that regard have been made by feminist
interpreters of the New Testament, who document at length the ways in
which Jesus' own relating to women defied the cultural expectations and
patterns of his time. Long before the day of the technically trained special-
ists, however, thinking women saw that, with respect to women, Jesus
represented something new:

> Perhaps it is no wonder that the women were first at the Cradle
> and last at the Cross. They had never known a man like this
> Man—there never has been such another. A prophet and
> teacher who never nagged at them, never flattered or coaxed or
> patronised; who never made arch jokes about them . . . ; who
> rebuked without querulousness and praised without con-
> descension; who took their questions and arguments seriously;
> who never mapped out their sphere for them, never urged
> them to be feminine or jeered at them for being female; who
> had no axe to grind and no uneasy male dignity to defend; who
> took them as he found them and was completely unself-
> conscious. There is no act, no sermon, no parable in the whole
> Gospel that borrows its pungency from female perversity;
> nobody could possibly guess from the words and deeds of Jesus
> that there was anything "funny" about woman's nature.
>
> But we might easily deduce it from his contemporaries,
> and from his prophets before him, and from his Church to this
> day.[11]

Important as Dorothy Sayers's insight is, however, it is not enough.
For an underlying individualism in the theological imagination will still
result in an account even of this so-called feminist Jesus as standing
alone, needing to receive nothing from women in order to achieve his

extraordinary capacity to enter into right relationship with them. More-over, it does not touch the problem that the creator God is imaged in the male and female, but the redeemer God only in the male.

THE CONFUSION OF THEOLOGY

The double current visible in the writings of Paul takes a new form in the subsequent history of Christian anthropology. While for Christian men the old Adam has been put off in Christ, no such assurance obtains about the old Eve.[12] There is Mary, of course, but theologians determined that God has not been made flesh in her *being* but only in her womb. Owing to the confrontation of biblical religion with Greek philosophical thought forms and very different creation myths, speculations arose about the nature of men and women. Theologians who had no doubt about the image of God in man questioned the image of God in woman and constructed a view of her biological, social, intellectual, and even spiritual inferiority. It should be known that there were theologians who advanced the thesis that women were not really human.[13]

Although the church never officially adopted the position that denied the humanity of women, the most influential theologian for Catholic Christianity from the Middle Ages to modern times, Thomas Aquinas, held quite clearly that the male sex was normative for humanity and that the female was a defective instance of human being. This anthropology underlies Aquinas's argument for forbidding priestly ordination to women as well as other considerations of her role in the church. At the same time, however, Aquinas reached a different conclusion with respect to the "state of glory": "If women burn with greater charity, they shall also attain greater glory from the Divine vision: because the women whose love for our Lord was more persistent . . . were the first to see Him rising in Glory."[14]

As late as the 1950s this theology perdured in popular form in the maxim "It's a man's world, but it will be a woman's heaven."[15] It is no wonder that Mary Daly called the history of the church and the second sex a "record of contradictions."[16]

It appears to be the case, then, that the freedom for which Christ has set human beings free, the new being that is available through baptism in his name, the new law that is the spirit of Christ poured out into the very heart of the human, the new power to teach and rule and sanctify in the community of the new covenant itself is applicable fully only to men. While men are not only permitted but encouraged to tame the earth

whose resistance to effort is the source of pain in labor, women are socialized to love the rule of men and to see any attempt at its overthrow as deep
infidelity to God's will for them.[17] There develops a vision of woman's
nature as essentially different from that of a man, one that fits her for certain occupations and renders her unfit for others. Right into the twentieth
century extraecclesial efforts at the emancipation of women are met with
staunch resistance on these theological grounds. Take, for example, the
reasoning of Pope Pius XI against coeducation: "There is not in *nature
itself, which fashions the two quite different in organism, in temperament, in abil-
ities,* anything to suggest that there can be or ought to be promiscuity, and
much less equality, in the training of the two sexes."[18]

Such thinking and teaching leads to a two-nature anthropology, a
vision of human being as divided into two distinct kinds, each with iden-
tifiable differences that become normative for the sex. This anthropology
of complementarity, as it came to be known, posits a theology in which
the sexes complete one another, not only on the level of reproduction, but
in the full range of human existence: social, intellectual, psychological,
spiritual. There is a male way of being and a female way, and these can be
known from an examination of the bodies of the two and given a fair
degree of specificity. Thus men are supposed to be, by nature, active,
rational, willful, autonomous beings whose direction goes outward into
the world; women are to be passive, intuitive, emotional, connected beings whose natural inclination is inward. This bipolar vision of the sexes
leads to an equally bipolar understanding of their respective places, namely,
the world and the home.[19]

In essence, the contemporary movement for the liberation of
women can be seen as a powerful reaction against this version of women's
destiny and, with it, of men's. As women came into the field of theology
and as they reflected on the tradition in light of their own experiences,
they challenged the theological validity of an interpretation of the sexes
as complementary, especially as it so often meant that women were
evangelized to sacrifice themselves for the wholeness of men and not
vice-versa.[20]

Out of the debate have come new models for understanding human
nature and the relationship between the sexes. The idea that there is a single human nature shared by women and men now does combat with the
notion of two distinct human natures, one superior and the other inferior.
At the same time, there is debate over how to image that single human
nature. Strong currents in contemporary culture opt for an androgynous

or a unisex ideal, and this results in images that are incompatible with the ancient creation stories of Genesis.[21]

For the contemporary Roman Catholic church in the West, nothing has so focused these questions of anthropology as the movement for the ordination of women. Here the nature question comes to the fore and ways of doing theology stand out in sharp contrast to one another.

Theologians who oppose the ordination of women do so on the basis of a dual anthropology that depends on belief in the unchanging structures of nature, and on an understanding that revelation, tradition, theology, and ethics are oriented toward the past. As Anne E. Carr puts it, this theological anthropology insists that "what is, has been given in nature by God and must not be changed. New knowledge of the human person, derived from the biological and human sciences, is irrelevant to theological discussion since the goal of theology is to preserve the past order as natural, as the order of creation, and therefore as revealed by God."[22]

On the other hand, the theology undergirding arguments for the ordination of women most often assumes a single anthropology. This theological anthropology emphasizes history and experience rather than nature and is open to dialogue with other human sciences. Revelation, tradition, theology, and ethics relate to the present and are conceived as dynamic realities.[23] I now think that for the Christian theologian the issue is not whether one adopts a two-nature or a one-nature anthropology; the notion of one nature or a common humanity has become so accepted that it was affirmed by the U.S. Catholic bishops right through the fourth draft of their proposed pastoral letter on the concerns of women. The issue is rather how to imagine the oneness that is to obtain between the sexes. Is it, in other words, a unity to be realized in an individual way or one that can be realized only in a community of persons, each of whom has gifts and limitations? The androgynous and unisexual images so prevalent in the culture, as well as the tradition of complementarity in the Roman Catholic church, assume a unity of humanity imagined after the model of the individual.[24] Androgyny advocates a development of the individual such that she or he includes within the self all that has been traditionally divided between male and female; the unisex approach takes one or the other sex as the ideal and sets about to accommodate the self to it, no matter what is given in nature; and the theology of complementarity has been based on the image of an individual body in which the male is the head and the female the lower part to be ruled over by the head, seat of reason and intelligence.

Directly contrary to this stands the revelation of Genesis and of the biblical tradition, properly understood, in which the unity of humanity is the unity of a communion of persons and the model of the person is not the autonomous and isolated individual but the covenanted one who is free because bound to others and to God. It demands an anthropology of mutuality in which the male/female difference becomes paradigmatic of human limitation and possibility and in which being like God can be achieved only by the gift of self to others and the reception of the gift of self from others. In such an anthropology, difference is not to be liquidated but delighted in, and personal development is the fruit of relationships as much as the reward for efforts of will.

To enter into a real relationship, however, requires a certain level of confidence in the way one is, in what one has to give, in the things one has come to value. Theologically, it requires deep assurance that one's way of being created is good and is indeed the image of God. In a tradition where the dominant images of God continue to be male; where the story of evil is told with emphasis on the role of the woman and the story of salvation is the record of the accomplishment of a lone male redeemer; where with respect to the sacraments—lifeblood of the community called Church—women need men for everything and men need women for nothing, this deep assurance can only be lacking and genuinely mutual relationships rendered impossible. Mutuality will be absent not only because women do not have the lived experience necessary to support belief in their being image of God, but because men too readily identify themselves with God.

THE CONTRIBUTION OF PIETY

There is another tradition. In poetry and song, in the visual arts, in the liturgical year and in the prayers of the faithful, in towering cathedrals and in wayside shrines there grew another account of salvation, one that gave the male redeemer a partner, that matched him with a coredemptrix. Marian piety has enjoyed a long and intricate development in the history of the church. Surely it was the imagination of women that saw in the figure of Mary one who was also a suffering servant. Her sorrows were the sorrows of women, and women were drawn to meditate on them. Her life was hidden, as was theirs, in the private places where children are born and raised, where whole traditions are passed on, where joys are celebrated and hurts are nursed as foundations of a lifetime are laid.[25]

In time, the meditation on her sorrows led to expectation of her victory as the Christian story was applied to the patterns of a woman's life and being. She was hailed full of grace, free of sin, powerful advocate, queen of heaven and earth.

Two dogmas were proclaimed of her: the Immaculate Conception and the Assumption. But in Roman Catholic intellectual circles today there is what seems to me great embarrassment over those outrageous declarations of Marian devotion. Since the Second Vatican Council, mainline Catholic theologians have appeared eager to associate Mary only with humanity and to put a stop to any tendencies to associate her with Christ except as his mother and "first disciple."[26] I know of no instance where the Marian dogmas are considered fundamental to a theological anthropology in anything like the way the christological dogmas are. Only the equally outrageous and original Mary Daly has seen the potential of Mary for the self-understanding of women, and this long after she decided that Christianity was bankrupt with respect to their real salvation: "The sometimes God-like status of Mary (always officially denied in Roman Catholicism, of course) may be, as Simone de Beauvoir suggests, a remnant of the ancient image of the Mother Goddess, enchained and subordinated in Christianity, as the 'Mother of God.' Yet, if it is a leftover, it may also be a foretelling image, pointing to the future becoming of women 'to the image of God.'"[27]

It should be said, of course, that the Marian tradition, no less than other traditions, has been affected by the androcentric bias of theology. There are ways of imagining Mary that thinking women consider damaging. One of my primary concerns is the way in which Mary, who clearly engaged in what is sexual experience—namely giving birth and breastfeeding—has been pictured in the theological tradition as being somehow preserved from what was considered to be the taint of sexual experience because she never had intercourse.

There is no question, then, that the Marian theological tradition needs critical examination. But Mary Daly has espied exactly what needs to be developed now: that in the figure of Mary, Christians are given the redeeming image of God in female being, an image that is salvific for men as well as for women.

SANCTIFICATION IN THE BODY

At the end of this overview of the theological terrain, we are left with the following: Human beings are created in the image of God, male and female. That creation entails limitations and possibilities for each. Both male and female are responsible for the injury inflicted by sin on human creatures and, through them, on the rest of creation. They are both responsible for the long, sad history of evil that has distorted the relationship between the sexes. Sin and its consequent damage can be overcome, so the Christian believes, by being baptized into Christ and living the Christian life. Jesus the Christ is the image of God sent to restore humanity to union with God and to establish a community in which such restored humanity is embodied for the world as a sacramental sign. The life of Christ is, then, the model for women as well as men.

Yet women may not image Christ in a sacramental way, for, according to current church teaching, they cannot: Christ was a male and so must be the priest who represents him in a personal way in the sacrament of orders. In this respect, women are urged to be like Mary, whose dignity, it is said, lies in her motherhood.

Seen in this way, the theological anthropology of the church cannot apply in practice to both male and female all that it says about the dignity of humanity.[28] The sacramental system teaches a different anthropology based on an androcentric soteriology: women must be saved in and through the ministrations of men; men are not saved in and through the ministrations of women. Attempts to reconcile such contradictory theological assertions end up recommending a notion of priesthood that discounts embodiment or that subtly implies the superiority of male embodiment because it enables the man to represent Christ and therefore God.

Pope John Paul II has provided, in my estimation, a way through the tangle of this theological knot. In a series of addresses entitled "The Theology of the Body," he sets forth a vision that, deeply meditated on, could liberate theology from its androcentrism and occasion a radical rethinking of the whole tradition.[29] First, Pope John Paul II puts the human body at the center of God's revelation. "The body, in its masculinity and femininity, is called from the beginning to become the manifestation of the spirit," he asserts.[30] The body has, then, the "value of a sign—in a way a sacramental sign." Thinking about the human experience of conjugal union, the pope argues that what is revealed therein is the meaning of the differentiated human body, namely, the "nuptial meaning." I take him to intend by this, not that everyone is destined to conjugal union, but that in and through a hermeneutic of conjugal union believers can discover the deep meaning of the human body. The meaning of being embodied as male and female, he argues, is that it enables both women and men to exist as givers and receivers because in and through the body human beings have something to give to and something to receive from each other. Later, the pope specifies the twofold donation that all human beings are called to make with their bodies: the gift of life and the gift of love.

This is the vocation of human beings, and it is common to men and women; yet no single individual will accomplish it alone because it is also part of embodied experience, as revealed in what I have termed the hermeneutic of the conjugal, that neither of the sexes has all that it takes without the other. If the conjugal union is paradigmatic for all of human life, as I think it is, then this truth will apply more widely, but not always to the differentiation by sex. It will mean that, as a human being, one always has something to give and to receive from other times, cultures, races, classes—even, I would hold, from other experiences of being sinners. As Augustine knew, these experiences work toward good for those who love in different ways.[31]

In a second step, the pope answers a fundamental question: what is it that "makes" a person male or female? Setting himself against any naturalistic or deterministic answer to that query, John Paul II draws from the wellspring of Genesis the saving truth that being male or female is a matter of knowledge. In a line with profound ramifications for theological anthropology, the pope says this about the knowledge of oneself as female or male: "It is . . . a further discovery of the meaning of one's own body, a common and reciprocal discovery, just as the existence of man, whom 'God created male and female' is common and reciprocal from the beginning."[32]

One implication of the pope's thought is that one cannot know oneself as a sexually differentiated being without a relationship to the sexually differentiated other.[33] Girls raised in a single-sex world, then, would know themselves only as like the others and never as different with respect to the body; the same would hold for boys. The very knowledge of one's body and its sexual possibilities is, then, a gift from the sexually differentiated other. Fully human self-knowledge requires some form of relationship to members of the other sex.[34] Inasmuch as, in the Catholic church, such reciprocity between men and women has not been institutionalized, men have had the power to separate themselves from women and create a single-sex world, a world that inadvertently deprives them of this form of self-knowledge. Applying the pope's thought in this way throws new light on some of the deformations surfacing regarding male clerics and religious, deformations from which women are saved, in part, by the very inability to live a sacramental life without contact with men.

The third and final point to draw out from the pope's writings on the theology of the body concerns the meaning of being male and female, of giving life and love, in and out of marriage. The pope says that "by means of the body, the human person is 'husband' and 'wife.' At the same time, in this particular act of 'knowledge,' mediated by personal femininity and masculinity, also the discovery of the 'pure' subjectivity of the gift: that is, mutual self-fulfillment in the gift, seems to be reached."[35]

Inasmuch as, for the Catholic Christian, marriage is a vocation and not an ordinance, it cannot be held that marriage is necessary to the fully human Christian life. Yet the self-giving that is characteristic of marriage is necessary and needs be learned, for, as I argued above, all of us are called to give the gift of life and love. The pope's insight thus challenges a narrow interpretation of "mutual self-fulfillment in the gift."

CORRECTIVES TO A CHRISTIAN ANTHROPOLOGY

This is the point to return to the figures of Jesus and Mary. Without Mary, theologians are forced to develop an androgynous Christology or a docetic one. By androgynous, I mean a Christology in which Jesus is imagined as complete in himself, embracing the possibilities of female as well as male being. By docetic, I mean that his body is not considered to be a real human body and that it in no way affects his being. If what the pope says about human self-knowledge and self-giving is true, and if an assertion of Jesus' true humanity requires that this reciprocity of being apply to him as well, he must have received his knowledge of himself as a man, as male, as masculine, from women.[36] Since it seems that he spent the better portion of his life either at home with Mary or with John the Baptist, Mary becomes much more important to the development of the personality of Jesus than can be accounted for by biological motherhood. She must have made it possible for him to become what he became and do what he did. To say this is to say that she shares, essentially, in his mission and in his being.

There is another dimension of the revelation that comes to us through the two of them. Although embodiment as male or female represents limitations, loving interaction with the other can open up undreamed-of possibilities. Jesus, as far as we know, begot no children, yet he gives life and love with his body through the Eucharist. Mary gave birth and fed with her body, yet she remains a virgin. Only the two figures together can reveal the radical saving truth about being male and female, virgin yet procreative, lover and life giver in the new age ushered in by the coming of the promised one. Only a hermeneutic of the two figures, male and female, and of the traditions that have interpreted them, can allow for the discovery of the common and reciprocal story of salvation.

The problem is that no human life, not even that of Jesus, can embrace both sides of the human experience at the same time. One cannot be both male and female, nurturer and nurtured, actor and audience, the one to undergo suffering and the one to feel the suffering of the other all at the same time. The androcentric bias in theology has repeatedly cast the spotlight on the one who acts but has left in the shadows the one who taught him so to act. Take the great miracle of the wedding feast at Cana (Jn 2:1–11). Whose miracle is it? The one who notices the need or the one who, challenged and corrected, acts to fill it? Seen this way, it becomes a false question. The miracle is the result of receptivity and activity, questioning and answering, preparing and being prepared. Only when we have a theology that appreciates the one as much as the other—as index of the salvific action of the divine in human life—will men as well as women be truly free to give whatever gift lies in their capacity for each other and the world.

This insight does not associate one way of being with women and the other with men. Mary is as much a model for men as Jesus is for women. But one without the other will result in a truncated theological anthropology. Christians who hold the two together will have revealed to them the mystery of human development, the pattern for which is always the paschal mystery. At times, suffering, death, and resurrection will be experienced directly, in the first person. Often they will be experienced vicariously, in the second person.[37] One way is not better than the other. Nor is one way more divine, for it is all in the image of God.

In many ways, the movement for the liberation of women has brought theological anthropology to the brink of a new era. There is great promise for discovering, not only possibilities for the humanity of women to embrace ways of being and works traditionally reserved for men, but also the reverse. The humanity of men is equally capable of giving life and love; Catholic pedagogy must reveal that to them. The talk should be as much about fatherhood as about motherhood, as much about unwed impregnation as about unwed pregnancy, as much about fathers bringing up the child as mothers bringing the fetus to term. Most of all, Catholics should be led to discover in the *ecclesiola,* as the Second Vatican Council called the family, a life as sacramentally real as that in the parish church. To do that, the church will require fathers as well as mothers in the home, mothers as well as fathers at the altar. Some time ago, having been invited to address a parish group on the topic of women in the church, I asked the audience, "Can you think of a single role in the church that cannot be filled by a man?" One woman shot back, "Yes. The Mother of God." Undaunted, I pressed ahead. "And how is that role symbolized in the official life of the church?" "It isn't," she replied, clearly pondering the import of what she had been led to say.

In a church that places as much emphasis on the body as Catholicism does, in a church that defends what is called the "sacramental principle," the absence of the "woman" has grave consequences. If the body itself has the value of a sacramental sign, if the human body is a text to be read, there is much to be anticipated as theologians let in the female and look for the inbreaking.

It is all ahead as theologians enter and reflect upon a new stage in the mystery of being human together. The salvation of the world depends on an openness to discern the empowering mandate and the limiting word spoken by God in the creation, redemption, and sanctification of human beings, male and female, in the image of God.

NOTES

1. Graham Leonard, Iaian MacKenzie, Peter Toon, *Let God Be God* (London: Darton, Longman and Todd, 1989), 55–56.

2. For an explanation of the rise of theological anthropology, see Edward Farley, "Toward a Contemporary Theology of Human Being," in *Images of Man,* ed. J. William Angell and E. Pendleton Banks (Macon, GA: Mercer Univ. Press, 1984), 55–56.

3. Phyllis Trible has shown conclusively that sexual differentiation and all it entails arises simultaneously with the creation of the "other." Before that, there is an "earth creature," but no male or female. "His sexual identity depends upon her even as hers depends upon him. For both of them sexuality originates in the one flesh of humanity." See *God and the Rhetoric of Sexuality* (Philadelphia: Fortress Press, 1978), 98–99.

4. I am indebted here to the work of Paul Ricoeur in *The Symbolism of Evil* (Boston: Beacon Press, 1967). The discussion of the "dizzying" effect of the interdiction is found on p. 252–55.

5. For a time feminists sported bumper stickers that said, "Adam was a rough draft."

6. See Phyllis Bird, "Images of Women in the Old Testament," in *Religion and Sexism,* ed. Rosemary Radford Ruether (New York: Simon and Schuster, 1974), 49.

7. Phyllis Trible has argued that a vision of this restored relationship is given in the Song of Songs. See "Love's Lyrics Redeemed," in *God and the Rhetoric of Sexuality,* 144–65.

I have repeatedly discovered in college classrooms that students rarely have any acquaintance with the Song of Songs and often are amazed when required to read it.

8. There are others who read this experience in a more "positive" way. Ricoeur, for example, suggests that "sin represents a certain advance in self-consciousness" that begins "an irreversible adventure, a crisis in the becoming of man, which will not reach its denouement until the final process of justification." See *Symbolism of Evil,* 253.

9. This way of presenting the case throws new light on the debate over calling sexism a sin. Sexism would be one of the concrete realizations of original sin. For a powerful analysis of the effect of this on sexual relationships and behavior, see Catharine A. MacKinnon's chapter, "Sexuality," in *Toward a Feminist Theory of the State* (Cambridge: Harvard Univ. Press), 126–54.

10. I owe this insight to the work of Julia O'Faolain and Lauro Martines, who, in their work *Not in God's Image* (New York: Harper & Row, 1973), pointed out what they call the "double current" in the apostle Paul; see pp. 128–29.

11. Dorothy L. Sayers, *Are Women Human?* (Grand Rapids: Eerdmans, 1971), 47. The essay was originally published in 1947.

12. See Bernard P. Prusak, "Woman: Seductive Siren and Source of Sin? Pseudepigraphal Myth and Christian Origins," in *Religion and Sexism,* ed. Rosemary Radford Ruether, (New York: Simon and Schuster, 1974), 89–116.

13. See Alvin John Schmidt, *Veiled and Silenced: How Culture Shaped Sexist Theology* (Macon, GA: Mercer Univ. Press, 1990), 69–95, for a review of this history. For an opposing view, see Maryanne Cline Horowitz, "The Image of God in Man: Is Woman Included?" *Harvard Theological Review* 72 (July–Oct. 1979): 175–206.

14. Thomas Aquinas, *Summa Theologiae* III, q. 55 a. 1, trans. Fathers of the English Dominican Province (New York: Benziger Brothers, 1947).

15. The answer given me by a teacher when, as a child, I asked why girls could not serve at the altar.

16. See chap. 2 of Mary Daly, *The Church and the Second Sex* (New York: Harper & Row, 1968), 32–75.

17. Women were even socialized by the church to love the pain of their labor in delivering children. Thus Pius XII to Women of Catholic Action: "Even the pains that, since original sin, a mother has to suffer to give birth to her child only draw tighter the bond that binds them: she loves it the more, the more pain it has cost her." Cited by Daly, *The Second Sex,* 72.

18. *Divini Illius Magistri,* Dec. 31, 1929. Cited in Daly, *The Second Sex,* 67, emphasis added.

19. See Elizabeth Janeway, *Man's World, Woman's Place* (New York: Dell, 1971), for an analysis of the causes and effects of such thinking.

20. See Catherine Mowry LaCugna, "Catholic Women as Ministers and Theologians," *America* 167, no. 10 (Oct. 10, 1992): 238–49.

21. I have expanded on these currents in comparison with the anthropology of complementarity in "Toward a Renewed Anthropology," *Theological Studies* 36, no. 4 (1975): 734–36 and in "Imagine Being Human: An Anthropology of Mutuality," in *Miriam's Song II: Patriarchy, A Feminist Critique* (West Hyattsville, MD: Priests for Equality, 1988), 45–48.

22. Anne E. Carr, *Transforming Grace: Christian Tradition and Women's Experience* (San Francisco: Harper & Row, 1988), 125.

23. For a more extensive analysis of these theological differences, see *Research Report: Women in Church and Society*, ed. Sara Butler (Mahwah, NJ: Catholic Theological Society of America, 1978).

24. For this insight, I am indebted to conversations with Catherine M. LaCugna, whose work on the Holy Trinity presents a theological challenge to the individualistic way of understanding the human person.

25. When I was a student at Vanderbilt, I was often asked by Protestant women's church groups to lecture. With amazing regularity, by the end of the evening, women would begin "confessing" to me that they prayed to Mary, despite the fact that their ministers railed against such practice. They prayed to her, they told me, because she was a mother and understood what mothers go through. There is much to learn from this, I think.

26. For a review of the contemporary literature on Mary, see Elizabeth Johnson, "Mary and the Female Face of God," *Theological Studies* 50, no. 3 (1989): 500–26.

27. Mary Daly, *Beyond God the Father* (Boston: Beacon Press, 1973), 83–84.

28. This was one of the fundamental theological flaws in the pastoral letter of women's concerns attempted by the U.S. Catholic bishops. The theological anthropology with which the document began (retained even into the infamous fourth draft) was contradicted by the view of life in the church expressed in the rest of the document.

29. The "theology of the body" was developed in a series of Wednesday afternoon audiences given between 1979 and 1981. The talks have been published in three volumes by the Daughters of St. Paul (Boston): *Original Unity of Man and Woman: Catechesis on the Book of Genesis* (1981); *Blessed Are the Pure of Heart: Catechesis on the Sermon on the Mount and Writings of St. Paul* (1983); *Reflections on* Humanae vitae: *Conjugal Morality and Spirituality* (1984).

30. Oct. 22, 1980. I am dependent on the translation published in *Sacred in All Its Forms*, ed. James V. Schall (Boston: Daughters of St. Paul, 1984), 125.

31. This realization opens up new ways of talking about the Mystical Body or the Communion of Saints.

32. March 12, 1980, in *Sacred in All Its Forms*, 137.

33. The pope thus teaches in his reflections the same truth that Phyllis Trible discovered through her exegetical work. See n. 3 above.

34. Theology is only beginning to consider the effects on the believer of relating to God through male imagery. For men, this way of imaging results in an identification with God without an accompanying experience of sexual differentiation; men readily see themselves in the language about God. On the other hand, such imagery limits women to a relationship to God modeled on a relationship with the sexually differentiated other without the experience of identification. Thus women have had great difficulty seeing themselves in the language about God. It is too strong to say that one who cannot find the other in God, cannot love the other as she or he is? I think not.

35. *Sacred in All Its Forms*, 138–39.

36. I am assuming here that Catholic belief about the perfection of Jesus' humanity would require such a self-knowledge; for Jesus not to know himself as male would represent a deficiency.

37. I am thinking here of Paul Ricoeur's felicitous phrase "death in the second person," by which he means the death of the beloved other. See *Freedom and Nature: The Voluntary*

and the Involuntary, trans. Exrahim V. Kohak (Chicago: Northwestern Univ. Press, 1966), 460.

FOR FURTHER READING

Carr, Anne E. *Transforming Grace: Christian Tradition and Women's Experience.* San Francisco: Harper & Row, 1988. Noted for an excellent explanation of theological anthropology, this work carefully considers the range of issues implied in the subtitle.

Cunneen, Sally. *Mother Church: What the Experience of Women Is Teaching Her.* New York: Paulist Press, 1991. In this unusual book, Cunneen distills the wisdom from her experience of teaching mothers beginning or returning to college and applies it deftly to the church.

Fiorenza, Elisabeth Schüssler. *In Memory of Her: A Feminist Theological Reconstruction of Christian Origins.* New York: Crossroad, 1987. A ground-breaking work, this reading of Christian origins challenges the whole church to rethink the way the story is told.

John Paul II. *Original Unity of Man and Woman: Catechesis on the Book of Genesis.* Boston: Daughters of St. Paul, 1981. In this first of three volumes collecting the pope's Wednesday afternoon talks on the theology of the body, John Paul II lays the groundwork for a theological anthropology based on original unity subordination.

MacKinnon, Catharine A. *Toward a Feminist Theory of the State.* Cambridge: Harvard Univ. Press, 1989. No theologian can afford to ignore this stunningly original analysis of sexism's effects on the modern state.

Maitland, Sara. *A Map of a New Country: Women and Christianity.* London: Routledge & Kegan Paul, 1975. This book, written by one who is writer, feminist activist, and wife of an Anglican priest, carves out a vision of Christianity radically changed by the inclusion of women.

Ranke-Heinemann, Uta. *Eunuchs for The Kingdom of Heaven: Women, Sexuality, and the Catholic Church.* Translated by Peter Heinegg. New York: Doubleday, 1990. No one else has amassed the evidence for an underside to the idealization of women in the Catholic church as Ranke-Heinemann has.

Ruether, Rosemary Radford, ed. *Religion and Sexism: Images of Women in the Jewish and Christian Traditions.* New York: Simon and Schuster, 1974. This collection of essays is an indispensable classic of feminist theological thought.

Rosenblatt, Marie-Eloise, ed. *Where Can We Find Her? Searching for Women's Identity in the New Church.* New York: Paulist Press, 1991. This more recent collection of essays engages the questions taken up by the now failed attempt of the United States Council of Catholic Bishops to write a pastoral letter on the concerns of women.

Schmidt, Alvin John. *Veiled and Silenced: How Culture Shaped Sexist Theology.* Macon, GA: Mercer Univ. Press, 1989. The best work to date on the history of the sociocultural attitudes that have deformed the Christian tradition with respect to women.

Trible, Phyllis. *God and the Rhetoric of Sexuality.* Philadelphia: Fortress Press, 1978. In this scholarly and creative study of primary texts that shape subsequent attitudes toward sexuality, Trible reveals the enduring power of the word to provoke new readings.

CHAPTER SEVEN

COMMUNITY FOR LIBERATION

— Church —

MARY E. HINES

ECCLESIOLOGY IS PERHAPS the most difficult area of systematic theology to treat from a feminist perspective within the Roman Catholic tradition. Church traditions and structures seem intractably patriarchal and hierarchical. Church documents continue to legitimize the exclusion of women from important areas of church life, especially from leadership roles, simply because they are women. Discouraged and alienated, some women have found it necessary to move outside the Catholic church to other Christian traditions more open to women's full participation or into what some consider to be the more women-centered Goddess traditions or Wicca.[1]

Other Catholic feminist women, however, have committed themselves to work for change and structural reform within the church. In fact, the continued exclusion of women from many spheres of the active ministry has forced them to devote themselves with greater intensity to the task of providing the theological groundwork for revisioning the church.[2] Catholic feminists join their voices with those of other marginalized groups to call clearly and loudly for a restructuring of the institutional dimensions of the Catholic church in the light of the church's liberating mission. The task, then, is both theoretical and practical. In common with other liberation theologies, feminist approaches to ecclesiology begin primarily at the grass-roots level with a reflection on the church as experienced in small intentional communities. This leads both to critique of present church structure and to constructive proposals for change.

Although there is more to the church than its institutional dimension, this came to dominate the church's self-reflection in the second millennium of its history and gave rise to assertions of power and authority not only internally but in the state as well. This institutional ecclesiology climaxed with Vatican I's definition of papal infallibility.[3] The church became largely identified with its centralized leadership in Rome, which asserted increasing control over the local churches through the various documents emanating from the papacy and its curial offices.[4] More and more the laity came to be viewed as the passive recipients of the official church's teaching, with little or no input into its formulation. Although this overly institutional ecclesiology had not gone unchallenged previously,[5] the historical and theological research of theologians such as Karl Rahner, Henri de Lubac, and the great French ecclesiologist, Yves Congar, in the first half of this century seriously called it into question and laid the groundwork for the renewed ecclesiology of Vatican II.

The Council contextualized the church's institutional aspects within its retrieval of a *communio* ecclesiology[6] and its emphasis on the powerful biblical image of the church as People of God. Vatican II's Dogmatic Constitution on the Church, *Lumen Gentium,* indicated with these images a major shift in the understanding of church, even in its very construction. Equally significantly, the Pastoral Constitution on the Church in the Modern World, *Gaudium et Spes,* signaled important changes in the official church's attitude toward the world. *Gaudium et Spes* moved beyond the world-denying approach characteristic of the nineteenth-century church. By this document's encouragement to "read the signs of the times," the official church indicated its willingness to be in dialogue with the modern world and its movements, among which are the changed role of women in society and the rise of feminist consciousness.

The conciliar texts refer to these societal changes among the signs of the times that must have an impact on the church's self-understanding. It is recognized that "where they have not yet won it, women claim for themselves an equity with men before the law and in fact" (GS 9). Women are to be included in every area of life and "should be able to assume their full proper role *in accordance with their own nature*" (GS 60, my emphasis). The dual anthropology of this text, however, reflects the dangerous conclusion that women are different by nature from men and that this distinct nature determines their appropriate social and ecclesial roles.[7] The most powerful conciliar text for the full and equal inclusion of women in all aspects of the church's life is the strong statement that "every type of discrimination, whether social or cultural, whether based on sex, race, color, social condition, language or religion is to be overcome and eradicated as contrary to God's intent" (GS 29). Such individual textual references, however, remain a problematic resource for women, who are mentioned in their own right only rarely and ambiguously.

A critical feminist theology of the church can find a more serviceable ecclesial starting point in Vatican II's contextualization of the church's institutional dimensions within its primary understanding of the church as the community of God's people journeying in history toward ultimate fulfillment in the realm of God. This dynamic and historical understanding of church captured the imagination of Catholic people following the council. The laity, and particularly women, began to believe and act on the conviction that "we are the church." This belief, joined with the reawakening of feminism in the 1960s, has led women to expect and demand full participation in all aspects of the church's life, particularly in areas of ministry and moral decision making where their experience has been most excluded but where decisions affect their lives dramatically. The critical voices of women and other marginalized groups have begun to transform the church "from below."

Excluded from ordained priesthood and other decision-making roles in the church, women and other laity gather in grass-roots movements to reflect on their experience, to ponder the Scriptures, and to imagine a new reality of church in today's world. This reflection has led many to the conviction that merely including women in the ordained priesthood as it now is exercised is not the solution. A massive transformation of the church's structures is needed to free them from the patriarchal, hierarchical, and clerical assumptions that prevent the church from becoming a prophetic community of equal disciples committed to the task of liberation for all people. If this transformation is too long delayed there exists the serious possibility of a definitive split between the church as community and the church as institution. Already many find the church's structures and its teaching office sadly irrelevant to their lives. Those who insist on the unchanging relevance of existing church structures are engaged in a key debate with those who insist that structures function to serve the church's mission. Such structures can and must be changed to facilitate the church's mission in the changing world.

In this chapter I will consider first the mission of the church in the world and its implications for a feminist critique of church structures. Second, I will reflect on the nature of the church and offer constructive proposals from various sources for a restructuring of the church to express better its reality as a liberating community for mission.

THE MISSION OF THE CHURCH IN THE WORLD

Past ecclesiologies often began with a description of the nature and structures of the church. Since Vatican II, however, with its emphasis on the church in the world, it has seemed more appropriate to consider the mission of the church first and then to understand the church's nature and structures in relation to its mission. The church has taken various postures in its relationship to the world, from one that saw the world and the visible church so closely and integrally related as to leave no room for an independent exercise of worldly autonomy, to an attitude that saw the world and church as completely separate and opposed. Vatican II sought a middle ground between these extremes.

In the years preceding Vatican I and to the eve of Vatican II, the official church had adopted an attitude of deep suspicion toward the world, consistent with its negative evaluation of modernity. Pius IX's "prisoner of the Vatican" posture in protest against the seizure of the Papal States epitomized this attitude of salvation through withdrawal from the world. The world, and particularly the modern thinking symbolized by the theories of Freud, Marx, and Darwin, was viewed as evil and dangerous, even an occasion of sin. The world of grace and the world of human history were viewed as separate realities. The church was the realm of grace, sometimes even identified as the kingdom of God on earth. Consecrated religious, people who "left" the world most definitively, seemed the more perfect Christians and religious life intrinsically a more perfect state. The resulting ecclesiology was fearful and defensive with respect to the church's relationship to the world.

A clear shift was signaled by Vatican II. *Gaudium et Spes* announced its intention to embark on an extended conversation with this ambiguous world (*GS* 3), which it saw as a world of both sin and grace. In many ways this reevaluation of the relationship of church and world was the most foundational change of the Council. It had important implications for understanding the church's mission. It also provided a starting point and an impetus for a new understanding of the roles and tasks of the laity and especially of women in the church. This Constitution announced that the church is to be a player in the theater of human history. The church will no longer stand apart from but must be involved in the massive social and cultural transformations of modern times. How to act out of this new stance has occupied much of the discussion about the church's mission and nature in the post–Vatican II period.

Theological underpinnings for this dramatic shift can be found in the writings of the great German theologian Karl Rahner. He proposed that the history of the world and the history of salvation are coextensive. Salvation is worked out in the joys and struggles of life in *this* world. The world, he insisted, is a world of grace![8] Rahner's theology and the secularization theologies[9] in vogue at the time influenced the Council's positive assessment of the possibilities of dialogue with the world. It even suggested, in a remarkable reversal of its previous position, that the church can learn from the world. This optimistic view has since been tempered by "political" theologians who remind us that the world is also a place of sin, oppression, and exploitation. The church can learn from the world. But it is also called, in light of the utopian vision of the future realm of God, to stand in prophetic opposition to all that is not yet fully the justice and peace of God's promise. This vision of God as the future of humanity radically relativizes all human solutions to the world's problems.[10]

Latin American liberation theologians share the conviction that the church's mission to the world includes challenging unjust political and social structures that oppress and marginalize human beings. While previous theologies focused on salvation as essentially future and otherworldly, liberation theologians share an eschatology, sometimes called "presentist," that summons the church to be the agent of the inbreaking of the signs of God's realm in this world. Although acknowledging that salvation includes freedom from personal as well as social sin and that the realm of God is God's free and future gift, liberation theology redresses the imbalances of the past with its emphasis on human involvement in creating the conditions of God's realm in this world. While tempering the earlier easy optimism about the world, both political and liberation theologies insist that there is no backing off from the dialogue with the world begun with Vatican II. Edward Schillebeeckx, for example, rewords the traditional "no salvation outside the church," to read, "no salvation outside the world."[11] Christians will find positive elements in the world. They also will find it necessary to be prophetically critical of much that is worldly, yet flight from the world should no longer be viewed as an authentic Christian option.

Church documents since the Council also reflect the conviction that the world is the arena of salvation. The 1971 Synod document, *Justice in the World,* states in the strongest terms that action on behalf of justice is a constitutive dimension of the church's mission.[12] Papal social documents since the Council have consistently emphasized the church's responsibility in the world.

This emphasis seems to be in some conflict with the conviction of John Paul II that clergy should refrain from direct involvement in politics. The papal position reflects the increasingly problematic position that the laity are primarily responsible for the church's mission in the world, while clergy and members of religious communities are to attend to the church's inner life and its more institutional aspects. While this does reflect the view of Vatican II (*LG* 31), the experience of the past twenty-five years calls this paradigm into question. Many laity have offered and prepared themselves professionally for inner church service such as parish work or chaplaincy, while clergy and members of religious communities currently minister in a wide variety of social and political situations, some not explicitly church connected. The Vatican II revisioning of the close relationship of church and world simply does not support a facile division of labor based on a prior structural classification of the members of the church into laity and clergy.[13]

The division of clergy and laity rests either on the division between sacred and secular that supported the previous radical separation of church and world or on the other fundamental dichotomy of previous theologies, between nature and grace. This implies a separation between the church's religious and social mission, while the close connection between church and world, referred to above, would see them as inextricably connected. The proper mission of the church is to be in the world creating the signs of the realm of God. Inner church ministry is in service to that fundamental goal. If *all* are called by baptism to participate in the mission of the church and its ministry, as Vatican II clearly states (*LG* 33), then allocation of ministries must be governed by charism and competence rather than by any static classifications based on "state in life." Those who, permanently or for a time, are called to the service of church ministry or community leadership must continually reevaluate the effectiveness of the church's structures to carry out this mission. Service within the church must, therefore, include the voices, experience, and gifts of all, since internal church structures exist to facilitate the liberating mission of the church for all people. Precisely the exclusion of the voices and experience of the laity from the inner dimensions of the church's life has resulted in the increasing irrelevance to their lives of the institutional church and its authority and structures. The church's mission is not well served by its present structures.

FEMINIST CRITIQUE OF CHURCH STRUCTURES

Among all liberation theologies, feminist theology is the strongest voice calling for the church to apply its concern for liberation and empowerment for all people to its own internal structures. Recognizing the connection between the church's mission and its structures, feminist theologies reiterate that to call for justice in the world the church must itself first be just.[14] If church structure is in service of mission, then without just internal structures the church's mission in the world will not be credible.

Rosemary Radford Ruether is one strong feminist voice challenging the church to become a community of liberation for all people, especially liberation from patriarchal oppression of women. Ruether calls the church to become an agent and support system for the process of conversion from patriarchy. Such a conversion requires community; it cannot be done alone.[15] Whether the church, itself deeply marked by patriarchy, can be such an agent for change is a serious question for Catholic feminists. Ruether contends that such a transformation is not likely to come from the top down but rather from the communal experience of feminist base communities. "A feminist base community is an autonomous, self-gathered community that takes responsibility for reflecting on, celebrating, and acting on the understanding of redemption as liberation from patriarchy."[16] She understands liberation from patriarchy as dismantling the clerical power structure that prevents women from exercising free, responsible adulthood in the church.[17] In feminist base communities women reappropriate the sacramental life that has been the preserve of the clerical caste.[18] These communities vary in their relationship to the institutional church and in what role they play in the lives of their members. Some may provide the communal support required to continue to participate in and work to transform a church in which they often feel alienated and rejected. Others offer a more complete church experience including worship, study, and political and social action. Participants in these communities, which are sometimes called Women-Church,[19] recognize that they can no longer wait for the institutional church to become aware of and redress its historic repression of women and their experience. Ruether writes,

> Women in contemporary churches are suffering from linguistic deprivation and eucharistic famine. They can no longer nurture their souls in alienating words that ignore or systematically deny their existence. They are starved for the words of life, for symbolic forms that fully and wholeheartedly affirm their personhood and speak truth about the evils of sexism and the possibilities of a future beyond patriarchy.[20]

It is characteristic of Women-Church to incorporate into life and worship not only usable elements from the Christian heritage such as its prophetic tradition, but also liberating elements from other traditions that affirm the experience of women. Many participants hope that their experience of Women-Church as Spirit-filled egalitarian community can eventually transform the historical institution. In the meantime, Women-Church provides a place where faith can be nurtured and women's experience validated. "Women-Church means neither leaving the church as a sectarian group, nor continuing to fit into it on its terms. It means establishing bases for a feminist critical culture and celebrational community that have some autonomy from the established institutions."[21] Although the formal Women-Church movement may be small, it typifies other less formal gatherings of feminist women and men who together imagine a new church order better able to image the egalitarian human relationships that are the goal of the church's mission.

Out of the experience of such gatherings arises a critique of present church structure and a call for the church to rethink its structures in the light of the "signs of the times" to facilitate its liberating mission in the world. Two particularly problematic areas are the church's teaching office and its hierarchical church order.

Contemporary experience challenges any simple division of the church community into teachers and learners.[22] Such a division is particularly troublesome since the authoritative teachers (bishops) are all celibate males. The limitation of experience this restriction entails, in all areas but especially in the area of sexuality, has led many Catholic women to question the relevance of the teaching of the magisterium to their lives. A static understanding of truth allows the magisterium to assume that one small group of the church's members has the truth and that the much larger and diverse remainder of the community must conform their experience and beliefs to that truth. This understanding makes it an enormous ongoing struggle to actualize the belief that the Spirit is with the whole church as *Lumen Gentium* states so clearly: "The body of the faithful as a whole, anointed as they are by the Holy One (cf. Jn 2:20, 27), cannot err in matters of belief. Thanks to a supernatural sense of the faith which characterizes the People as a whole, it manifests this unerring quality when, 'from the bishops down to the last member of the laity,' it shows universal agreement on matters of faith and morals" (*LG* 12).

Admittedly, the process of ascertaining the sense of the faithful is difficult, but it is a creative task worth grappling with. Church teaching will not call forth the assent of all until the voices of all have been included in its formulation.[23] The methods of composing the pastoral letters on peace and the economy of the American bishops, who consulted with a wide representation of the church in their preparation, are an encouraging beginning. But these methods must also be applied to documents that affect the inner life of the church and to documents concerning sexual morality.

Much contemporary discussion has focused on the relationship of bishops and theologians in developing the church's teaching and on working out conditions for dissent from authoritative church teaching.[24] A truly inclusive view of the church in which all are teachers and learners would make such a discussion unnecessary. An image of the church as a human community of people struggling together toward the truth challenges present understandings of assent and dissent that imply oppositional postures. Church teaching might rather be viewed as developing within a community of dialogue. The dialogue must necessarily include the experience and "sense of the faith" of the many who are neither professional theologians nor bishops but whose lives make up the very fabric of the church, for example, the poor, members of the variety of racial and ethnic groups, women, married persons, homosexuals, divorced Catholics. It is an impoverishment that those who make up by far the majority of the church's population have been so marginalized that their voices have been excluded from the church's ongoing self-reflection as articulated in its official teaching function.[25]

The exclusion of many Catholics from decision making in general, as well as from the teaching function in the church, is perpetuated in large part by the continued exclusion of women from ordained ministry, since, from early in the church's history, leadership in the community has been tied to ordination. Early in the women's movement in the Catholic church there was a focus on admission of women to priesthood. As women began, in the post–Vatican II church, to minister in settings previously restricted to the ordained, they became frustrated by being unable to complete a pastoral process of reconciliation or care for the sick with the celebration of the appropriate sacrament. The First Women's Ordination Conference in Detroit in 1975 arose largely out of this experience. The conference awakened in many participants a recognition that ordination to the priesthood, as presently understood, was an inadequate solution to a problem that was deeper and more complex than first imagined. The problem was not merely the exclusion of women from the church's ministerial structures but a deep-seated injustice deforming the very structures themselves. The conference was soon followed by the Vatican declaration *Inter Insigniores* (1976), which stated that the church did not consider itself authorized to admit women to ministerial priesthood.[26] This had the effect of further radicalizing the conversation.

While the first effort toward ordination bore the stamp of equal rights or liberal feminism,[27] calling for equal access for women within the existing structures, post–*Inter Insigniores* discussions call for a radical revisioning of the priesthood and the ministerial structures of the church. Such structures must be transformed by the experience of women and other marginalized groups. Present church order is hierarchical, commonly defined as a "system with grades of status or authority ranking one above another in a series."[28] References in the rite of ordination to the raised rank and status of the ordinand undermine any suggestion that this definition does not apply to the church's understanding.[29] In light of this, most feminist Catholics no longer view being ordained into such a system as an ideal. The struggle for ordination has been decentered in favor of working for systemic change. It cannot be denied, however, that the continued exclusion from ordination remains a potent symbol of women's wider exclusion in the Roman Catholic church.[30]

The feminist critique now challenges the very system of hierarchy itself. To question the hierarchical ordering of church ministry seems to some to be questioning the need for structure and indeed the rootedness of the church in Jesus. This position holds that the hierarchical structure is divinely ordained, given to the church by Jesus, and cannot be changed. Biblical and historical studies, however, challenge this position and propose that while Jesus may have foreseen that his teaching would be carried on by a community of his disciples, the community's structure has developed in response to changing social and cultural circumstance.

Discussions of church structures often focus on identifying changeable and unchangeable elements in the church and trying to link certain church structures to the intentionality of the earthly Jesus.[31] Yet, to ascertain Jesus' intention is notoriously difficult. Contemporary hermeneutical theory would suggest that all the possible legitimate consequences of one's actions are not necessarily consciously apprehended at the time of the action. Later historical circumstances or questions may draw forth other unforeseen but legitimate implications.[32] Francis Schüssler Fiorenza has proposed that whatever Jesus' conscious intention may have been with respect to the foundation of the church and its structures, the more important question is whether the church today can be demonstrated to be carrying on the mission and ministry of Jesus. This judgment can be based on criteria of continuity disclosed in the pages of the New Testament as the testimony of the early Christian communities. "Something is divinely instituted to the degree that it mirrors the relation between Jesus and the Church as normatively described in the New Testament."[33] At stake is a dynamic question about continuity and credibility rather than a static question about a once-for-all foundational event. The church's mission is central. Church structures exist to facilitate the doing of the mission and therefore are changeable and contingent.[34] Although the church's official organs continue to maintain the permanent validity of its hierarchical structures, discussion of alternative structures is well under way at the theological and grass-roots level.

THE NATURE OF THE CHURCH: FROM DESCRIPTION TO IMAGE

The search for alternative structures can find a resource in Vatican II's move from description to image to understand the nature of the church. The variety of images for the church used by Vatican II effectively undermined the supposition that the church can be adequately explained or defined by its visible, institutional dimensions and set the imagination free to bring to the fore other facets of the church's reality. Current discussion builds on this conciliar foundation.

Coming out of a period where the church was described primarily with respect to its institutional aspects, Vatican II chose to relativize and contextualize this dimension of the church's reality by picturing the church with a variety of evocative images drawn largely from Scripture and the fathers of the church. In a dramatic reversal of earlier concentration on the visible aspects, the Council first imaged the church as mystery, unable to be tied down or defined completely by human language, possessing a certain transcendent dimension, open to be understood in new and surprising ways (*LG* 1). Its visible and invisible facets are suggested by the image of sacrament, understood as "sign of intimate union with God, and of the unity of all [humankind]" (*LG* 1). The traditional image of the body of Christ appears, but there is no effort to harmonize it explicitly with the institutional elements of the church as had Pius XII's encyclical *Mystici Corporis* (*LG* 7). The focus is more on communal dimensions and the interdependence among the members implied by the Pauline texts from which this image is drawn.

Perhaps more significant than any single image is the plurality of images employed in *Lumen Gentium*. As mystery, the church cannot be defined by any absolute conceptualization. This said, however, it cannot be denied that the image most immediately and popularly received by the church was the empowering picture of the church as People of God. While chapter 1 of *Lumen Gentium* had opened with the transcendent reality of the church as mystery, or, "church from above," chapter 2 focused on its human dynamic actuality as a community of people journeying together in history toward the realm of God, or, "church from below." The slogan "We are the church!" captured the excitement of a laity newly awakened to their baptismal power and responsibility as part of this evolving human community. This conviction, likely taken more seriously than the Council participants foresaw, grounds the summons from the laity and particularly women for a restructuring of the church so that their voices may be heard and their contributions acknowledged. It also helps to explain the tenacity with which many women and other marginalized groups continue to define themselves as Catholic Christians in spite of disagreement with and exclusion by the official structures of the church.

These are only a few of the central images of the church encountered in the documents of Vatican II. In an article written shortly after the Council, Karl Rahner enumerated several more. The church appears as a church of the poor and oppressed, a sinful church, a communion of faith, hope, and love, a church of the free charismata, a pilgrim church.[35] This plethora of images indicates that the Council truly intended to set a new direction for the church,[36] a direction that makes clear the inadequacy of an ecclesial self-understanding drawn from its institutional dimensions and conceptualized as a "perfect society," visible, self-sustaining, and parallel in structure to the state. Rahner writes, "All this [that is, the institutional elements] is . . . subsumed and made subordinate to a more basic understanding of the Church, in which the Church is viewed as the people of God gathered together by God's grace. . . . The Church appears not primarily as she who acts upon us, but rather as she whom we all *are* in virtue of the fact that the grace of God has moved and inspired us and bound us together into a unity."[37] The picture of the church as a pilgrim people journeying through history toward its eschatological future radically decenters the church as an end in itself and rejects any triumphalism as to its present existence.

Rahner suggested shortly after the Council that the most lasting and significant new image of the church might well come from the tentative introduction of the idea of the local church in *Lumen Gentium*. While retaining the universalist ecclesiology of the recent past, *Lumen Gentium*, in its recognition of the importance of the local church, Rahner suggested, pointed the direction toward the future reality of the church. "We should consider the future that presses in upon the Church, a future in which the premium set upon the characteristics present in the local Church, her poverty, smallness and 'diaspora' mode of existence will perhaps be higher even than it is in the present. . . . The Church in the new form which it will acquire in the future will first, and by anticipation, be experienced *here* in the local Church."[38] Rahner's words, written in 1966, sound strangely prescient in light of the contemporary grass-roots development of small intentional or basic Christian communities.[39] In later years the idea of local church became even more central in Rahner's thought, as a central motif of his later ecclesiology.

NEW IMAGES, NEW STRUCTURES: CONSTRUCTIVE PROPOSALS

These diverse images that significantly altered the face of the church reflect a legacy of Vatican II only now being recognized as problematic. Vatican II dramatically reenvisioned the nature of the church without providing for the structural change required to realize that vision.[40] The institutional aspects of the church are contextualized and relativized by these many images but otherwise left unchanged. The increasing discomfort of trying to live a new vision within old structures has turned attention today, at least at the grass-roots level, to imagining and modeling new forms in which a new reality of church can be realized. Feminist Catholics join with others in the church who envision a renewed, participative, and just community. Three particular, not mutually exclusive, directions will be explored: the church as discipleship of equals, the church as democracy, and the church as "world-church."

One compelling image for a restructured, nonhierarchical church order comes from Elisabeth Schüssler Fiorenza. In her feminist reconstruction of the Jesus movement and early Christianity she detects a challenge to the prevailing patriarchy in the egalitarian gathering of female and male disciples around Jesus.[41] Women figure prominently among the marginalized of society with whom Jesus associated, and there is evidence that women exercised leadership in the early community. In its ongoing spread and development, Christianity capitulated to the prevalent patriarchal ordering of society, but the "dangerous" memory of a community of equal disciples constitutes a summons to the church to recapture its early egalitarian vision. For Schüssler Fiorenza, as for Ruether, Women-Church is the place where such a vision can be kept alive and nurtured.

> We have begun to gather as the *ekklesia* of women, as the people
> of God, to claim our own religious powers, to participate fully
> in the decision-making process of church, and to nurture each
> other as women Christians. Baptism is the sacrament that calls
> us into the discipleship of equals. No special vocation is given,
> no more "perfect" Christian lifestyle is possible.[42]

In such a community, all women and men are called to ministry and to full participation on the basis of their different gifts rather than on the basis of any ontological sacramental status. While not endorsing this functional view of ministry, theologian Avery Dulles also finds the image of equal discipleship the truest expression of the reality of the church and its ministry.

> Discipleship is the common factor uniting all Christians with
> one another, for no one of them is anything but a follower
> and a learner in relation to Jesus Christ. As disciples, all must
> help, using their own talents for the benefit of the rest. All

are ministers and all are ministered to. The concept of discipleship undercuts the illusion that some in the Church are lords
and masters.[43]

Imaging the church as a discipleship of equals undermines the pervasive influence of patriarchy epitomized in the hierarchical structures of the
church. Since all are followers of Jesus and sharers in his liberating ministry, there is no room for an absolute centralizing of power and authority
in the hands of the dominant few males. Structures that legitimate relationships of dominance and subordination have no place in a community
of equal disciples.

In a different but related approach, the self-evidence of the presumption that the church is not and cannot be a democracy is being questioned.[44] Edward Schillebeeckx argues that the church has repeatedly
adapted itself to the social structures of the time and even borrowed from
these structures. He attributes its resistance to democracy to the fact that
"the hierarchical articulation of the church is supposed, in accordance with
a divine plan, not to allow any democratic structures in the church."[45]
This view, already undermined by scriptural and hermeneutical studies, as
noted above, is a serious source of alienation for today's Catholics, who
are accustomed to the democratic structures of the modern state and who
harbor a deep suspicion of any kind of monarchial absolutism.[46]

The church's history in fact is not devoid of democratic elements.[47]
In modern times, however, the institution has been resistant to the
influences of modern democracy and has claimed divine sanction for its
hierarchical structures. Those who advocate the democratization of the
church are careful not to romanticize the democratic ideal or to identify
it with its American incarnation as conflated with free market capital-
ism. Rather, they encourage a return to the roots of modern democratic
theory, "which sought to create more just societies based on the consent
of the governed."[48] The democratic ideal should inspire the restructuring of the church, not a reduplication of any particular democratic social
order.

A key element of reformed church structure would include broad-
based participation in calling forth church leadership on every level,
whether by election or by other participative processes. In this respect,
increased use of synods, councils, and assemblies of the people for church
decision making can provide a historically grounded way of more clearly

imaging the church as discipleship of equals. These groups, however, must have decision-making power and be truly inclusive of the church throughout the world. Such inclusivity will not be achieved until women are active participants in all dimensions of the church's life, especially in decision-making roles.

Bianchi and Ruether suggest five principles, rooted in the church's history, for a democratic restructuring of the church: participation, conciliarity, pluralism, accountability, and dialogue.[49] To effect change, these principles would require concrete strategies. Such strategies might include: nonviolent resistance to oppressive uses of authority and to those structures that impede the church's mission in the world, educational programs, and the exercise of alternative ministries within the church.[50]

Proposals for structural change are still at an early stage and remain necessarily somewhat vague. The disjunction between the grass-roots communities where such ideas are born and the apparently intractable power structure of the Roman Catholic church grows wider. Although a corrective focus on the local church emerged in the period following Vatican II, there appears today a growing emphasis in Rome on the universal church and its centralizing control over the local churches. This is in marked contrast to a growing consensus at the grass-roots level and among many theologians that new life, new vision, and new structures will emerge out of the experience of church at the local level.

Rahner, for one, was convinced that Vatican II, in its retrieval of the place of the local church, brought the church just to the brink of its future reality. In his later ecclesiological writings he became preoccupied with the evocative symbol of the "world-church" that for him epitomized what he finally came to view as a "qualitative leap" in the church's consciousness of itself.[51] By *world-church* he meant a communion of local, indigenous churches, each wholly church, whose combined reality would make up the whole, or universal, church.

At Vatican II, Rahner says, the church entered only the third great phase of its history. The first age was the very short period of Judeo-Christianity; the second, the accommodation of the early church to Hellenism, which eventually led to its identification with European culture and civilization—the very long period often called Christendom. In this second period, he says, Christianity became so identified with its western European expression that adoption of Christianity involved adoption of a Western lifestyle as well as cultural and social mores.[52] With the new period that began at Vatican II, Rahner suggests that there is to be no longer a "European and western [and he includes North America here] Church with European exports to the whole world."[53] In the world-church the living space for Christianity is truly the whole world, but it must come to be authentically *within* the diversity of cultures in which it is incarnated. There must be a truly African, Asian, and North American Christianity, for example. Assumed in this notion of world-church are a number of presuppositions. Clearly the church is seen as embedded in history, not above it or outside it. The church is imaged as coming to be within a concrete historical reality, in a particular time and place. This signals the end of a kind of ecclesial docetism that sees the church identified with the kingdom of God, only thinly disguised as an earthly, historical reality.

Rahner enumerates some characteristics of this new church. The world-church is a diaspora church existing in places where it is and will continue to be a minority community. It is in the world as a visible *sign* of God's gracious will to save and liberate all people, but it no longer is the only locus of that salvation. It exists in the midst of enormous social and cultural plurality. It may no longer rely on general agreement with a single view of social reality that can be expressed in a single philosophy or theology, such as neoscholasticism. It can no longer rely on universal acceptance of a natural law with which it could assume all right thinking and reasonable persons would agree.

The world-church is in the first instance local church, wholly and truly church in each particular locality. It is a communion of communions, a church from the ground up in which the universal church comes to be through the gathering of the local churches, a diverse and pluralistic community characterized by a unity that is not uniformity. This coming church will no longer be well served by the kind of hierarchical authority structure that characterized the previous epoch. Rahner suggests that the new ecclesial situation will need a more collegial or democratic form of governance. "In a real world-Church something of the kind is necessary, since a world-Church simply cannot be ruled by that Roman centralism that was usual in the time of Pius XII."[54]

Rahner believed that this more egalitarian and democratic ecclesial structure might best be initiated in networks of grass-roots communities. This conviction is widely shared.[55] Ruether and Bianchi note, "Perhaps a much simpler structure, in which church takes primarily the form of intentional communities gathered amid a variety of social relations . . . needs to be imaged. . . . Simple forms of networking, linking such communities together in a sense of a common identity as the Christian church, while retaining pluriformity of organization and cultural expression, might be more appropriate than a vast state-like superstructure."[56]

Latin American liberation theologians have long insisted that authentic ecclesiological reflection must emerge out of the life of the community. Theology will follow practice. This suggests that the future starting point for ecclesiology should be the local church understood broadly as encompassing the diversity of lived reality of the Christian community. Feminist theologians endorse this direction, underlining that this new church must include the experience of women and other persons marginalized by the present power structure. For a new church to be born in fidelity to the original and ongoing inspiration of the spirit of Jesus, the gifts of all must be called forth and celebrated. Ideally this renewed church would be united around the unifying symbol of the Petrine ministry understood in a less juridical way than at present.

Whether the present, apparently intransigent, central structures will allow this transformation to take place remains a serious question. Schillebeeckx points out that the community of the church as historical reality will incarnate itself within human structures.[57] If the growth that is taking place at the grass-roots level, particularly among laity who are newly convinced of their full adulthood and responsibility as Christians, does not find a home in the Roman Catholic church, then laity and especially women may look for other communities where this growth can be nurtured. Belief in the church as Spirit-filled community, however, sustains hope that a new birth can take place and that the church may become within and for the world a place "where the good news of liberation from sexism is preached, where the Spirit is present to empower us to renounce patriarchy, where a community committed to the new life of mutuality is gathered together and nurtured, and where the community is spreading this vision and struggle to others."[58]

Sustained by this hope, Catholic feminists critique present patriarchal and hierarchical structures in the light of the church's liberating mission and propose alternative structures that will better embody the nature of the church as an egalitarian community of disciples. To achieve this a feminist vision of the church calls on what is liberating and prophetic in the Christian tradition, searches for other usable tradition, tries to free the tradition from the deforming influence of patriarchy, and includes the hitherto excluded experience of women so that the church may truly become a community of liberation for all humanity.

NOTES

1. Mary Daly, whose *The Church and the Second Sex* first thematized the critique of patriarchy and clericalism in the church, now considers herself postchristian. She today considers unrealizable and irrelevant her observation that "the reformed, democratized Church of the future is not yet here, although the seeds of it are present in the living faith, hope and courage of the Christian community" (213). For her, the church is so hopelessly deformed by patriarchy that it is incapable of being a liberating community for women. Those feminists who persist in the belief that there is hope for a renewed Catholic church continue to find in Daly's early work a valuable resource for reform and, unfortunately, still a relevant critique. *The Church and the Second Sex,* with the Feminist Postchristian Introduction and New Archaic Afterwords by the author (Boston: Beacon Press, 1968, 1975, 1985).

2. See Catherine Mowry LaCugna, "Catholic Women as Ministers and Theologians," *America* 167 (Oct. 10, 1992): 238–48. However, there is not a large body of literature on specific ecclesiological questions from a feminist perspective. After an initial spate of writing on the ordination question, many Catholic feminist theologians turned their attention to other questions foundational to a revisioning of Catholic theology. The clash of this feminist theology with seemingly impervious church structures may have contributed to a dearth of writing on the topic of the church.

3. For brief discussions of this institutional development and its consequences, see Avery Dulles, *Models of the Church* (New York: Doubleday, 1974), 31–42, and Edward Schillebeeckx, *Church: The Human Story of God,* trans. John Bowden (New York: Crossroad, 1990), 198–207.

4. Yves Congar, *Lay People in the Church,* trans. Donald Attwater (Westminster MD: Newman Press, 1965), 286.

5. For example, nineteenth-century Tübingen theologians, members of the Catholic Faculty of Theology, influenced by romanticism, developed a mystical and pneumatological ecclesiology. Johann Adam Möhler has been the most influential of these theologians.

6. This approach to ecclesiology understands the church in the first instance as a community or communion of persons united with one another and with Christ. It does not necessarily exclude institutional aspects but sees them as secondary to the church's communal reality. For further discussion, see Dulles, *Models of the Church,* 43–57.

7. See Mary Aquin O'Neill's chapter on anthropology for an extended discussion of this concept and the alternative proposals of feminist anthropology.

8. "History of the World and Salvation History," trans. Karl-H. Kruger, *Theological Investigations,* vol. 5 (New York: Seabury Press, 1975), 97–114.

9. This term applies to diverse theologies that arose between the two world wars and that gained interest among Catholic theologians influential at the Council, such as Yves Congar and Karl Rahner. Although diverse, these theologies shared a common conviction that humankind had "come of age." This raised the question of the ongoing need for a God, often understood as one who filled in the gaps when human ingenuity and effort failed. D. Bonhoeffer, the "death-of-God" theologians, and J. A. T. Robinson (*Honest to God*) popularized these theories. For further discussion, see *Encyclopedia of Theology: The Concise Sacramentum Mundi,* s.v. "secularization."

10. See Johannes Baptist Metz, *Faith in History and Society,* trans. David Smith (New York: Seabury Press, 1980).

11. Edward Schillebeeckx, *Church: The Human Story of God,* trans. John Bowden (New York: Crossroad, 1990), 5.

12. "Justice in the World" (Washington, DC: United States Catholic Conference, 1972), 34.

13. See Joseph Komonchak, "Clergy, Laity and the Church's Mission in the World," *Official Ministry in a New Age* (Washington, DC: Canon Law Society of America, 1981), 168–93.

14. This necessity is recognized in the 1971 synod document, "Justice in the World," 44.

15. Rosemary Radford Ruether, *Sexism and God-Talk* (Boston: Beacon Press, 1983), 193.

16. Ruether, *Sexism and God-Talk,* 205.

17. Rosemary Radford Ruether, *Women-Church: Theology and Practice of Feminist Liturgical Communities* (San Francisco: Harper & Row, 1985), 86.

18. Ruether, *Women-Church,* 87.

19. Ruether describes Women-Church as follows: "Women-Church is the Christian theological expression of this stage of feminist collectivization of women's experience and the formation of critical culture. It means that women delegitimize the theological myths that justify the *ecclesia* of patriarchy and begin to form liturgies to midwife their liberation from it. They begin to experience the gathering of liberated women as a redemptive community rooted in a new being. They empower themselves and are empowered by this liberated Spirit upon which they are grounded...." (*Women-Church,* 61). "Women-Church [is] a feminist counterculture to the *ecclesia* of patriarchy that must continue for the foreseeable future as an exodus both within and on the edges of existing church institutions" (*Women-Church,* 62).

20. Ruether, *Women-Church,* 4–5.

21. Ruether, *Women-Church,* 62.

22. Although the teaching church (*ecclesia docens*) and the learning church (*ecclesia discens*) are often interpreted, theoretically and in practice, as referring respectively to the magisterium (pope and bishops) and the laity, other interpretations see both teaching and learning as functions of the entire church in response to the Word of God. For further discussion, see Yves Congar, *Lay People in the Church,* 292–94, and Leonardo Boff, *Church: Charism and Power,* trans. John W. Diercksmeier (New York: Crossroad, 1985), 138–43. For a detailed study of the evolution and exercise of the church's teaching office, see Francis Sullivan, *Magisterium: Teaching Authority in the Catholic Church* (New York: Paulist Press, 1983).

23. See Schillebeeckx, *Church,* 209.

24. There are a number of theological studies of the possibility and conditions of dissent. See, for example, Sullivan, *Magisterium,* 153–73, and Patrick Granfield, *The Limits of the Papacy* (New York: Crossroad, 1987), 153–68. The American bishops suggested conditions for dissent in *Human Life in Our Day: A Collective Pastoral Letter of the American Hierarchy* (Washington, DC: United States Catholic Conference, 1968).

25. For a discussion of the impact on the church of including these "marginalized" voices, see Mary Ann Hinsdale, "Power and Participation in the Church: Voices from the Margins" (Warren Lecture Series, no. 13, The University of Tulsa, Oct. 28, 1990).

26. The arguments for this position are mentioned in several of the chapters in this volume.

27. Maria Riley, *Transforming Feminism* (Kansas City, MO: Sheed and Ward, 1989), 46–49.

28. *Oxford American Dictionary,* s.v. "hierarchy."

29. See "Ordination of a Priest," *The Rites of the Catholic Church* (New York: Pueblo Publishing, 1980), 2:62–63.

30. Anne E. Carr, *Transforming Grace: Christian Tradition and Women's Experience* (San Francisco: Harper & Row, 1988), 21.

31. See Karl Rahner, *Foundations of Christian Faith,* trans. William V. Dych (New York: Seabury Press, 1978), 326–35, and "Basic Observations on the Subject of Changeable and Unchangeable Factors in the Church," *Theological Investigations,* vol. 4, trans. David Bourke (New York: Seabury Press, 1976), 3–23.

32. Francis Schüssler Fiorenza, *Foundational Theology: Jesus and the Church* (New York: Crossroad, 1984), 108–22.

33. Fiorenza, *Foundational Theology,* 168.

34. See the discussion of the contingency of institutions in Schillebeeckx, *Church,* 230–31.

35. Karl Rahner, "The New Image of the Church," *Theological Investigations,* vol. 10, trans. David Bourke (New York: Seabury Press, 1973), 28–29.

36. In this period of attempted restoration there is a conflict of interpretation about the conciliar texts. The documents are the result of compromise between those holding to the interpretations of the past and those who felt impelled to set a new direction for the church. Read as a whole and in the light of available commentaries recounting the conciliar debates, the major documents in particular, such as *Lumen Gentium* and *Gaudium et Spes,* clearly seem to be attempting to set a new direction for the church.

37. Rahner, "The New Image of the Church," 27–28.

38. Rahner, "Image of the Church," 11.

39. It is important to note that Rahner had in mind primarily the understanding of local or particular church that the Council envisioned, namely the diocese. In later writings he extended his ideas to other small Christian communities formed at the grass-roots level and reflecting the social and cultural situation out of which they arise. See, for example, Rahner's *The Shape of the Church to Come,* trans. Edward Quinn (New York: Seabury Press, 1974), 108–18.

40. See John Beal, "Toward a Democratic Church: The Canonical Heritage," in *A Democratic Catholic Church,* ed. Eugene C. Bianchi and Rosemary Radford Ruether (New York: Crossroad, 1992), 60, and Schillebeeckx, *Church,* 207.

41. Elisabeth Schüssler Fiorenza, *In Memory of Her: A Feminist Theological Reconstruction of Christian Origins* (New York: Crossroad, 1983), 105–53.

42. Schüssler Fiorenza, *In Memory of Her,* 344.

43. Avery Dulles, *A Church to Believe In* (New York: Crossroad, 1984), 12.

44. See Rahner, *The Shape of the Church to Come,* 119–22.

45. Schillebeeckx, *Church,* 188.

46. Schillebeeckx, *Church,* 188.

47. Bianchi and Ruether, eds., *A Democratic Catholic Church,* 249–51.

48. Bianchi and Ruether, eds., *A Democratic Catholic Church*, 12.

49. Bianchi and Ruether, eds., *A Democratic Catholic Church*, 253–60.

50. Bianchi and Ruether, eds., *A Democratic Catholic Church*, 259.

51. Karl Rahner, "Basic Theological Interpretation of the Second Vatican Council," *Theological Investigations*, vol. 20 (New York: Seabury Press, 1981) 80.

52. Rahner, "Basic Theological Interpretation," *Theological Investigations*, 20: 83.

53. Karl Rahner, "The Abiding Significance of Vatican II," *Theological Investigations*, vol. 20 (New York: Seabury Press, 1981), 91.

54. Rahner, "Basic Theological Interpretation," *Theological Investigations*, 20:89.

55. A number of popular ecclesiologies draw their inspiration from the experience of small intentional communities. See, for example, Virginia Hoffman, *Birthing a Living Church* (New York: Crossroad, 1988); Vincent J. Donovan, *The Church in the Midst of Creation* (New York: Orbis Books, 1989); Bernard J. Lee and Michael A. Cowan, *Dangerous Memories: House Churches and Our American Story* (Kansas City, MO: Sheed and Ward, 1986).

56. Bianchi and Ruether, eds., *A Democratic Catholic Church*, 12–13.

57. Schillebeeckx, *Church*, 213.

58. Ruether, *Sexism and God-Talk*, 213.

FOR FURTHER READING

Bianchi, Eugene C., and Rosemary Radford Ruether, eds. *A Democratic Catholic Church: The Reconstruction of Roman Catholicism*. New York: Crossroad, 1992. Multiauthored collection of essays that explores, from a variety of perspectives, the possibility of a more democratic and participative church government.

Boff, Leonardo. *Church Charism and Power: Liberation Theology and the Institutional Church*. Translated by John W. Diercksmeier. New York: Crossroad, 1985. A strong call to the church for institutional reform in the light of insights from Latin American liberation theology. Suggests alternative church structures that emerge from reflection on the communal praxis of base ecclesial communities.

Carr, Anne E. *Transforming Grace: Christian Tradition and Women's Experience*. San Francisco: Harper & Row, 1988. Contains valuable essays on women in the church and on the question of ordination. Calls for a reform of ministerial structures away from patterns of domination to an inclusive ministry of service that would better express the nature of church as the "sacrament of the incarnation of Christ into all humankind."

Chopp, Rebecca S. *The Power to Speak: Feminism, Language, God*. New York: Crossroad, 1989. Focusing on the emancipatory power of the Word freely proclaimed, this work calls the church to become the community of emancipatory transformation. The alternative vision of Women-Church provides the place where this liberating dream can become a reality.

Daly, Mary. *The Church and the Second Sex: With the Feminist Postchristian Introduction and New Archaic Afterwords by the Author*. Boston: Beacon Press, 1985. Originally published in 1968, it remains a relevant critique of sexism and patriarchy in the Roman Catholic church. The postchristian introduction and afterwords give some insight into Daly's journey following the publication of this now-classic work.

Fiorenza, Elisabeth Schüssler. *Bread Not Stone: The Challenge of Feminist Biblical Interpretation*. Boston: Beacon Press, 1984. The insights of feminist biblical scholarship inform this collection of essays that include discussions of Women-Church as the hermeneutical center of feminist biblical interpretation and of the church understood as community of coequal disciples.

———. *Discipleship of Equals: A Critical Feminist Ekklesia-logy of Liberation*. New York: Crossroad, 1993. A collection of essays around the central motif of "discipleship of equals" that provides insight into the development of one of the most influential voices within the feminist community and an overview of the central ecclesial issues from a feminist perspective.

Hoffman, Virginia. *Birthing a Living Church*. New York: Crossroad, 1988. Written in popular style, this book offers a vision of a new, nonhierarchical, nonclerical church structure that is coming to birth in the experience of small, intentional communities.

Isasi-Díaz, Ada María, and Yolanda Tarango. *Hispanic Women: Prophetic Voice in the Church*. San Francisco: Harper & Row, 1988. Contributes the important voices and experiences of Hispanic women to the call for radical change in oppressive church structures. These prophetic voices interpret the church primarily as the community of the people in which women play a central role.

Ruether, Rosemary Radford. *Sexism and God-Talk: Toward a Feminist Theology*. Boston: Beacon Press, 1983. Envisions a new image of church, born from the experience of feminist liberation communities, in which ministry is exercised as mutual empowerment. Includes a liberation Mariology that understands the church as symbolically female and reveals the conviction that God is on the side of the poor and the oppressed, among whom women are numbered in every society.

———. *Women-Church: Theology and Practice of Feminist Liturgical Communities*. San Francisco: Harper & Row, 1985. Describes the emergence of Women-Church from historical and theological perspectives. Calls for the development of intentional communities of faith where the vision of church as a community of liberation from sexism can be actualized.

Russell, Letty. *Church in the Round: Feminist Interpretation of the Church*. Louisville, KY: Westminster/John Knox, 1993. Drawing on her long experience of participation in and shaping of communities of liberation, Russell reimagines the church using the central symbol of the table, a round table where leadership is shared and inclusive, a hospitable table where diversity is welcomed and justice served.

Schillebeeckx, Edward. *The Church with a Human Face: A New and Expanded Theology of Ministry*. Translated by John Bowden. New York: Crossroad, 1985. A largely historical study of the origins and development of ministerial structures in the church, this work contextualizes contemporary critiques within this history and maintains that structures that developed through history in response to specific circumstances can and must continue to change in the light of the gospel to meet new social and ecclesial needs.

———. *Church: The Human Story of God*. Translated by John Bowden. New York: Cross-road, 1990. Asserts that the church, in its development of authoritarian and hierarchical structures, has gotten away from its true nature as embodying the liberating freedom of Jesus Christ. Offers theological arguments for a more democratic and participatory exercise of authority in the church to better realize its liberating mission in the world.

CHAPTER EIGHT

GOD'S EMBODIMENT AND WOMEN

— Sacraments —

Susan A. Ross

Did the woman say,
When she held him for the first time in the dark of a stable,
After the pain and the bleeding and the crying,
"This is my body, this is my blood"?

Did the woman say,
When she held him for the last time in the dark rain on a
    hilltop,

After the pain and the bleeding and the dying,
"This is my body, this is my blood"?

Well that she said it to him then,
For dry old men,
brocaded robes belying barrenness,
Ordain that she not say it for him now.

—*Frances Croake Frank*

THIS PROVOCATIVE POEM evokes many powerful images—the words of consecration, the blood of childbirth and death, the anger and pain of women excluded from sacramental ministry—and it raises many important theological issues. In the Catholic tradition, the "sacramental principle" affirms that all of created reality reveals God. And because God has chosen to live with humanity in the flesh, all of human life has been transformed. Sacraments in particular are those events through which God is communicated in the church, when the community responds to the offer of God's grace, and which symbolize the presence of God. Sacramentality thus takes physical reality very seriously. For feminist theology, the crucial question is whether human physical differences ought to carry the theological significance they have come to bear. The poem that opens this essay raises four issues that will be central to my feminist approach to sacramental theology: the incarnation, the centrality of embodiment and all that it implies, women's lived experience, gender roles, and "real presence." In this chapter I will not be arguing for a sacramental theology "influenced" by feminism, as if feminism suggested a few minor alterations in the existing structure. I will rather rethink the meaning of the Christian sacramental vision where women's experience is taken into account and then show how this reflection challenges some of the basic assumptions of mainstream sacramental theology.

In an essay on sacraments it is important to mention the issue of ordination in an essay on sacraments at the outset because women's exclusion from ordination serves as a kind of "negative criterion" for what constitutes a uniquely Catholic feminist theology and a Catholic feminist sacramental theology in particular. But by the same token the prohibition of ordination does not close off discussion of women and the sacraments. Rather, it pushes the discussion to deeper levels, such as the meaning of embodiment and sexuality, of symbolic representation, of the distinction between secular and sacred reality. Ironically, because the current official

Catholic position on ordination rules out the presence of women in the priesthood, Catholic feminist theologians have the opportunity to take a more creative approach to the sacraments than simple inclusion in the present system. With decreasing numbers of clergy, and consequently increasing numbers of laity serving in ministerial capacities in the liturgical life of the church, the implications of sacramental theology from a feminist perspective reach beyond the academy and into the everyday lives of Catholics in the United States and elsewhere.

Because feminist theology is both critical and constructive, I first spell out some of the main issues that have emerged in the history of the sacramental tradition. These issues are in many ways closely connected to those involved in women's participation in the sacramental life of the church, since the emergence of the most recent women's movement and the Second Vatican Council occurred during the same decade. Second, I will discuss feminist thought as it impinges upon sacramental theology and practice. While feminist scholarship in this area is not as extensive as in some other areas (for example, Christology or spirituality), there is nevertheless a growing body of work that draws on fields such as psychoanalysis and literary criticism and both criticizes mainstream sacramental theology and also suggests new and creative approaches to the sacraments.

Finally, I will suggest some areas for further thought and practice. Bringing feminist thought to bear on this very important area of theology does more than "add women and stir" to the already existing reality. It may be that a theology that comes to terms with both feminism and sacramentality will look very different from sacramental theology as it presently exists.

TRADITIONAL CATHOLIC SACRAMENTAL THEOLOGY

Sacramental theology has a long and complex history. Not until the late Middle Ages was it even agreed that there were seven sacraments. But the evidence from the early church shows the frequent practice of the Lord's Supper, the baptism of new members, the laying on of hands for leaders, and practices of public repentance. These liturgical practices came to be known as sacraments. *Sacrament* is a Latin translation for *mysterion,* a Greek term meaning mystery, or a secret revealed by God; it was also used for the oath taken by Roman soldiers in loyalty to the emperor.

Women are mentioned in the letters of Paul among the leaders of the early church, but there is some evidence that by the end of the first century a conservative movement against women's leadership roles had ended the earlier practices. This conservatism is especially visible in the Pastoral letters of the New Testament.[1] The *Didache,* the writings of Irenaeus of Lyon, and the *Apostolic Tradition* of Hippolytus offer further glimpses of the sacramental life of the early church.

The first systematic writing on sacramental theology came from Augustine of Hippo (354–430), who described sacraments as *signs* of God's grace, as opposed to a crude physicalist understanding of divine presence. Augustine located sacraments primarily within the church community. In his works against the Donatists, who had argued that the piety of the minister could affect the grace derived from the sacraments, Augustine emphasized the intrinsic power of the sacraments (later to be known as *opus operatum*).[2] His purpose was to affirm that the sacraments are the *church's* acts, not acts of the individual minister. It is also worth noting that, even though marriage had not yet been established as a sacrament, Augustine's understanding of sexuality and of the goods of marriage profoundly influenced the church's subsequent history. Sexuality, for Augustine, was that dimension of the person most affected by concupiscence, the desire of the self for its own gratification, which he considered the root of original sin. The role of sexuality in marriage was primarily for procreation; all birth control was therefore sinful. In addition, the growth of monasticism and the practice of clerical celibacy, along with the increasing institutionalization of the Roman Catholic church, resulted in the increasing separation of laity and clergy and an understanding of priesthood that emphasized its cultic dimension. The administration of the sacraments became increasingly the preserve of the clergy.

The Middle Ages were a time of controversy and development in sacramental theology. The issue of the "real presence" of Christ in the Eucharist was the focus of at least two major controversies that dealt with the symbolic nature of the sacraments. Are the sacraments "merely" signs of God's grace? If Christ is really present in the Eucharist, do we chew his very body with our teeth? Such questions during this period suggest an increasing division between the real and the symbolic, a division not intended in Augustine's writings. Against the background of such questions, Thomas Aquinas's (1225–1274) use of the Aristotelian categories of causality and substance to understand sacraments was to have a deep and lasting effect on sacramental theology and practice. By defining sacraments *instrumentally* rather than *symbolically,* in terms of their function rather than what they represented or expressed, sacraments increasingly became disconnected from their personal and ecclesial dimensions.[3] That is to say, the philosophical categories used in this theology were *abstract* and thus taken out of their context within Christian life. Aquinas's great gift was the scientific clarity he brought to his reflection on every aspect of Christian life and thought. But this clarity carried a heavy cost, especially in the writings of his interpreters. The richly layered complexity of the symbolic, which resists clear and precise delineation, was nearly lost. Increasingly the juridical categories of canon law became the most significant ones for the sacraments, and a more physicalist interpretation of real presence became the norm.

The history of sacramental theology and practice, however, needs to be understood not only from magisterial documents and the writings of theologians, but also from the practice of lay people, including women. The late Middle Ages serve as a fascinating example of the contrast between official theology and lay belief and practice. During a time of rich and sometimes bizarre eucharistic devotion, the Eucharist, partly as a result of its theological objectification and partly because of ecclesiological developments, took on magical significance. The laity clamored to see the host at the elevation, and the host itself came to possess miraculous powers to convert infidels and to heal the ill. Carolyn Walker Bynum describes how women found in the Eucharist a confirmation of the importance of physicality—of God become human.[4] Since women had been told for centuries that they were more physical, and therefore less spiritual than men, the Eucharist, where the body and blood of Christ are really and truly present, became extremely important for women's piety. Some, like Catherine of Siena, subsisted on the Eucharist alone (and died at an early age!). But most found in the Eucharist a confirmation of the sacred significance of the body which, to some extent, ran counter to the denigration of women's embodiment taught by the church.

The Reformation was a time of controversy for sacramental theology as well as for the entire Western world. Debates over infant baptism, the nature of priesthood, the number of sacraments, and the forgiveness of sin divided the Christian community. Regis Duffy has characterized this time as a "partial retrieval and an occasional (unintended) distortion of the classical teaching of previous periods."[5] The Reformers emphasized biblically based sacramental theology and the power of God to fulfill God's promise in the sacraments. The Roman Catholics emphasized rather the intrinsic and objective character of sacramental grace. By keeping the indulgence system, which was based on a legalistic understanding of sin and forgiveness, the Roman Catholic church continued to maintain a juridical mentality in relation to sacramental theology and practice.

While neither Reformers nor Roman Catholics made any explicit shift in their understanding of the role of women, certain theological positions carried implications that bore fruit centuries later. In his stress on the priesthood of all believers, Luther unwittingly paved the way for the ordination of women to the ministry by describing all people, women as well as men, as priests to one another.[6] In doing so, Luther also expanded the notion of vocation to include the domestic sphere. The minister was called to leadership by the congregation, not by any quality intrinsic to the individual minister. In the Roman Catholic tradition, the emphasis on the spiritual and corporal works of mercy provided an inspiration to women and men determined to carry out the ministry of the church to the wider world.[7]

The four hundred years between the Council of Trent (1545–1563) and the Second Vatican Council (1962–1965) saw little development or change in official sacramental theology and practice. Sacramental theology and the administration of the sacraments were largely left to the clergy; the hierarchical model of the church dominant during this period served to maintain a distance between the laity and the sacred mysteries. This distance was physically reinforced by altar rails and cloisters and psychologically maintained by a conception of separate spheres of sacred and secular reality. Perhaps as a consequence of this separation, popular devotions grew: novenas, the forty hours, benedictions, pilgrimages, devotions to Mary and the saints, along with the use of sacramentals such as scapulars, rosaries, holy cards, and icons. These devotions and holy objects provided a more immediate connection to the holy for the laity, and especially for women. While access to God's grace in the sacraments has taken place almost exclusively through the mediation of a male priest, devotional practices in Roman Catholicism (as in all the other major religious traditions of the world) have provided women with some sense of power as well as a preserve of religious piety not dominated by men.

TRANSITIONS IN TWENTIETH-CENTURY SACRAMENTAL THEOLOGY

During the first sixty years of the twentieth century, theologians such as Edward Schillebeeckx and Karl Rahner, along with the leaders of the liturgical movement, developed a new theology of the sacraments rooted in a more dynamic understanding of the divine-human relationship. Schillebeeckx's pioneering *Christ the Sacrament of the Encounter with God* (published in English in 1962) developed his basic insight that human life with God is rooted in our life in the world.[8] Strongly influenced by the philosophical movement of phenomenology, an early twentieth-century school of philosophy that stressed the description of concrete experience, Schillebeeckx stressed the embodied and historical character of the sacraments. God's ultimate self-revelation is found in Jesus of Nazareth whose experience of God as Abba made possible a new and much more intimate relationship with God. At the heart of Schillebeeckx's sacramental theology is the insight that the sacraments provide a point where we encounter God in and through interpersonal experiences. Sacraments are not mere "pipelines" of grace; they are, as he puts it in his later work, "anticipatory signs" of salvation, places where human beings live out in a symbolic way the life of the gospel.

Karl Rahner, also influenced by newer interpretations of Aquinas, developed a theology of symbol based in the intrinsically expressive character of human existence.[9] In his article "The Theology of the Symbol," first published in 1959, Rahner argued that this expressiveness is rooted in the Trinity and in God's self-expression in the Incarnation. The use of symbolic language in sacramental theology had been seen as suspect, from as early a time as the Middle Ages, as the symbolic was increasingly distanced from the "real." Rahner's contribution was to show that the sacramental nature of the church was rooted in the Incarnation and that symbolic expression is at the heart of human knowing and loving. The effect of both of these theologians' work was to transform the language of sacramental theology into more personal and dynamic terms, to challenge the radical distinction between the sacred and the secular, to reintroduce the language of symbol, and to make sacramental praxis the action of the whole church and not just of the clergy.

Many of the changes of Vatican II were indebted to the work of Schillebeeckx and Rahner, and the changes were already well under way by the time the Council opened in the fall of 1962. The first major document of the Council, *Sacrosanctum Concilium,* began the massive task of transforming the liturgy by allowing the use of the vernacular and encouraging the participation of the laity in the liturgy.[10] Over the following years, all of the sacraments were affected to a greater or lesser extent by the changes of the Council. Perhaps the most important change, developed in two constitutions of the Council, *Lumen Gentium* and *Gaudium et Spes,* was the new understanding of the church as People of God. While the hierarchical distinction between clergy and laity was retained, the primary stress now fell on the entire community of the church as ministering together. The sacramental dimension of the church received renewed emphasis.

The breakdown of distinctions between clergy and laity, sacred and secular, had a profound effect on sacramental theology in the years following Vatican II. The older instrumental understanding of the sacraments gave way to an enhanced recognition of the sacramental character of all of human life. The work of Schillebeeckx and Rahner deeply influenced the present generation of sacramental theologians. Certain sacraments were substantially changed: the older sacrament of penance became "reconciliation," symbolizing a pastoral rather than punitive approach to human sinfulness. The Rite of Christian Initiation of Adults reintroduced the catechumenate to church membership using a developmental approach.

THE WOMEN'S MOVEMENT
AND SACRAMENTAL THEOLOGY

In addition to Vatican II, the women's movement of the 1960s and 1970s raised awareness of the pervasive sexism within Christian theology and of the injustice of women's exclusion from nearly every position of power and decision making in the church. In the 1970s, with the establishment of the Women's Ordination conference and the decision of many Protestant denominations to ordain women, many Catholics hoped that the Vatican would change its position on the issue. But the Vatican Declaration of 1976, *Inter Insigniores,* while acknowledging the spiritual equality of women and men and the difficulty of grounding historically its decision, stood firm in its opposition to women's ordination by appealing to an "unbroken tradition" of ordaining only males and to a sacramental theology of "natural resemblance."[11] Based on an interpretation of Thomas Aquinas's sacramental theology, this document argued that the difference of sex, unlike race or ethnicity, is an "essential" difference. Because of Jesus' maleness and his "decision" to "choose" only males for the twelve apostles, the church was "not free" to change its position. The maleness of Christ was thus seen as essential to the theology of the priesthood.

Few contemporary feminist theologians now argue for the inclusion of women in the existing structures of the church's ministry. But contemporary Catholic feminists find themselves in a dilemma: whether to abandon participation in the male-dominated sacramental life of the church in favor of a nonsexist worship life or to continue participating in a male-dominated sacramental system and to work for change from within.

Rosemary Ruether, in her book *Women-Church,* argues that "women in contemporary churches are suffering from linguistic deprivation and eucharistic famine."[12] Her sourcebook is intended to help usher in a new church—Women-Church—as a community of equals. While not reject-ing the Jewish and Christian heritages, Ruether seeks "both to go back behind biblical religion and to transcend it. Women-Church embraces a liminal religiosity."[13] The book provides guidelines for worship spaces and liturgies to celebrate events in women's lives such as first menstrua-tion, pregnancy loss through miscarriage and abortion, healing from pain-ful experiences. Taking a position between those who reject the church altogether and those who try to work within church structures, Ruether suggests that these rituals can provide women with the strength needed to persist in a world and church still dominated by sexism.

Christine Gudorf makes the case that sacraments are, at their heart, celebrations of what women do naturally—give birth, feed, and comfort—physical experiences that have been taken up by men and sacralized.[14] Men can then do what women do, but on a higher, more spiritual plane; women's bodily experience is now seen as less holy than men's. Her pro-posed solution is to reconnect the sacraments with ordinary life so that men can become better accustomed to the experience of the concrete and to recognize the ritual power of women.

Mary Collins has suggested that contemporary women can learn from the medieval women whom Bynum describes: their refusal to receive or understand the sacraments from a hierarchical or neoclerical perspective led them to redefine their own experience.[15] By focusing on the ways in which these medieval women used the sacraments to deepen their own appreciation of their humanity, Collins points out that women need not let the sacraments be co-opted by the clergy as their own; the sacraments belong to the whole church, and this challenge to the impoverishment of the Eucharist is one of women's contributions to the present situation.

But the dilemma remains. Part of the difficulty for a feminist sac-ramental theology is that the issues are practical as well as speculative and academic. Like every other area of feminist theology, a feminist per-spective on the sacraments involves rethinking the bases for our under-standing of these issues from the perspective of women's experience. It also involves the more radical questions of whether the sacramental system is intrinsically sexist and whether a feminist sacramental theology is even possible, much less necessary.

FEMINIST ISSUES IN SACRAMENTAL THEOLOGY

All feminist theorists ask, with a few variations, the same questions: How are women accounted for in a given area of study? How is the experience of women integral to a particular field? In sacramental theology, since its transformation involves not only the practical dimensions—for example, who can be a minister—but also deeply entrenched symbolic associations, a feminist approach must start by looking at the bases of human experience out of which the sacraments emerge. Since Vatican II, the recognition of the anthropological basis of human ritual activity has by now become standard. The theories of Arnold van Gennep and Victor Turner on rites of passage and of Paul Ricoeur and Hans Georg Gadamer on human symbolism are widely drawn upon.[16] Feminist theory has challenged some of the most widely held assumptions about human activity and thought by pointing out how many theories rely only upon the experience of men. So too a feminist sacramental theology cannot simply assume that the predominant understandings of human experience on which sacramental theology has drawn provide an adequate basis for a sacramental theology for women. Instead, we must begin at a deeper level and ask what dynamic lies at the root of human symbolic and ritual experience.

NATURE AND HISTORY

Many traditions base their rituals and symbols on the cyclical processes of nature and, by extension, on the process of human development. Rituals mark the beginning of new life in spring and the harvest and (temporary) death of nature in autumn. The Christian tradition, while acknowledging a connection with nature, has usually found its basis for ritual and symbol in God's action in *history* rather than in the cycles of nature.

In Christian sacramental theology, as in the whole of the Judeo-Christian tradition, the emphasis has been on God's entry into history and the historical transformation of nature. Human beings are no longer tied to the closed and cyclical system of nature. Sacraments are to be distinguished from their so-called pagan counterparts, Christians are told, since the celebration is not simply of the natural but the natural as transformed by God.

Feminist theology challenges this contrast between the natural and the historical and argues that such a split has been part of a dualistic system that has opposed men and women, spirit and nature, history and nature, soul and body.[17] Feminists point out that the nature religions to which Judaism and Christianity are opposed have been oriented around fertility and the Goddess, both of which are symbolically associated with women. Goddess feminists in particular have sought a return to an earth- and nature-based tradition and charge that the historical religions have sought to erase a sense of the intrinsic sacrality of women.

Dualisms such as nature/history, body/spirit, female/male are oppositional—one side is seen over and against the other—as well as hierarchical—one side must control the other. Violence against women, children, and nature, that is, the animal world and the fragile ecosystem that supports all life on the planet, can result when one side rejects the other as evil. A Catholic feminist perspective bases its critique of these dualistic conceptions on a retrieval of the Incarnation, seeing God's taking on the condition of humanity as God's own self-expression. Sacramentality grows out of human embodiment and its connection to the natural world, not in contrast to it. Feminist theology thus argues for a closer connection between nature and history, body and soul.

Many of the reforms in sacramental theology have given greater recognition to the connections between nature and history and are indebted to the work of anthropologists, sociologists, and psychologists of religion. Feminist theologians caution, however, that these theoretical bases are all too often uninformed by women's experience and carry with them unexamined assumptions about relations between the human and the natural, and Christianity and so-called pagan religions. The appeal of Goddess religions, which are self-consciously rooted in the natural cycles of the seasons, can be better understood against these perceptions.

PSYCHOLOGY AND FEMINISM

The role of the human developmental process has proven to be another fruitful area for post–Vatican II sacramental theology. The recognition that conversion is a *process* has influenced renewed practices such as the R.C.I.A. (Rite of Christian Initiation of Adults), the rite of reconciliation, and, to some extent, the sacrament of marriage, especially in the ways that changes in annulment practices have occurred over the last twenty-five years. By now it has become essential to acknowledge the maturation processes human beings undergo and to connect them with sacramental celebrations. Influenced by developmental psychologists, scholars in the psychology of religion point to recognizable stages in the development of a mature faith.[18]

Recent work in feminist literary and psychoanalytic theory has suggested some new ways of looking at the developmental process that focus on the experience of women, raising some provocative questions about the role of symbols. Theories of human development, especially in this century, have relied heavily on the work of Freud and his followers. While there are few "pure Freudians" around these days, the influence of the Viennese thinker remains pervasive. Even the work of a respected documenter of the human condition such as Erik Erikson is deeply indebted to the kinds of maturation turning points first outlined by Freud.[19]

One area that has appealed to feminist theorists is object relations theory, which focuses primarily on the relationship between the child and the mother.[20] Briefly put, object relations theorists point out that Freud and his successors focused on the experiences of boys and modeled human development on that of males. In addition, they largely ignored the very early relationship between mothers and infants. Object relations theorists show how boys and girls undergo the process of gender identification in different ways. Separation becomes key for boys, who learn that they are not like their mother (who is most often the primary child rearer). Girls learn instead that one day they too may be mothers and come to see their primary relationship (with the mother) in terms of identification. As a result of distinguishing themselves from their mothers, boys come to see themselves and their world in terms that are clear-cut and objective. Boys' activities are rule-bound; studies show that when boys experience conflict in game playing, they resort to rules. In psychologist Carol Gilligan's well-known (but also controversial) studies, boys resort to abstract principles of rights and justice in trying to resolve moral dilemmas.[21] The key concept here is *separation:* in order to develop his identity as a boy, and later as a man, the male child must separate from his mother and, indeed, all that symbolizes her.

Girls, on the other hand, have more permeable ego boundaries and are socialized to be more empathic and other-identified than boys. Being a tomboy is a normal occurrence for many girls. When girls experience conflict in games, they more often abandon the game in favor of preserving relationships instead of resorting to rules, which are perceived as objective and impersonal. In resolving moral dilemmas, Gilligan's work proposes, girls value caring and relationship and are uncomfortable with using only theories of rights or justice. The key concept here is *identification*, in which the girl comes to a sense of her self by identifying with her mother and by being other-oriented in her relationships.

From these theories emerge some patterns that can be correlated with sacramental theology and practice. One is the significance of clearly delineated boundaries: between male and female, public and private, spiritual and material. Gudorf points out that when the sacraments are seen to be the preserve of meaning and power (and not the ordinary physical activities from which they are derived), there is much at stake in preserving the distinction between the sacramental and the ordinary.[22] A related pattern is the valuing of the symbolic over the literal: what is seen as truly real is not what is concrete, but what *represents* the concrete. In addition, the emphasis on individuality and autonomy that characterizes the ideal for manhood can be correlated with an understanding of the church community as a gathering of independent, autonomous persons whose interpersonal relationships are not as intrinsic to their selfhood as is their individual relationship to God.

By raising these questions of human development and the role of symbolic representation, it is possible to ask whether there are connections with the way that sacraments have come to represent key moments in the lives of the Christian community. To what extent has the concern with canonical validity obscured the power of the presence of Christ in the Eucharist or the sacramental power and presence of Christ in the nonordained? An even deeper question is whether symbolic and ritual activities have taken on a role for men that they do not have for women. In other words, is it necessary to set aside certain moments, actions, and places that are sacred? If object relations theorists are correct about women's psychological experience of more permeable ego boundaries, of connections between personal and political, private and public, does this call into question the very basis for sacraments as ritual activity set apart from ordinary life? Or does it suggest that we need a different approach to the presence of God in human life?

Asking these questions strikes at the very heart of the Christian message. If Christian sacramentality is, at its heart, expressive of male separation, along with alienation between the sacred and secular dimensions of human life, then a feminist sacramental theology is impossible. But if sacramentality expresses the mystery and presence of God-for-us in the Incarnation, and if God's becoming human, formed within the body of a woman, is central to Christian faith, then women's experiences cast a different light on sacramental theology and practice. Perhaps even the number and content of the sacraments might change, but they would not be dismissed altogether. Women's relationships to the sacred and to the everyday would broaden and deepen sacramental theology and would act as criticism and corrective to the sacramental tradition.

I will take the latter route in the rest of this chapter, basing it on the conviction by many Catholic women that the gospel message is radically inclusive, nonhierarchical, and directed against oppressive structures; that women as well as men have been shapers of the tradition; and that the call to reform church structures of their sexism challenges women and men to reenvision the symbolic expressions of their faith.

A FEMINIST SACRAMENTAL THEOLOGY

The poem that opens this chapter evokes the centrality of embodiment for the sacraments. While sacramentality is not unique to the Christian tradition, the radical and, to some, scandalous conjunction of divine and human in the Incarnation is at the root of sacramental theology. Once God has elected to dwell among us, sharing our human condition, all of creation is profoundly affected: the radical distinction between divine and human is no longer unsurpassable.

The challenge of feminism to Christian theology is the expression of the full humanity of women and men, not only "in Christ," but in society and in the church. What has hampered this realization in Catholic theology in particular is a historical reliance on a theology of natural law that regards biological sex differences as essential factors in the significance of human nature, resulting in differential treatment of women and men. Women's "nature" is understood (as in the writings of John Paul II) to be primarily oriented toward childbearing and rearing, thus relegating women to the sphere of the home.[23] The vocations of religious women are sometimes seen as extensions of this maternal role, as Pope John Paul II points out. In addition, the almost primeval character of religious symbolism has been infected by the pervasive influence of sexism. The resistance not only by many men but by many women to use feminine imagery for God suggests that our language and vision need reeducation.[24]

Where a sacramental feminist theology begins, then, is in the basic conviction of the full humanity of women and the recognition that the meaning associated with sex differences over the centuries is highly suspect. This meaning, usually seen as complementarity, is rooted in history and culture and therefore its claim to understand women's supposedly essential and timeless nature is without an adequate basis. In addition to this challenge comes the conviction of the interconnectedness of human life and of human and nonhuman life. Much of feminist thought over the last twenty years has pointed out the distinctive nature of women's experiences and has thus opened itself to criticism that these distinctive elements look suspiciously like stereotypically feminine qualities attributed to women by men. But what distinguishes these efforts are, first, the concern to know and value women's experiences and not to model expectations for women on male experience alone; and, second, a recognition of the *ambiguity* of women's experience. That is, because women have been both included in and excluded from the category *men* and have been included in the structures of society as domestic shapers of culture yet excluded from public positions of power, women have developed a dual consciousness, an awareness of "twoness"—in short, a sense of radical ambiguity that does not lend itself easily to strategies of separation and isolation.[25]

What some psychologists label as the greater permeability of women's ego boundaries, and what some ethicists have labeled as the inability of women to make clear moral distinctions, have been understood to handicap women. But women's sense of ambiguity, reluctance to make separations, and tendency to identify with the other are closer to the heart of Christian sacramentality than the strict separations that have become pervasive in much sacramental theology and practice. Such a sense of interconnection and an appreciation of the often conflicting realities that co exist in such interconnection is characteristic of much of contemporary feminist theory in psychology, literary theory, history, and ethics. These ideas have important implications for sacramental theology as well.[26]

How might we conceive of a feminist sacramental theology, informed both by the central Christian belief that God has come to dwell in our humanity and by the conviction that women's experience of the connections between body and soul, physical and spiritual, represents a significant resource for expressing this belief? Beginning with the existing sacraments provides an opportunity for both critical and constructive suggestions.

Baptism and by tradition *confirmation* (originally a part of the baptismal ceremony) are intended to introduce and confirm the person into Christian life. Baptism has also signified the cleansing away of original sin, dying and rising with Christ, incorporation into a liturgical community. Confirmation emphasizes the gifts of the Holy Spirit and the continued commitment to witnessing to the gospel.

The "new life" that the Christian community provides has often been seen in distinction from, and sometimes in contrast to, "merely physical" birth. Such ideas have served to suggest, as Gudorf notes, that the ordinary activities on which the sacraments are modeled have lesser value than their spiritual counterparts. A feminist perspective is critical of these distinctions and their effects on women's lives and struggles to reconnect sacraments with ordinary, biological life. In contemporary practice, all too often these sacraments are performed as a matter of course, without their concrete implications being sufficiently realized. Confirmation classes are routinely taught in grade eight, and young people are confirmed with little awareness of the sacrament's meaning. Or so much attention is given to sacramental administration that insufficient attention is paid to the *continuing* challenge of sacramental life. If we are to see the sacraments as intensifications of human experiences in their physical form, then the processes of human birth and growth in maturity need greater emphasis. For example, if the symbolic association between the amniotic fluid and the water of baptism as bringing new life were made clearer in sacramental theology and practice, then the sacrament's connection with the physical act of birth would become explicit. In sacramental practice, while the moment in which the sacrament is received tends to be the main focus, what is equally significant is the day-to-day living of the demands of Christian life. Greater attention to religious education (a field, not surprisingly, dominated by women) would help to intensify sacramental commitment in daily life. The essential element of baptism and confirmation is that one is now part of a new community, which bears the promise of the message of Jesus.

The sacraments of *reconciliation* and *anointing* touch on those parts of human existence where we are wounded and ill. The purpose of the sacraments is to reconcile us to God, to others, and to the church so that our fractured lives may receive some healing. Feminist theologians have been critical of much of the theology and practice of the church with regard to sin. The understanding of sin as *pride,* or *hybris,* is, as Valerie Saiving wrote over thirty years ago, more applicable to men than to women who have been encouraged to be self*less.*[27] Women's sin may well lie more in an underdevelopment of the self and a too-great reliance upon the opinions of others.

In addition, a disproportionate amount of space in the traditional manuals of moral theology, which counseled confessors, was devoted to sins pertaining to sexual morality. This focus, as Johannes Baptist Metz has charged, has tended to privatize sin: it keeps the stress on Christian living within the home and not in the wider society.[28] Even in recent years, while the Catholic church has a long record in recognizing the social dimensions of the faith, much of the burden of living one's faith has been placed on sexual, rather than social, morality. The social character of sinfulness is something that feminist theology has emphasized. Human sexuality and social practices are intrinsically linked; "the personal is the political" is one of the key statements of the women's movement. Thus the practice of reconciliation needs to become more attentive to all of the dimensions of human sin and suffering. In the ancient church, penances often involved restitution of stolen goods, and public penances exemplified the fact that the sin was an offense to the entire Christian community. While a return to these ancient practices has much merit, at the least a greater recognition of the social character of much of human sinfulness and a greater appreciation of the positive role of human sexuality would help to continue the transformation of the sacrament of reconciliation.

The sacrament of the sick has already benefited from a realization of the healing power of prayer and a greater attentiveness to touch. Here again, the participation of all people in the reconciling and healing role of the church would work against the privatization that has haunted the practices of these sacraments. Gudorf points out how men have often been the scientific decision makers rather than the caregivers in human sickness and healing. The lesser value given to caring underscores the asymmetry of our understanding of sin and woundedness.

The sacraments of commitment, *marriage* and *holy orders,* have been the most affected by an asymmetric understanding of gender roles and, in their theologies, have most excluded the experiences of women. Women have been encouraged to subsume their individuality into the roles of wife and mother and have been the most hurt by an androcentric theology of sexuality. Women have much to contribute to a more adequate theology of marriage grounded in the mutuality of persons and to a more adequate theology of sexuality attentive to women's embodied and social experience. The traditional theology of marriage, upheld in Vatican documents until Vatican II, taught that the man was the "head" and the woman the "heart" in a marriage. Grounded in the relationship of Christ the Bridegroom to the Church as Spotless Bride, Catholic marriage theology was essentially hierarchical. That Catholic ecclesiology has also frequently resorted to this metaphor to characterize the relationship between the clergy and the laity should come as no surprise.[29]

A theology of marriage marked by dialogue, in which each partner is valued, is needed at a time when women are still far too often the victims of violence in the home. For too long the Christian churches have supported a hierarchical theology of marriage that has presumed the superiority of men over women and, in effect, has given men permission to abuse their wives and children. This theology has the additional disadvantage of freezing gender roles. A dialogical understanding of marriage would allow for the development of each partner, their growth in relationship to each other, to their children, and to the community. A developmental theology of marriage is especially needed since human life expectancy has nearly doubled within this century.

The church's theology of sexuality, usually understood in the context of its marriage theology, is also in need of the voices of women. The few attempts that have been made to listen to women's own experience of their sexuality—such as Archbishop Weakland's listening to women on the issue of abortion—unfortunately have met resistance. The most recent (fourth) draft of the American bishops' pastoral on women's concerns omits the direct quoting of women's voices.[30] The sacramental dimension of sexuality is recognized in the designation of marriage as a sacrament, but the church's concern for sexuality seems to be narrowly focused on the immorality of contraception and abortion and not on the wider dimensions of the goodness of human sexuality and the responsibility to care for one's body. Seeing the marital relationship as a partnership of equals suggests a different model for the church than the traditional hierarchical one where the "active" groom and "receptive" bride exist in an asymmetric relationship.[31]

Efforts by the magisterium to close off discussion on ordination notwithstanding, the issue remains a powerful reminder of the injustice of women's exclusion from sacramental ministry. An all-male priesthood reinforces the common assumption, mistaken even on traditional grounds, that sacramental grace is always mediated by men. The understanding of the priest as *in persona Christi* (acting "in the person of Christ") continues the long-standing association of maleness with divinity.

The experience of many parishes and other religious communities is that women *are* serving as effective pastors in all ways except the celebration of the Eucharist. The numbers of women who serve as pastoral administrators and hospital and campus chaplains are growing. Many Catholics who experience the ministry of women in various capacities such as counseling and preaching are coming to question the wisdom of an all-male priesthood and the deprivation of the wider community of the full exercise of women's gifts.

Moreover, the connection between maleness, priesthood, and divinity has been challenged repeatedly by many theologians in recent years who have sought to remind the Christian community of the metaphorical nature of all religious expressions (stated eloquently by Thomas Aquinas in the *Summa Theologiae*[32]) and of the historical, social, and political factors in the development of an all-male priesthood. The theological adequacy of the 1976 statement has been questioned by eminent theologians such as Rahner and Schillebeeckx.

The nature of priesthood has undergone much serious examination in recent years. The return to the sources advocated by Vatican II has resulted in a greater awareness of the factors that influenced the development of a cultic conception of priesthood, which concerns the priest's role in worship. The more recent emphasis on the servant nature of the priesthood and the priest's relation to the community have begun to transform the self-conception of the priesthood. While this has been a painful experience for many priests whose seminary education relied on a hierarchical model, the possibilities for a transformed priesthood are only beginning to be realized.

A feminist theology of ordained ministry takes seriously human embodiment, in all its various forms, as the place where humans encounter God. The example of Jesus' inclusive, destabilizing, and nonhierarchical ministry[33] serves as a model. This understanding of ministry is inclusive, in that distinctions of sex, race, and class are irrelevant. Many are called to ministry, although some have gifts for certain roles, such as leadership or preaching. This approach to ministry is destabilizing, in that it questions the usefulness of all human structures. The extent to which structures and institutions serve the message of the gospel is the measure of their value. And this ministry is critical of hierarchy for its tendency to concentrate power in a few. A feminist theology of ministry is one of empowerment, serving to energize the community, not to rule over it.

This new vision of ministry has already begun to take shape: in the voices of women who preach, in the small base communities of men and women, in the exercise of women's leadership in nonpriestly capacities. But the vision will remain unfulfilled as long as women are excluded from ordination. For in the deeply sacramental tradition that is Catholicism, the message remains that women cannot fully represent Christ and that although women's bodies may bear the Incarnation, women cannot serve as priests.

In the meantime, the exercise of the ministry of the nonordained and the greater visibility of women in the church has already effected a major shift in consciousness among many in the church (a majority of whom now favor the ordination of women). What effect this will have on the future church is yet unknown, but the revolution in the awareness of and about women cannot be ignored. The ordination of women would be a recognition of the fundamental equality of the sexes before God and in the church and in the sacrality of the human body.

The theology of the *Eucharist* is, in many ways, inseparable from the issue of ordination. Religious communities of women as well as groups of lay women have come increasingly to find the Eucharist a source of pain and anger as much as a source of grace and unity. Groups of women must "import" a priest, often unknown to the community, to ensure the "valid- ity" of the Eucharist. That the sacrament of unity is a symbol of sexual inequality causes many to question its centrality in their own spiritual lives. Many lay and women's groups have, in effect, taken the Eucharist into their own hands. Recalling the ancient tradition of the presence of Christ being found in the local community, groups gather together for communal sharing of bread and wine and reflection upon scriptural (and other) texts. What many groups miss, however, is the connection with the universal church. Collins's argument that women can learn from medieval women to refuse to accept a hierarchically dominated understanding of the Eucharist is helpful here. Her point is not to dismiss the question of or- dination but rather to point out that the Eucharist is not encompassed by the clergy or hierarchy.

At its heart, the Eucharist symbolizes the extravagant self-gift of Christ and the unity of the community in all its diversity and ambiguity. For Collins, "symbolic reductionism" takes place when limited realities are equated with the reign of God; this is a mentality that "finds it unbeliev- able that what is humanly incoherent coheres in God, a crucible of dark concealment and blinding light."[34]

The feminist critique of eucharistic theology and practice charges that the Eucharist itself has become a symbol of power, to be held tightly by a male clerical caste. A feminist eucharistic theology has its center in the ecclesial assembly not in the presider. When the focus is on the assem- bly, the Eucharist is a lavish gift to be shared, not scarce gold to be parceled out piecemeal only to those who qualify. Like the multiplication of the loaves and fishes, the eucharistic feast ought to be a living symbol of the openness and generosity of the Christian community. That it so often fails to live up to this generosity is a scandal.

Furthermore, the connection of the Eucharist with the hunger of the world is a point that has been developed by liberation theology. Our bodily hunger for food cannot be separated from our spiritual hunger for the word of God. Women's role in the feeding of the world is a point that cannot be ignored.

Finally, the unofficial ways in which women exercise a priestly awareness of the holiness of the body and of everyday human life should be mentioned. In an important 1981 essay, Sandra Schneiders described the flip side of women's exclusion from leadership roles and its effect on women's spirituality. That this exclusion has been painful for women and that the church has lost much is readily acknowledged by Schneiders. But there are unintended positive consequences—a flip side—to these practices. While there are negative effects that flow from women's exclusion from official ministry, there are nevertheless some positive dimensions to be found as well, such as women's greater experience in the private sphere and willingness to create egalitarian structures. Drawing on her insight, one could argue that because women have not had the experience of official priestly ministry, women are in a position to have a greater appreciation for the sacrality of the everyday, to be aware of the real presence not just in the Eucharist but in the ordinariness of preparing daily meals, to convey a healing touch to a sick child, to do the daily work of reconciling parents and children, spouses, and friends. This insight is not, however, meant to suggest a complementary notion of women's common priesthood but rather to suggest that the different experiences and gifts women would bring to the priesthood would inevitably change the office. Like the chef Babette in the Isak Dinesen novel and in the film *Babette's Feast,* whose cooking became the sacrament of community among those she served, women *have* exercised sacramental ministry throughout the church's entire history although it has rarely been recognized. The time has now come to join more closely the public and private expressions of Catholic sacramentality.

CONCLUSION

In this chapter I have surveyed some of the major issues in Roman Catholic sacramental theology as they concern women and have begun the construction of a feminist sacramental theology. Certain issues remain critical in any continuing reflection on women and the sacramental life of the church.

1. The meaning of the Incarnation and its connection with theological anthropology are at the core of sacramental theology. The recognition that God took on *human* (not specifically *male*) flesh is central, as is the recognition that the historical and social constructions of gender have played crucial roles in maintaining assumptions about women's so-called proper role in the church. The threats to women's full humanity have been recognized especially in the last one hundred and fifty years. While differences between men and women remain a controversial subject, traditional notions of complementarity are no longer adequate. Differences have most often been seen from a male perspective, so that women's awareness of their own experience has only recently begun to emerge. The postmodern focus on the multiplicity and diversity of human experience offers one way of accounting for difference without the stereotyped categories of complementarity. This focus also opens up the consideration of human experience from the perspectives of race and class as well as gender.

2. The influential role of symbolic expression and the recognition of the ways in which gender is an unacknowledged dimension of that expression require careful interdisciplinary analysis. Literary, psychoanalytic, and social critiques have revealed hidden biases in so-called universal expressions of human experience in novels, in psychological analyses of human development, and in the dynamics of social groups. Theologians need to be especially attentive to the contributions of their colleagues in these fields, since they can shed needed light on central theological questions. Sacramental theology, because of its reliance on studies of symbol and metaphor and its rootedness in human developmental processes, can especially benefit from such collaborative work.

3. The connection between sacramental praxis and social justice has received renewed emphasis since the rise of the liberation movements of the 1960s. Tissa Balisuriya writes that "the Eucharist has to be related positively to human life if it is to be faithful to its origins and its performance."[35] In more traditional language, sacraments must effect what they signify. The disjunction between social praxis and ecclesiology maintained in *Inter Insigniores* will no longer suffice as an adequate explanation for "sacramental sex discrimination." As long as sacramental theology continues to privilege the experience of men over women, there will not be a just sacramental praxis.

To a great extent, reflection on women and sacraments is at a very early stage. The depth of symbolic meaning precludes rapid change or change by fiat, but the realization that the structures of the imagination are deeply rooted should not be allowed to inhibit all changes. Openness to new developments, continuing reflection on women's experience, and careful scrutiny of our theological and symbolic heritage will work to transform the ways in which we live out the Christian belief that Christ lives among us, in the flesh and blood of the church.

NOTES

1. Elisabeth Schüssler Fiorenza, *In Memory of Her: A Feminist Theological Reconstruction of Christian Origins* (New York: Crossroad, 1983).

2. Augustine, *Letters* (Washington, DC: Catholic Univ. Press, 1966), 2:100–2.

3. Thomas Aquinas, *Summa Theologiae,* III, qq. 60–63.

4. Carolyn Walker Bynum, *Holy Feast and Holy Fast: The Religious Significance of Food to Medieval Women* (Berkeley and Los Angeles: Univ. of California Press, 1987), and Bynum, *Fragmentation and Redemption: Essays on Gender and the Human Body in Medieval Religion* (New York: Zone Books, 1991).

5. Regis Duffy, "Sacramental Theology," in *Systematic Theology: Roman Catholic Perspectives,* ed. Francis Schüssler Fiorenza and John Galvin (Minneapolis: Fortress Press, 1991), 198.

6. Martin Luther, "The Pagan Servitude of the Church," in *Selections from the Writings of Martin Luther,* ed. John Dillenberger (New York: Doubleday, 1961), 345ff.; but see also "The Estate of Marriage," in *Luther's Works,* ed. Walter I. Brandt (Philadelphia: Muhlenberg Press, 1959).

7. See, for example, *Journey into Freedom: Mary Ward, Essays in Honour of the Fourth Centenary of Her Birth* (London: The Way, 1985).

8. Edward Schillebeeckx, *Christ the Sacrament of the Encounter with God,* trans. N. D. Smith (New York: Sheed and Ward, 1963).

9. Karl Rahner, "The Theology of the Symbol," in *Theological Investigations,* vol. 4, trans. Kevin Smyth (New York: Seabury Press, 1974).

10. Walter M. Abbott, ed., *The Documents of Vatican II* (New York: Guild Press, 1966).

11. The text can be found in Arlene Swidler and Leonard Swidler, eds., *Women Priests: A Catholic Commentary on the Vatican Declaration* (New York: Paulist Press, 1977).

12. Rosemary Radford Ruether, *Women-Church: Theology and Practice of Feminist Liturgical Communities* (New York: Crossroad, 1985), 4.

13. Ruether, *Women-Church,* 4.

14. Christine Gudorf, "The Power to Create: Sacraments and Men's Need to Birth," *Horizons* 14 (1987): 296–309.

15. Mary Collins, "Women in Relation to the Institutional Church" (Lecture given at the Leadership Council of Women Religious 1991 National Assembly, Albuquerque, NM, August 26, 1991).

16. Arnold van Gennep, *Rites of Passage,* trans. Monika B. Viaedom and Gabrielle L. Caffe (Chicago: Univ. of Chicago Press, 1969); Victor Turner, *The Ritual Process: Structure and Anti-Structure* (Ithaca: Cornell Univ. Press, 1969); Paul Ricoeur, *The Symbolism of Evil,* trans. Emerson Buchanan (Boston: Beacon Press, 1967); Hans Georg Gadamer, *Truth and Method* (New York: Seabury Press, 1975).

17. See Rosemary Radford Ruether, *New Woman/New Earth: Sexist Ideologies and Human Liberation* (New York: Seabury Press, 1975); Carol Christ, "Rethinking Theology and Nature," in *Weaving the Visions: New Patterns in Feminist Spirituality,* ed. Judith Plaskow and Carol Christ (San Francisco: Harper & Row, 1989).

18. James Fowler, *Stages of Faith: The Psychology of Human Development and the Quest for Meaning* (San Francisco: Harper & Row, 1981).

19. Erik Erikson, *Identity and the Life Cycle* (New York: Norton, 1980).

20. Nancy Chodorow, *The Reproduction of Mothering: Psychoanalysis and the Sociology of Gender* (Berkeley and Los Angeles: Univ. of California Press, 1978); Dorothy Dinnerstein, *The Mermaid and the Minotaur: Sexual Arrangements and Human Malaise* (New York: Harper & Row, 1976); Margaret Homans, *Bearing the Word: Language and Female Experience in Nineteenth Century Women's Writing* (Chicago: Univ. of Chicago Press, 1986).

21. Carol Gilligan, *In a Different Voice: Psychological Theory and Women's Development* (Cambridge: Harvard Univ. Press, 1981).

22. Gudorf, "The Power to Create," 304.

23. John Paul II, "*Mulieris Dignitatem:* On the Dignity and Vocation of Women," *Origins* 18, no. 17 (Oct. 6, 1988).

24. Margaret Miles, *Image as Insight: Visual Understanding in Western Christianity and Secular Culture* (Boston: Beacon Press, 1985).

25. See Elizabeth Fox-Genovese, *Feminism Without Illusions: A Critique of Individualism* (Chapel Hill: Univ. of North Carolina Press, 1991).

26. See Susan A. Ross, "Sacraments and Women's Experience," *Listening* 28 (1993): 52–64.

27. Valerie Saiving, "The Human Situation: A Feminine View," in *Journal of Religion* 40 (1960), reprinted in *Womanspirit Rising: A Feminist Reader in Religion,* ed. Carol Christ and Judith Plaskow (San Francisco: Harper & Row, 1979), 25–42.

28. Johannes Baptist Metz, "Messianic or Bourgeois Religion?" in *The Emergent Church: The Future of Christianity in a Postbourgeois World,* trans. Peter Mann (New York: Crossroad, 1981).

29. Susan A. Ross, "The Bride of Christ and the Body Politic: Body and Gender in Pre–Vatican II Marriage Manuals," *Journal of Religion* 71 (July 1991): 345–61.

30. The U.S. bishops voted to table the fourth draft of the pastoral letter amid much discussion and controversy.

31. For an argument *against* women's ordination by a woman who appeals to this understanding of bride and groom, see Sara Butler, "The Priest as Sacrament of Christ the Bridegroom," *Worship* 66 (1992): 498–516.

32. Thomas Aquinas, *Summa Theologiae,* I, q. 13.

33. These are Sallie McFague's terms, from her *Models of God: Theology for an Ecological, Nuclear Age* (Philadelphia: Fortress Press, 1987).

34. Collins, "Women in Relation to the Institutional Church," 8.

35. Tissa Balisuriya, *The Eucharist and Human Liberation* (Maryknoll, NY: Orbis Books, 1979), 86.

FOR FURTHER READING

Bynum, Carolyn Walker. *Holy Feast and Holy Fast: The Religious Significance of Food for Medieval Women*. Berkeley and Los Angeles: Univ. of California Press, 1987. Explores how medieval women developed a distinctive spirituality oriented around the Eucharist, showing how it represented a way for women to exercise control over their religious lives.

Chodorow, Nancy. *The Reproduction of Mothering: Psychoanalysis and the Sociology of Gender.* Berkeley and Los Angeles: Univ. of California Press, 1978. One of the most influential works in feminist psychology and philosophy; argues that as long as women remain the primary child rearers, the present sexist social system will be perpetuated.

Gudorf, Christine M. "The Power to Create: Sacraments and Men's Need to Birth." *Horizons* 14 (1987): 296–309. Argues that sacraments represent an institutionalized and male-dominated version of what women do in ordinary life (give birth, feed, comfort).

Fiorenza, Francis Schüssler, and John Galvin, eds. *Systematic Theology: Roman Catholic Perspectives*. 2 vols. Minneapolis: Fortress Press, 1991. A comprehensive overview of the current "state of the question" in Roman Catholic theology. Contains a chapter on the sacraments in general and separate treatments of the individual sacraments. Fiorenza's chapter on marriage is especially helpful in raising gender issues.

Procter-Smith, Marjorie. *In Her Own Rite: Constructing Feminist Liturgical Tradition*. Nashville: Abingdon Press, 1990. A clear and coherent feminist critique of liturgy that focuses largely on preaching and God-language and the need for new styles of presiding that incorporate the body. The Protestant focus is limited to baptism and Eucharist, but she provides a useful critique of the present system.

Rahner, Karl. *Theological Investigations*. Vol. 4, trans. Kevin Smyth. New York: Seabury Press, 1974. Contains four important essays that represent the significant impact Rahner had on the sacramental theology of Vatican II.

Ruether, Rosemary Radford. *Women-Church: Theology and Practice of Feminist Liturgical Communities*. San Francisco: Harper & Row, 1985. Both a critique of current ecclesiology and liturgical practice and a sourcebook for their transformation, including suggested rituals for women's experiences and for seasonal celebrations.

Swidler, Leonard, and Arlene Swidler, eds. *Women Priests: A Catholic Commentary on the Vatican Declaration*. New York: Paulist Press, 1977. Contains the declaration against women priests, the report of the biblical commission, and forty-six responses by Roman Catholic theologians on the biblical, historical, and ethical implications of the church's continued prohibition of the ordination of women.

Walker, Barbara G. *Women's Rituals: A Sourcebook*. San Francisco: Harper & Row, 1990. A helpful resource for understanding the emerging movement in women's spirituality and the use of Goddess imagery. Provides a "how to" for women's rituals.

CHAPTER NINE

FEMINISM AND CHRISTIAN ETHICS

— Moral Theology —

LISA SOWLE CAHILL

FEMINIST ETHICS IS immensely significant for the future of Catholicism, precisely because so many of the moral teachings that have formed Catholic identity have been directly related to gender expectations and roles of women and men. These same dimensions of morality, having to do with sex and gender but also with the social opportunities available to women and men, are issues within Christian ethics generally that have undergone drastic and rapid revision, especially in modern Western societies. These changes reflect corresponding shifts in the culture; as women gain access to public roles, men discover the importance of domestic ones, and Christianity adapts to respond to these new social realities. In ethics, feminist theology finds its most concrete and perhaps its most challenging expression.

In the past three decades, Roman Catholic ethics as a whole has become more biblical, more historically conscious, and in some ways more flexible. These changes have necessitated a revision of the theory of natural law, the moorings of ethics built by Thomas Aquinas. One very significant turn in Catholic ethics, or moral theology, has been the inclusion of social and ethical perspectives that had been barely acknowledged in the dominant traditions, especially perspectives of economically marginalized peoples and classes and of women. This inclusive move has also signaled the growing globalization of ethics, especially under the impact of liberation theology. A feminist theological ethics maintains that human nature is not adequately understood without full attention to the personal and social experience of women. It advances scriptural arguments in favor both of expanded models for Christian women and of the affirmative inclusion of other oppressed groups. It also insists that issues of so-called personal ethics, such as sexuality, cannot be understood apart from their social contexts and that social institutions, like male and female gender roles, have direct and deep influence on individual decisions and actions.

The central, most direct, and most obvious way that feminist theology has influenced ethics is in its advocacy for women's concerns and women's perspective, expressed ethically as justice for women. Justice for women means to regard women as the moral and social equals of men and to support their equal participation in the social roles that contribute to the common good, as well as their equal share in those benefits comprised by it. For instance, the U.S. Catholic bishops in their recent pastoral letter on the economy[1] were explicitly concerned with the situation of women. The social and economic marginalization of many women and its attendant ill effects on women, their children, and their families were directly addressed in that document as they had not been in earlier Catholic social teaching. Previous documents, by contrast, had tended to speak generically of the rights and duties of "man."[2] Women's perspectives are also more important in traditional areas of so-called personal ethics. While abortion, for instance, was once simply treated as a simple matter of an unborn child's right to life versus the mother's interests, such as her own life or other lesser values, which could be objectively assessed, the woman's situation is now more frequently seen as lending a distinctive texture to the complexity of the abortion situation. Pope John Paul II writes sympathetically of the unwed·mother, abandoned by the father of her child, who is pressured into an abortion.[3] More importantly, women themselves are seen as indispensable contributors to the moral analysis of abortion.[4]

In addition, feminism has influenced moral theology at a more fundamental level by shaping its questions and methods. At this level, feminism's influence is distinctive, though not unique. In other words, the characteristic contributions of feminist thinking are reflected in other, related approaches to ethics, especially that of liberation theology, of which feminist theology is usually understood to be a part.

These more fundamental contributions of feminism to theological ethics can be placed in three interdependent categories: (1) a revision of natural law as the basis of ethics; (2) an emphasis on the social and histori-cal contexts of ethics, including a cross-cultural perspective; and (3) a renewal of Scripture as a source for ethics. Feminism's special contribution of advocacy for women's liberation and these three fundamental but shared contributions to ethical method will be developed in turn. Then I will explore the contributions of feminism to Christian ethics at the prac-tical level through discussing two areas of applied ethics: sex and gender, and war and peace.

CHRISTIAN FEMINISM AND FUNDAMENTAL ETHICS

Anne E. Patrick has defined feminism as endorsing "(1) a solid con-viction of the equality of women and men, and (2) a commitment to reform society, including religious society, so that the full equality of women is respected, which requires also reforming the thought systems that legitimate the present unjust social order."[5] Feminist theology is never merely theoretical but is also always practical. The integral relation of theory and practice (or, to use the Marxist term, *praxis*) is a premise of all political and liberation theologies. These theologies arise out of an experienced situation of oppression and have as a primary aim the decon-struction of unjust social structures and institutions. Thus, by definition, liberation theology is at the same time ethics.

Feminist theology emerges from women's experience of exclusion from social opportunity and power; it also aims at social change. The dis-tinctive characteristic of liberation theology in its feminist variety is that it identifies with women as an oppressed group (as well as with men as also constrained by narrow gender-derived definitions of human identity) and that it seeks to introduce into the social agenda the importance of women's cause. Feminist theology begins with women's concrete reality, which it uses to critically address received traditions viewing women primarily in the service of institutionalized male dominance (patriarchy). As Margaret Farley asserts, "Feminist ethics traces its origins to women's growing awareness of the disparity between received traditional interpretations of their identity and function and their own experience of themselves and their lives." As such, it also claims a special "vantage point in a focus on women's experience precisely as disadvantaged."[6] The moral test, from a feminist point of view, is the effect of an ethical position, moral decision, or policy on the actual lives of women. The feminist moral ideal is to transform persons and societies toward more mutual and cooperative relationships between women and men, reflecting their equality as human persons.

Natural Law as a Basis for Ethics: The Feminist Revision

Feminists often appeal to the full human stature of women as their moral criterion and call for its recognition. Farley insists that the "most fundamental" principle of feminism is that "women are fully human and are to be valued as such."[7] This claim is also foundational to Rosemary Ruether's ethics. "The critical principle of feminist theology is the promotion of the full humanity of women. Whatever denies, diminishes, or distorts the full humanity of women is, therefore, appraised as not redemptive."[8] This criterion, especially as proposed by these two prominent Catholic theologians, serves as an important point of contact with the natural law tradition and also suggests resources for its renewal.

The most distinctive characteristic of the Roman Catholic tradition of ethics is its foundation in the natural law morality of Thomas Aquinas. In the thirteenth century, Aquinas combined the theology of Augustine with Aristotelian philosophy to locate morality within creation and redemption, and he also gave great importance to reason and human experience in discerning specific moral values and actions. The natural law he defined as humans' innate inclination toward what promotes human fulfillment; it has been instilled in the creature by God and is knowable by reason. By reflecting on experience itself, the human person can understand what sort of personal and political life will be most fulfilling for humans and, with a somewhat lesser degree of certitude, what specific actions best fulfill in the concrete the universal moral values that can be generalized from human behavior. For instance, all human beings seek to preserve their own lives, procreate and educate their young, live in society with others, and know the truth about God.[9] By considering these general principles in relation to the specific requirements of life in society, we may arrive at moral rules about issues such as self-defense, war, capital punishment, or monogamous marriage, contraception, and abortion. Even though the exact formulation of such rules and their application may vary among cultures or situations, Aquinas's natural law morality provides a base on which to build a community of moral discourse that transcends cultures and unites individuals and societies. In this sense, the natural law morality is a reasonable and objective morality.

It is important to realize that while Aquinas himself took an inductive and flexible approach to natural law, exhibiting caution about the absoluteness of specific conclusions from the general principles, some of his neoscholastic heirs (under the influence of Cartesian and Kantian philosophy, with their ideals of clear concepts and absolute norms) turned the morality of nature into a rigid, ahistorical system, which functioned to control and sanction experience rather than to reflect it. Treatments of sexual morality and bioethics illustrate this point. Ethical reflection tended to stake its authority on absolute principles, such as the primacy of procreation or the inviolability of all innocent human life, and then to derive from them specific conclusions (the immorality of all contraception and abortion), upon which were conferred the same absoluteness. What ethicists overlooked was the fact that this process of derivation, as well as the formulation of the starting principles, always takes place within a historical setting in which the perspectives of some will be privileged over those of others and in which the perceived need to address social and moral problems can result in distortions of ostensibly universal values.[10] Yet both Aquinas and his more recent interpreters allow that objectivity is attained historically and inductively and therefore always partially. The natural law approach is of lasting value for today in that it grounds an experiential morality while holding to an ideal of shared human truth, and manifests a confidence that God's will for persons is revealed in creation as an ongoing process of discovering God in human life.

Feminists who speak of "full humanity" as an ethical norm or test share the confidence of the natural law tradition in several areas: in seeing ethics as an objective enterprise; in building an understanding of basic and shared human characteristics through reflection on human life itself; and in viewing the fulfillment of human characteristics as imbued with moral value.

Feminists also claim that women and men share one human nature and that, whatever their functional biological differences and the exaggerated gender roles that have separated them historically, the commonality of that nature warrants similar moral treatment. Men's and women's virtues and vices are like enough so that their fundamental social contributions, duties, and claims may also be equal. Most feminists reject "two natures" theories that result in separate spheres dividing men and women and securing the dominance of one sex by the submission of the other. On the contrary, they believe it is possible to build on agreement about human purposes, goals, and values in order to challenge and begin to change sinful social structures perpetuating inequality.

While the concerns of many Roman Catholic feminists coincide with the natural law approach, they also introduce some new emphases. According to feminists, the patriarchal model of virtue that dominated neoscholastic ethics emphasized rationality, control, and certitude over affectivity, relationality, and dialogue. It also focused on the individual to the detriment of interdependence and community. Although few feminists today would want to argue that women are *intrinsically* more prone to affective relationships and men to individualist rationality, they would recognize that *historically* different qualities have been socially encouraged in men and women and that the perspectives of women can introduce into ethics a more complete view of human moral capacity. For Christian feminists, virtue consists not only in the integrity and rectitude of the rational self. It also requires a relational concern for building communities in which all can contribute to mutual fulfillment, communities secured on a base of justice and ascending toward the completion and transformation of love.

Just as feminists avoid a two-natures theory of women's and men's emotional, cognitive, and moral characteristics, so they reject the idea that justice and love mean something essentially different for women than for men. Ruether has written of a "cult of true womanhood" that followed nineteenth-century industrialization in Western countries, an ideology that both idealized women and confined them to the home and domesticity. Women were seen as more religious, spiritual, and moral than men, and it was their destiny to sacrifice themselves for husband and children.[11] This separation of women's and men's spheres and the subordination of women's talents to the family were reinforced by a particular Christian ideal of love as self-sacrifice—an ideal that was applied unevenly to women and men. In a landmark essay, Valerie Saiving pointed out that the prevalent Christian definition of sin as self-assertion and virtue as self-sacrifice was addressed more to the male situation in history than to the female and that women may face different temptations, against which they need to cultivate different virtues. Ideally, all Christians should experience a sacrificial and self-transcending love. At the same time, the cult of maternal and wifely sacrifice encourages in women the sin of self-negation rather than that of will-to-power. As she puts it, "A woman can give too much of herself, so that nothing remains of her own uniqueness; she can become merely an emptiness, almost a zero, without value to herself, to her fellow men, or, perhaps, even to God."[12]

Christian ethicists today seek ways of defining love that retain its aspect of self-offering while giving new emphasis to a mutuality or reciprocity that makes possible and completes the genuinely interpersonal and relational dimensions of love.[13] The reconceptualization of love has had far-reaching effects in moral theology. For instance, John Paul II, even in defending the traditional ban on contraception, does not claim that women's proper role is at the heart of the family but instead appeals to the "total reciprocal self-giving of husband and wife."[14] Although the fact that he also alludes to women's "true femininity," which should not be diluted by roles outside the home,[15] introduces a note of ambiguity into his endorsement of mutuality in marital love, the pope still exemplifies a notable shift in the premises of moral theology regarding one of its central virtues. This shift is carried through by authors like Christine Gudorf, who uses her own experience as a parent as a point of departure for arguing that Christian love is not disinterested but involved. All love requires sacrifice but also aims at mutuality, at the extension and sharing of the love relationship.[16]

Christian ethics today is considering anew whether shared and even universal human values are able to provide any sort of a reasonable and objective base for morality. This question is all the more urgent given heightened awareness of cultural and historical pluralism, as we shall see clearly in the next section. Feminist thought helps to clarify that all claims about what is natural to persons arise out of limited, partisan, and provisional experiences. The particularity of experience and of moral insight does not invalidate them as sources for an objective ethics; however, it does require that any proposal about a universally human or Christian morality be subjected to critical scrutiny and revision in light of the testimony of persons and groups of which natural law theorists may not have taken full account. For example, feminists have reexamined moral theology's tradition of assigning special virtues to women, especially self-sacrifice as wives and mothers, which in fact worked to exclude women from full humanity. Natural law ethics is not dead, but it is certainly more inductive, dialectical, and cautious in its method, thanks to feminism and other critical social movements that have unmasked the partiality of false universalisms whose proponents presented their own experiences and interests as absolute. A revised natural law method in Christian ethics bases morality on goods for persons, such as freedom, mutual love, justice, and association in the common good. However, it will constantly reexamine the status quo in light of the concrete requirements of these goods and, in particular, will enter into dialogue with diverse interpretations of the fundamental human goods.[17]

The Social Context and Content of Ethics

All ethics is social ethics. Our discussion of natural law has already made evident that all ethics is socially situated; moreover, even so-called personal moral decisions and relations have a social dimension. In the feminist motto, "the personal *is* political." Attention to the moral agent or moral subject must be accompanied by recognition of the subject's social context. From the middle of the twentieth century, Catholic theology has been characterized by the "turn to the subject" influenced by the philosopher Immanuel Kant and demonstrated in the work of Karl Rahner. In Rahner's thought, the person as free subject in relation to God is the reference point of a theological anthropology that portrays morality, especially love of neighbor, as the response of the individual to the ever-present summons of the divine love. But in recent ethics, this stress on the free, acting subject has been complemented by a revived interest in the social nature of the person. Social structures and expectations impinge on all persons and all their ethical decisions, whether in the areas of economics or sex, just war or the termination of medical treatment.

Feminism highlights the social side of all morality by critically evaluating sexual and family practices in the light of patriarchy and showing their economic and political ramifications. Thus it furthers this general movement in Christian ethics to integrate personal decision making with the social location of the agent and the social reverberations of action. The common good, interdependence, and sociality have all been used to counteract strains of liberal individualism in Christian ethics. In Catholic feminist writing, this emphasis on the communal and social dovetails with the Thomistic tradition of posing social issues in terms of the common good rather than in terms of individual rights. Human persons are "essentially relational as well as autonomous and free."[18]

In an essay on method in Christian ethics, June O'Connor draws together themes of sociality with those of a revised natural law epistemology. The fact that ethics is consciously experiential means that it must recognize both that there are sources of insight in addition to reason and also that experience and moral insight are communal. O'Connor notes that contemporary religious ethics attends to noncognitive capacities for moral insight, such as the affections and emotions. Contemporary ethics also acknowledges that many of our visions of reality operate prereflectively and hence their social sources and implications must be critically examined. "Feminist critiques of society detail ways in which attitudes about women shape personal behaviors and social policies."[19] Feminist thought also exemplifies an increasing trend to acknowledge that "communities of shared faith" (whether religious or not) shape values and visions of life and to commend "a cross-cultural consciousness" to the ethical enterprise.[20]

When the social dimension of all morality is adequately recognized, it also becomes possible to view moral norms in relation to their social conditions and effects rather than as abstract absolutes. In Catholic social teaching and social ethics, it has long been recognized that general moral principles may demand an application that is nuanced to particular sociopolitical settings. In writings about political organization, the economy, or war and peace, normative ethics has offered a general framework rather than systems of specific absolutes. For instance, workers may be said to have a right to a living wage, without specifying the precise amount of a minimum salary or whether it is up to employers or the government to guarantee it or how to accommodate the fact that some households will include more than one wage earner. Similarly, just war theory stipulates several criteria of legitimacy for armed conflict (for example, defense of the common good, last resort, right intention, proportionality, immunity of civilians) without trying to specify exactly which concrete policies, actions, or decisions meet or do not meet these criteria. But in areas of so-called personal, especially sexual, morality, Catholic ethics has operated on the basis of absolute norms about specific physical acts. This inconsistency of approach has been widely noted by moral theologians,[21] and a sexual morality that is more nuanced to situations has been proposed.

Another angle on the same problem is provided by the revival of "virtue" ethics, replacing the manualist focus on individual moral acts.

The manuals of moral theology that were the staples of seminary education in the first half of this century tended to isolate decisions from the full texture of the moral life. An ethics of virtue stresses the continuity of one's moral character, as expressed in decisions and actions. A feminist vision supports the cultivation of virtue understood in relational terms, not only as the righteousness of the agent as such. Moral acts find their meaning in the character of an integral moral life, realized in community with others, and consisting in the cultivation of personal, social, and religious values.

In summary, Catholic ethics today incorporates the importance of the social on at least two levels. First, it acknowledges that moral thinking always occurs within a sociohistorical context. This context shapes one's moral point of view, insights, and conclusions. Moral principles, norms, and decisions have a speicial relevance to this context, developing in response to its needs and standing to be enlarged or redefined when the relevance of other contexts of experience and thought become clear. Second, Catholic ethics now recognizes that there is no such thing as purely individual or even interpersonal morality. All morality is social, not only because it arises from the social context, but also because individual choices and relationships always affect and are affected by social practices, institutions, and the common good. The old dualism of personal and social morality was a false one. Still needed in Catholic ethics is a coherent moral methodology that would recognize in both personal and social life the need for norms, as well as the need to nuance their application sensitively to situation and context, and to place specific applications within an integrally virtuous life.[22]

Scripture and Feminist Ethics

A revisionist, iconoclastic, and subversive approach to images and roles of women in the Bible has been a mainstay of Christian feminism.[23] Feminist biblical interpretation, like feminist theology, is inherently political in its inspiration and aims, and hence it is also ethical. Feminist ethics reflects the renewed interest in Scripture that has made gradual headway in Catholic moral theology since Vatican II.

Since Catholic ethics has been primarily an ethics of the natural law, the inclusion of biblical resources has presented to it two special challenges. The first is to confront the fact that Jesus' teachings about discipleship may be at odds with the most "obvious" conclusions of rational, objective ethical thinking. No doubt the clearest examples are

Jesus' commands to love one's neighbor and even enemy and his example of nonviolence (see the Sermon on the Mount, Mt 5–7). In general, Jesus summons his hearers to a new way of life in the kingdom of God, even if the result for those who follow him is rejection or persecution. The ethical implications of the New Testament call into question any morality based on individual rights, self-defense, or even justice in the usual senses of equal regard or equal treatment.

A second and related challenge lies in the fact that the Bible takes sides. Jesus establishes a radically inclusive community in which the sinner, the poor, the outcast, and the marginal (including women) have a new place and are even preferred in God's eyes. Once more, the Bible calls into question the objective and universal ethics of the natural law tradition. Instead, the Bible seems to function ethically in providing models of how the early Christian communities undermined the reigning power relations of their day by establishing inclusive communities of reciprocity, forgiveness, and even love. This is not to say that the early Christians embodied the kingdom of God perfectly in their lives. However, many scholars use sociology and social history to illumine the settings of biblical texts and to read through the text the relation of the early churches to their surrounding cultures. As a result, they can claim that the nonviolence and sharing of goods practiced by early Christian communities may have offered critical alternatives to societies structured by the dominance of the wealthy over the poor and torn by revolutionary movements, hatred among religious and racial groups, and blood vendettas for redressing wrongs.[24]

The appropriation of these challenges in Catholic ethics is an ongoing process, as yet incomplete. Catholic moral theologians tend to want to preserve both the community of moral discourse guaranteed by natural law and the special inspiration of Jesus' teaching. Hence they maintain that, while religious commitment provides a unique motivation for fulfilling the moral law, "human" and "Christian" morality are substantively the same. The Christian will not behave differently in the concrete than the morally sincere and prudent atheist, though he or she may locate moral agency against the transcendent horizon of God's redeeming love.[25]

Liberation theology, as a movement within Catholicism, has, however, introduced into the mainstream a somewhat different response to the biblical challenges by means of the theme of a "preferential option for the poor." This preemptive special concern for those who are least well off is certainly reinforced by feminist theology. The preferential option has appeared particularly in economic ethics (for instance, in the U.S. bishops' pastoral letter, "Economic Justice for All"), and is often applied first of all to women and children, who, among the poor, suffer most. Moreover, as the U.S. bishops noted, since there are a greater number of women and children than men in poverty, Jesus' preference for the excluded must be directed in a special way to them.

In summary, the Bible has been important in the renewal of post–Vatican II Catholic ethics. A biblical ethics places more emphasis on conversion, on the transcendent meaning and aim of all moral activity, and on the importance of responding compassionately to those in need rather than on adherence to abstract moral rules. The New Testament also seems to challenge some of the central principles of the natural law and to propose radical gospel-based communities of mercy and love. An unresolved problem in Catholicism is how to combine a genuine attentiveness to the biblical kingdom witness with the traditional natural law commitment to moral universality and objectivity.

CHRISTIAN FEMINISM AND APPLIED ETHICS

We have seen that feminist ethics adopts an advocacy stance for women; it builds on the experiential base of natural law ethics; it highlights the social nature of personal relationships; and it turns to Scripture to heighten compassion and solidarity as moral values. Now we will explore the ways in which these contributions are influencing Roman Catholic approaches to the ethics of sex and gender and to the problem of war.

Sex and Gender

The area of sex and gender is without a doubt the one in which the ethical influence of feminist thought has been most conspicuous. Very important here is the "turn to experience," especially the experience of women. Up until the 1960s, Catholic ethics continued to define the primary purpose of sexuality as procreation and to understand women's role primarily in relation to motherhood. The basis of this teaching was the "nature" of sex, understood in terms of its physical function of procreation, to which the potentials of sex to give pleasure and to enhance companionship and love were subordinated. The isolation of the procreative meaning of sex as its moral key occurred under the influence of a variety of historical factors, among the most important of which were the need for Christianity to defend sex and procreation from attack by ancient and medieval dualist philosophies and religions, which denied the goodness of the body and discouraged sexual relations and childbearing. Also, theologians worked within a cultural framework that valued marriage, childbearing, and women in relation to patriarchal kinship and inheritance patterns. These contingent factors were obscured when the resulting sexual ethic was expressed in abstract definitions of the "nature" of sex that absolutized one particular aspect of human sexual experience.

During the Second Vatican Council and subsequently, Catholic sexual teaching responded to the modern possibility that marriage could be a partnership, not only of economic and domestic cooperation and parenthood but also of love. It was the incipient recognition in Western culture of women as equal in dignity to men that made it possible to view men and women as entering into authentic friendship in marriage, which sexual union can augment. Both the Council's *Pastoral Constitution on the Church in the Modern World* and the "birth control encyclical," *Humanae vitae,* presented sex and marriage as having two equal purposes, love and procreation. Even though the magisterium continues to defend specific sexual norms based originally on the old procreative focus (like the ban on artificial contraception), so fundamental a change has occurred in the understanding of sexuality that its concrete effects have no doubt not yet been fully realized. [26]

Another major development in the Christian attitude to sex is that it is not now understood so much in terms of sex acts as in terms of sexuality and of sexual relationships, of which genital expression is only one part. This development reflects the general ethical shift away from a morality of acts governed by stringent norms and toward a personal and social morality guided by the integration of a virtuous Christian life. Philosophers and theologians such as Paul Ricoeur and André Guindon have characterized sex as a "language," [27] and even official teaching has incorporated the new formulation. Sex, in papal writings, is "the 'language of the body' [which has] an important interpersonal meaning, especially in reciprocal relationships between man and woman." [28]

Women's writing about sexuality clearly reflects an interest in placing sexual expression within the totality of an ongoing relationship or friendship. Christian feminists tend to see sexuality as above all a relational capacity undergirding intimacy and commitment, not just as consolidating economic, kinship, and procreative relationships. "At the heart of sexual intimacy . . . is the desire to wholly express and nurture the mutuality of committed relationship. Commitment . . . requires the same kind of vulnerability, openness, risk-taking, and trust at the level of genital sexuality as it does within every other dimension of the partnership."[29]

The displacement of the procreative purpose of sex by its affective and communicative ones also has signaled increased openness toward lesbian and gay relationships, although moralists vary in the interpretation given to them. However, even ethicists who regard the significance of shared parenthood to be a cross-cultural human meaning of sex, entailing a privileged status for heterosexual marriage, may regard the committed sexual relationships of homosexual couples as morally acceptable. Neither condemnation of gay persons nor the demand that they remain celibate is easy to reconcile with the fact that sexual orientation is a deep component of personal identity and the realization that gay persons are as capable as heterosexual ones of manifesting a range of human and Christian virtues in their lives.[30]

The relationship between sex and gender is one area in which the ability to know a moral "law of nature" has been called radically into question. The contemporary perception that definitions of nature are perspectival and hence must be held broadly accountable to experience is crucial here. As we have seen, the twentieth century has witnessed a remarkable change in Christian (and philosophical) understandings of the meaning of sex, since the potential of sex to express affection, friendship, and commitment has moved into the foreground. The old biologist standard of procreative sex, contained within a marital union seen as a vehicle for the education of children, has widely been judged inadequate to the full human experience of sexuality.

But an unfinished agenda for a contemporary Christian sexual ethics is to relocate parenthood positively in relation to sexuality. Parenthood, despite inevitable distortions in reality, is a fulfilling human relationship that unites a sexual couple and binds the generations. Yet many personalist interpretations of sex, in displacing procreation as the normative meaning of sex, lose sight of it altogether. If procreation is not to be seen as the absolute norm for sex, then what legitimate moral role should it in fact play?

The first step toward reintegrating parenthood with sexual morality is to take conception and childbearing out of the old "act" morality and to place them in a new relational one. Bearing and nurturing children are not reducible to biogenetic procreation but involve *parenthood* as an enduring and demanding *relationship*. Although the fundamental human paradigm for the parental endeavor may be children conceived sexually and raised by two parents committed to one another, many analogous forms of parenthood are morally commendable, especially adoption. One issue for the new sexual morality is how to define which forms of parenthood are morally desirable and which, however well intentioned, come into conflict with other important values, such as the integrity of the marital bond. This issue is relevant in light of new reproductive technologies and infertility therapies, especially those that use "surrogate mothers" or "donors" of eggs, sperm, or embryos.

Feminist thinking has been important in the evolution of a sexual-parental morality. Feminists have especially inspected, criticized, and reinterpreted the human meaning of motherhood, revealing how women's experience of parenthood has been institutionalized in patriarchal cultures. Feminists not only question whether parenthood is a natural role for women more than for men, but also unveil how constricting social interpretations of it have narrowed women's contributions in other areas. Many feminists seek ways to offer positive construals of the actual experience of being a mother, while breaking the bonds of a "biology is destiny" ideology.

A philosopher offering a creative reconsideration of motherhood is Sara Ruddick, whose work has been noted by many Christian ethicists. She advances what she calls a "practicalist" conception of knowledge akin to Catholic moral theology's inductive reformulations of a morality of nature. Ruddick examines the practice of motherhood, drawing on her own experience, in order to illuminate its salient qualities, especially the virtues that it requires. "Maternal practice begins with a double vision—seeing the fact of biological vulnerability as socially significant and as demanding care."[31] Although women's appreciation of this "demand" may be heightened by pregnancy and labor, Ruddick seems to see "maternal work" as the calling of all parents. The mother's special works are preservative love, nurturance, and training, the distinguishing virtue of which is the "attentive love" of "maternal thinking." Attentive love can degenerate into self-loss and can be contradicted by motherhood's peculiar vices—"anxious or inquisitorial scrutiny, domination, intrusiveness, caprice, and self-protective cheeriness." But at its zenith, attentive love is (in the words of Simone Weil) an "intense, pure, disinterested, gratuitous, generous attention."[32] The virtues cultivated through the parental relationship are a valuable moral education for other spheres of life.

Noting the oppressive situations of women cross-culturally, Christine Gudorf laments that conditions are far from adequate for a positive ethic of motherhood worldwide, since in many cultures women lack the opportunity to reflect on their most essential experience of motherhood and to shape their parental and social roles accordingly. Too often it is still the case that women "are given and taken in marriage, seized for rape and battery, mutilated and sterilized as matters of policy, and assigned more work than men." Necessary conditions for the development of an acceptable practice of motherhood include respect for women's bodies, sexuality, and decisions about them; the opening of alternative female roles in addition to motherhood; equal responsibility of men in the care of children and the home; social support like maternity leave and day care, which would allow all parents to undertake both domestic and public roles successfully; social initiatives to alleviate the poverty that affects women and children most of all.[33]

In summary, the ethics of sex and gender demonstrates the commitment of contemporary Catholic ethics to reexamining natural law categories on the basis of experience and to incorporating the testimony of those engaged practically in the relevant areas, especially when their voices have been in the past neglected or excluded. Current understandings of sexuality also emphasize its relational over its procreative capacity, although the weaving into the sexual relation of a morally attractive notion of parenthood for women and for men is an ongoing task. This project has been furthered by feminist readings of motherhood as an important human relationship whose value transcends patriarchal social institutionalizations.

Ethics of War and Peace

Not surprisingly, a feminist approach supports the greater attentiveness to the pacifist witness of Christianity that surfaces in the U.S. bishops' peace pastoral, *The Challenge of Peace*.[34] Although the pastoral's major agenda item was probably to address the dangers of nuclear deterrence and to insist on the principle of noncombatant immunity, it also took a biblical turn by elucidating the biblical ideal of peace. It reinforced Catholic tradition's support for the justifiability of limited, defensive war, but it also recognized pacifism as an indispensable witness within Christian history.

As Rosemary Ruether points out, connections between feminism and peace extend back as far as the abolitionist feminists of the 1830s.[35] Ruether also draws a connection between patriarchy and war. "In macho mythology, women stand for a feared weakness, passivity, and vulnerability which must be purged and exorcised from the male psyche through the rituals of war. Feminists have pointed out the close connection between military indoctrination and sexism typical of the U.S. Army's basic training."[36]

Not all feminists have abandoned just war theory, and most would be cautious about crediting women with a higher morality than men as if women would be able to avoid conflict were they to attain comparable positions of political power. However, the relational and empathetic values of feminism, along with its advocacy for history's victims, creates an affinity with pacifist values. Sara Ruddick identifies in maternal practice evidence of "an ongoing attempt to renounce and resist violence, to reconcile opponents, and to keep a peace that is as free as possible from assaultive injustice."[37]

In a recent treatment of theological perspectives on war and peace, Richard Miller locates the point of contact between just war theory and pacifism in their presumption against causing harm, "implying compassion for those who are victims of harm, a bias against suffering, an intolerance of cruelty."[38] It is notable that the values of empathy and identification with those on the underside of power, embraced by feminists, are here identified as the inception of just war theory rather than the values of a right to self-defense or a principled limitation of the damage of war.

The central social tradition of Catholicism on war and peace is just war theory, not pacifism, despite the greater accommodation of the pacifist option. Catholicism has always been committed to responsible public participation and has never been characterized by the sectarian ecclesiology that absolute pacifism might seem to demand.[39] Yet, generally speaking, the Roman Catholic ethics of war has moved toward an ever greater caution about allowing exceptions to the presumption against war grounding the just war criteria. Pope John XXIII set the mark in 1963 by calling just war "hardly possible to imagine" in the nuclear age.[40] Even with the passing in the 1990s of the mutual nuclear terrorization of the two superpowers, the threat of nuclear weapons is hardly negligible, and uses of armed destruction on a massive scale continue worldwide.

Christian ethics reflects feminist values when it exercises a "hermeneutics of suspicion" on all applications of so-called just war theory, as was done widely in the wake of the Persian Gulf war. In this and other cases, ethicists press for greater scrutiny of claims that military ventures with astounding "collateral" consequences for civilians and whole populations can meet criteria of last resort, proportionality, right intention, and real necessity for the common good. As the noted Catholic pacifist Gordon Zahn observes, ingenuity in just war theorizing can be an intellectual exercise with deadly practical results. "Those same individuals or agencies which are the least likely to be influenced by the limits the ethician would impose on military decisions will always be ready and eager to exploit every ethical loophole or exception (even, one might suggest, the very implications of a concept like 'just' war) as justification for some new escalation of war's inhumanity."[41]

Furthermore, ethicists encourage citizens to hold public officials and military leaders accountable for decisions that may be more opportunistic than moral. All but abandoned is the theory—in sway from Augustine through World War II—that citizens must support any war initiated by a legitimate authority. Religious leaders and theologians now urge citizens to object conscientiously to wars that can only be regarded as suspicious, even in light of standard just war criteria.[42]

Two further characteristics of today's Christian ethics of war and peace reflect the shared agenda with feminism. First, a global and not merely national perspective informs the discussion; second, the definition and effects of violence are pursued into social structures and networks that extend far beyond war itself. As we saw earlier, feminism is highly sensitive to the social and historical contexts within which moral viewpoints are sculpted; and feminism recognizes that no particular moral issue, policy, or decision can be isolated from what might seem to be its secondary social ramifications. The global and the structural angles on violence are implied by this social approach.

First, war can no longer be considered the business of nation-states that act analogously to individual moral agents. The decision of heads of state to wage war takes place within a global balance of power; its effects are multinational as well. The modern papal social encyclicals have moved gradually to recognize that "common good" is a global concept, and they now employ the term "universal common good." It was on this basis that John XXIII took such a highly critical approach to war and even to the arms race, for he noted that even without an outright conflagration, the military consumption of resources exerts an oppressive effect on all peoples of the world, especially citizens of developing nations. From the global perspective, it is important to ask why certain countries are militarily strong; why some become aggressors; and why they defend certain allies but not others or refrain from the defense of innocent populations in some of the nations most plagued by corruption, violence, and deprivation.

Related to our heightened consciousness of the global meaning of war is our awareness that violence—even lethal violence—takes myriad forms. Some of these are closely attendant on the waging of war, as when whole populations, within which the poor usually undergo the most agony, are deprived of basic necessities of life, such as food and medical supplies, through economic sanctions that are the modern equivalent of seige warfare. Others are forms of structural violence, decried by liberation theologians, by which the well-off peoples of the world exploit the impoverished ones and perpetuate their suffering and early demise. A feminist perspective fills in relationality and interdependence as the background of any particular action or policy. It is attuned to the full social dimensions of moral problems and understands that violence is not isolable as war, for it filters through global economic and political alignments, which also kill.

Once more, Scripture and its concern for those who suffer and are persecuted characterizes a feminist liberationist approach to violence, whether experienced directly as war and political massacre, or as deprivation of the conditions necessary for life to thrive or even to survive. Catholic peace activist Eileen Egan recalls us to the power of the Beatitudes and especially to the works of mercy that war obliterates.[43]

The answer to structural violence goes beyond nonviolence to aggressive action for social change. A Costa Rican feminist asks, "How can the name of Christian be claimed by the stockholders in the great corporations or by those who monopolize the means of production and exploit workers in such deadly ways; or by those who talk of human rights but at the same time approve shipments of military aid to dictatorial regimes so that the latter may open the door to multinational corporations?"[44] The gospel demands that the Christian strive to live in the kingdom of God initiated in Jesus, a kingdom that does not exist only in some distant and supernatural realm, but in the midst of human life, where Christians resist oppression and struggle toward an inclusive community of liberation from material as well as spiritual sufferings.

In summary, mainstream Catholic tradition, retaining its commitment to moral involvement in the political realm, admits violence as an occasionally necessary means to defend the common good and protect the innocent. However, it is now less likely to accept governmental authority as the final moral arbiter of war, and it encourages a healthy skepticism about whether just war criteria have in fact been honestly met in any particular instance. Further, it comprehends pacifism as a part of the

Christian witness and indeed as a catalyst toward a more just international order. Both just war criteria and pacifism are increasingly characterized in contemporary ethics as rooted in human compassion rather than in moral rules either proscribing violence or limiting while permitting it. In addition to sharing with feminist sensibilities an appreciation of the destructive effects of violent conflict on human lives, relationships, and communities, the ethical attempt to shelter both just war and pacifist thinking under the umbrella of a single tradition represents a serious consideration of the possibility that Scripture can and does challenge some of the ways of justice, strictly understood. Just as feminism employs biblical discipleship as a subversive agent against patriarchy and all domination, so Catholic pacifism, even when linked with just war permissions, undermines any assumption that resort to armed force is the unassailable prerogative of nation-states.

CONCLUSION

The defining characteristic of Roman Catholic ethics is its commitment to reasonableness and objectivity in moral discourse; these are the hallmarks of the tradition of natural law. In the second half of the twentieth century, this tradition has been qualified epistemologically by the emergent recognition of the contextual nature of knowledge. One result has been a very contemporary philosophical caution about the credibility of universalist claims, resulting in broader consultation and more provisional assertions. It has resulted also in a renewal of interest in Aquinas, for Aquinas himself recognized that absolute certainty was hard to come by in applying principles to very particular and contingent moral matters. More fundamentally, he began from the premise that society brings persons together for the common good and is ultimately rooted in God, and he emphasized virtue as the integral cultivation of humanity's highest natural capacities and as a response to divine love.

The specifically theological horizon of Roman Catholic ethics has also been renewed by Vatican II's mandate to recover the biblical inspiration of the moral life. The biblical renewal has modified natural law moral theology not only insofar as it complements reason with faith, but also in that it qualifies detached objectivity with a special commitment to those to whom Jesus most reaches out—people forgotten or downtrodden by those with prestige and status. Both the natural law and biblical reinterpretations of Catholic ethics reflect a more direct concern with the social setting of ethics. Human nature can be understood only in a global conversation; the preferential option for society's excluded must take on international dimensions.

The uniquely feminist thread in the Catholic ethical fabric is advocacy for women's experience and women's concerns, as is directly evident in sex and gender ethics. In other areas of ethics—bioethics, war and peace, or economics—feminism has had an indirect but important role in reinforcing themes of sociality, relationship, compassion, and affirmative action on behalf of power's victims.

NOTES

1. "Economic Justice for All: Catholic Social Teaching and the U.S. Economy," *Origins* 16, no. 24 (1986): 409–55.

2. The most important example is the modern papal social encyclicals, from *Rerum Novarum* (1891) onward. In *Rerum Novarum*, Leo XIII concludes that in order for economic justice to be served, "every one must put his hand to work which falls to his share," "masters and rich men must remember their duty," and "all men must be persuaded that the primary thing needful is to return to real Christianity.". . . (no. 45).

3. "*Mulieris Dignitatem:* On the Dignity and Vocation of Women," *Origins* 18, no. 17 (1988): 261, 263–83.

4. See Patricia Beattie Jung and Thomas A. Shannon, eds., *Abortion and Catholicism: The American Debate* (New York: Crossroad, 1988).

5. Anne E. Patrick, "Authority, Women, and Church: Reconsidering the Relationship," in *Empowering Authority,* ed. Patrick Howell and Gary Chamberlain (Kansas City: Sheed and Ward, 1990).

6. *Westminster Dictionary of Christian Ethics,* rev. ed., s.v. "feminist ethics," by Margaret A. Farley.

7. Margaret A. Farley, "Feminist Consciousness and the Interpretation of Scripture," in *Feminist Interpretation of the Bible,* ed. Letty M. Russell (Philadelphia: Westminster Press, 1985), 44.

8. Rosemary Radford Ruether, *Sexism and God-Talk: Toward a Feminist Theology* (Boston: Beacon Press, 1983), 18.

9. Thomas Aquinas, *Summa Theologiae,* I–II, q. 94, a.2.

10. John T. Noonan's *Contraception: A History of Its Treatment by the Catholic Theologians and Canonists,* enl. ed. (Cambridge: Harvard Univ. Press, 1986), proposes and impressively defends this thesis.

11. Rosemary Radford Ruether, "Home and Work: Women's Roles and the Transformation of Values," in *Woman: New Dimensions,* ed. Walter J. Burghardt (New York: Paulist Press, 1977), 71–83.

12. Valerie Saiving, "The Human Situation: A Feminine View," *Journal of Religion* 40 (1960): 108.

13. In the feminist literature, a theological base is offered for this ethical shift by Margaret Farley, who notes a movement from hierarchical patterns of relationship to more

egalitarian ones and who reconceives trinitarian symbolism correspondingly. See Margaret A. Farley, "New Patterns of Relationship: Beginnings of a Moral Revolution," in *Women: New Dimensions,* ed. Burghardt, 64–67.

14. John Paul II, "On the Family," Apostolic Exhortation, December 15, 1981 (Washington, DC: United States Catholic Conference, 1982), no. 32.

15. John Paul II, "On the Family," no. 23.

16. Christine E. Gudorf, "Parenting, Mutual Love, and Sacrifice," in *Women's Consciousness, Women's Conscience: A Reader in Feminist Ethics,* ed. Barbara Hilkert Andolsen, Christine E. Gudorf, and Mary D. Pellauer (Minneapolis: Winston Press, 1985), 175–91.

17. See Thomas L. Schubeck, "The Reconstruction of Natural Law Reasoning: Liberation Theology as a Case Study," *Journal of Religious Ethics* 20 (1992): 149–78.

18. Farley, "Feminist Consciousness," 45. See also Elizabeth Fox-Genovese, *Feminism Without Illusions: A Critique of Individualism* (Chapel Hill: Univ. of North Carolina Press, 1991), for a philosophical argument in favor of a more communitarian form of feminism.

19. June O'Connor, "On Doing Religious Ethics," in *Women's Consciousness,* ed. Andolsen, et al., 265.

20. O'Connor, "On Doing Religious Ethics," 276.

21. Among U.S. theologians, see especially the work of Richard A. McCormick, *The Critical Calling: Reflections on Moral Dilemmas Since Vatican II* (Washington, DC: Georgetown Univ. Press, 1989); and Charles E. Curran, *Transition and Tradition in Moral Theology* (Notre Dame: Univ. of Notre Dame Press, 1979) and *Tensions in Moral Theology* (Notre Dame: Univ. of Notre Dame Press, 1988).

22. See Jean Porter, *The Recovery of Virtue: The Relevance of Aquinas for Christian Ethics* (Louisville, KY: Westminster/John Knox Press, 1990).

23. Two important works by Catholic women are Elisabeth Schüssler Fiorenza, *In Memory of Her: A Feminist Theological Reconstruction of Christian Origins* (New York: Crossroad, 1983); and Sandra M. Schneiders, *The Revelatory Text: Interpreting the New Testament as Sacred Scripture* (New York: Harper San Francisco, 1991).

24. For a more complete discussion, see Lisa Sowle Cahill, "The New Testament and Ethics: Communities of Social Change," *Interpretation* 44 (1990): 383–95.

25. See Josef Fuchs, *Personal Responsibility and Christian Morality* (Washington, DC: Georgetown Univ. Press, 1983), especially chap. 6, "Autonomous Morality and Morality of Faith."

26. See Lisa Sowle Cahill, "Catholic Sexual Ethics and the Dignity of the Person: A Double Message," *Theological Studies* 50 (1989): 120–50.

27. Of special importance is André Guindon, *The Sexual Language: An Essay in Moral Theology* (Ottawa: Univ. of Ottawa Press, 1976).

28. John Paul II, *Reflections on Humanae Vitae: Conjugal Morality and Spirituality* (Boston: St. Paul Editions, 1984), 30.

29. Katherine E. Zappone, *The Hope for Wholeness: A Spirituality for Feminists* (Mystic, CT: Twenty-Third Publications, 1991), 82. See also Mary E. Hunt, *Fierce Tenderness: A Feminist Theology of Friendship* (New York: Crossroad, 1991).

30. For an overview of recent positions on homosexuality, see McCormick, *The Critical Calling,* chap. 17. For a nuanced example of Catholic gay advocacy, see Robert Nugent

and Jeannine Gramick, *Building Bridges: Gay and Lesbian Reality and the Catholic Church* (Mystic, CT: Twenty-Third Publications, 1992).

31. Sara Ruddick, *Maternal Thinking: Toward a Politics of Peace* (Boston: Beacon Press, 1989), 18.

32. Simone Weil, quoted in Ruddick, *Maternal Thinking*, 120.

33. Christine Gudorf, "Women's Choice for Motherhood: Beginning a Cross-Cultural Approach," in *Motherhood: Experience, Institution, Theology*, ed. Anne E. Carr and Elisabeth Schüssler Fiorenza, Concilium 206 (Edinburgh: T. & T. Clark, 1989), 61.

34. National Conference of Catholic Bishops, *The Challenge of Peace: God's Promise and Our Response* (Washington, DC: United States Catholic Conference, 1983).

35. Rosemary Radford Ruether, "Feminism and Peace," in *Women's Consciousness*, ed. Andolsen, et al., 63.

36. Ruether, "Feminism and Peace," 71.

37. Ruddick, *Maternal Thinking*, 161.

38. Richard B. Miller, *Interpretations of Conflict: Ethics, Pacifism, and the Just-War Tradition* (Chicago: Univ. of Chicago Press, 1991), 9.

39. Not all pacifists are sectarian in the sense of withdrawing from political involvement, but they put witness to nonviolent ideals above acceptance in the culture or effectiveness in changing the course of history. For a discussion of the Catholic just war tradition, see J. Bryan Hehir, "The Just-War Ethic and Catholic Theology: Dynamics of Change and Continuity," in *War or Peace? The Search for New Answers*, ed. Thomas A. Shannon (Maryknoll, NY: Orbis Books, 1980), 15–39.

40. John XXIII, *Pacem in Terris*, no. 127.

41. Gordon C. Zahn, "Afterword," in *War or Peace?*, ed. Shannon, 236.

42. See Eileen P. Flynn, *My Country Right or Wrong? Selective Conscientious Objection in the Nuclear Age* (Chicago: Loyola Univ. Press, 1985).

43. Eileen Egan, "The Beatitudes, the Works of Mercy, and Pacifism," in *War or Peace?*, ed. Shannon, 169–87.

44. Elsa Tamez, *Bible of the Oppressed* (Maryknoll, NY: Orbis Books, 1982), 80.

FOR FURTHER READING

Andolsen, Barbara Hilkert, Christine Gudorf, and Mary D. Pellauer, eds. *Women's Consciousness, Women's Conscience*. Minneapolis: Winston Press, 1985. Contains nineteen essays in three sections: women's experience as a source, specific normative claims, and feminist method in ethics. Some specific topics are economics, women, and class; Hispanic feminism; anti-Semitism; black spirituality and sexuality; Goddess religion; feminism and peace; women's friendship; abortion; parenting; bioethics.

Burghardt, Walter, ed. *Woman: New Dimensions*. New York: Paulist Press, 1977. Originally an issue of *Theological Studies*, this volume addresses some of the basic theological issues of feminism, including feminist theology as liberation theology, the redefinition of love as mutuality rather than sacrifice, historical Christian images of women and their encouragement of stereotypical gender roles, women in the New Testament, sexist language in theology, and theological anthropology.

Carr, Anne E., and Elisabeth Schüssler Fiorenza, eds. *Motherhood: Experience, Institution, Theology*. Concilium 206. Edinburgh: T. & T. Clark, 1989. This issue of the international series *Concilium* places the institution of motherhood in broad perspective, including European, American, Canadian, Latin American, and African contributions. Church teaching on motherhood is compared with women's experience and with social realities. Conceptions of motherhood are also linked to theological symbols, historical practices, and to the practical problems of reproductive technology, militarism, and ecology.

Curran, Charles E., ed. *Moral Theology: Challenges for the Future*. New York: Paulist Press, 1990. Some leading Catholic ethicists deal with fundamental issues (theology, Scripture and ethics, personalism, conscience, moral norms, and the teaching authority of the church) as well as applied ethics (sex, marriage, and divorce; abortion; death and dying; reproductive technologies; war and peace).

Farley, Margaret A. *Personal Commitments: Beginning, Keeping, Changing*. San Francisco: Harper & Row, 1986. Illustrates the meaning of commitment with anecdotal cases, in which relationships are undertaken and changed in response to new situations. Offers an experiential understanding of commitment, love, obligation, and fidelity, showing how these are transformed by religious faith and how the biblical model of covenant relationship can illumine human commitments.

Grimshaw, Jean. *Philosophy and Feminist Thinking*. Minneapolis: Univ. of Minnesota Press, 1986. Brings important work in philosophy and in feminist theory to bear on fundamental questions for theological and well as philosophical feminists: women and "male" intellectual traditions, experience and reality, human nature and women's nature, autonomy and individualism, and the idea of a female or maternal ethic. A key presupposition of the work is that, while all theory is historical and contextual, not all moral positions or theories are relative or equally valid.

Porter, Jean. *The Recovery of Virtue: The Relevance of Aquinas for Christian Ethics*. Louisville: Westminster/John Knox Press, 1990. Notes the difficulty of contemporary moral theory in attaining coherence, much less objectivity, in the wake of critical, historical consciousness; offers Aquinas as a possible base on which to take up reconstructive work.

CHAPTER TEN

TOWARD SPIRITUAL MATURITY

— Spirituality —

Joann Wolski Conn

CONVERSATIONS ABOUT SPIRITUALITY happen with unbelievers or nuns, at parties or retreats, with professors or hairdressers. People who never go to church anymore often say they are very interested in spirituality. Graduates of twelve years in Catholic school are surprised to discover that something in their ordinary lives qualifies as a "religious experience." Religious publishers are selling more books about spirituality than any other kind. To base theology on religious experience is now a dominant trend in theological method. Interreligious dialogue focused on spirituality is now the preference of many in conversations that try to bridge East and West. The Association of Spiritual Directors International increased its membership, in three years, from a few hundred to nearly a thousand. Why is spirituality capturing so much attention?

Because spirituality refers both to experience and to an academic discipline, in this chapter I will examine first the different ways the term *spiritual* can refer to life's experience. Then I will explore how the academic field that studies this experience has emerged recently. Finally, using the methodology of academic spirituality, I will examine issues and controversies in the field through one lens: the question of spiritual maturity.

SPIRITUALITY AS EXPERIENCE

Paul's letters describe reality under the influence of the Holy Spirit as "spiritual." There are spiritual blessings, spiritual gifts, spiritual persons. When Paul distinguishes the latter from natural persons he does not mean to contrast spiritual to material or evil, but simply to contrast those who act under the Spirit's influence to those who do not.[1]

This theological denotation for the adjective *spiritual* or the noun *spirituality* continued until the twelfth century when other meanings arose. In philosophy, the spiritual was opposed to the material. In church law, *spiritual* referred to ecclesiastical goods whereas *temporal* designated secular things. In the seventeenth century, *spirituality* came to refer to the interior life of Christians, but often with suspicious overtones of dubious enthusiasm or even heresy. The term *devotion* was preferred; it carried the sense of careful allegiance to the tradition and the exercise of piety within the bounds of standard church practice. By the eighteenth century, *spirituality* referred to the life of perfection that could lead to mysticism, in contrast with the "ordinary" life of faith. By the nineteenth and mid-twentieth centuries, *spirituality* automatically meant the interior life of those striving for perfection. Since the 1950s the meaning of *spirituality* has expanded far beyond a Christian or even religious denotation to refer to the whole realm of experiences and practices involving the human spirit and the soul dimension of existence.

Spirituality is now used in three ways. First, it refers to a general human capacity for self-transcendence, for movement beyond mere self-maintenance or self-interest. Some philosophical, psychological, or anthropological studies use this term. When Jungian psychologists speak of "care of the soul" and of masculine or feminine spirituality, they use the term in this generic sense. When business consultants want to assist personnel to maximize their potential for productive relationships they sometimes speak of a spirituality of work. These uses *may* intend some religious overtones; therefore, it is wise to clarify any meanings that extend beyond the generic. Second, the term *spirituality* can refer to a religious dimension of life, to a capacity for self-transcendence that is actualized by the holy, however that may be understood. Third, it may refer to a specific type of religious experience such as Jewish, Christian, Muslim, or Buddhist.

Self-transcendence is at the core of any definition of spirituality. This does not mean that one transcends or escapes being one's self or stops attending to oneself or caring for oneself. Rather, one acts out of the center or heart of one's self in a way that reaches out in love, freedom, and truth to others and to the unrealized dimensions of one's own capacities. One does this within the horizon of whatever one imagines or judges to be ultimate. Spirituality, then, depends on what is judged to be of ultimate value. Christian spirituality presupposes that ultimacy is God revealed in the death and resurrection of Jesus, known in the sanctifying power of the Holy Spirit poured out in the community. Humanistic spirituality derives from the ultimacy of the individuated self. The definition of spirituality in terms of self-transcendence fits the full range of spirituality, nonreligious as well as religious.

Although the definition of spirituality may be generic, there is no generic spirituality. All spirituality is concrete, embedded in the particularities of experience. These include, for example, symbols and stories, bounds of social awareness, focus of personal authority, modes of knowing and feeling, and range of expectations regarding gender and race. Even though this chapter is focused on Catholic Christian spirituality, there is no generic or uniform Catholic spirituality. Spirituality as experience includes all the complexity and richness of each person's historical and cultural location as well as the particularities of gender, race, class, and psychological development and the unique operation of divine grace within human personality. I will specify these further as I discuss the issues and controversies that are examined by spirituality as an academic discipline.

SPIRITUALITY AS AN ACADEMIC FIELD

Until the High Middle Ages all theology was spiritual theology in the sense that it was reflection upon life "in the Spirit." All theology arose in monastic or pastoral settings as an attempt to convey the experience of faith expressed in Scripture, liturgy, private prayer, communal life, or pastoral care.

When the university rather than the monastery became the primary home of theology, "sacred science" gradually moved away from its explicit foundation in spiritual experience and focused on a foundation in philosophy, logical argumentation, or even in controversy. Reformation theology of the Eucharist, for example, seldom aimed to explicate the religious experience of union or division in Christ; rather, it tried to expose contradictions in its opponents' use of Scripture.

Explicit reflection upon religious experience did continue in monastic and pastoral settings, but this was not considered academically reputable. Julian of Norwich in the fourteenth century gave years of careful attention to her experience of the Trinity and described this in her *Revelations,* yet her book was not studied in the religious academy until recently. Throughout history many careful and even systematic accounts of the spiritual life were written outside of formal theology in many different literary genres: religious rules, commentaries on Scripture, autobiography, letters of spiritual advice, poetry, sermons.

In the eighteenth and nineteenth centuries, academic credibility was finally granted to the study of the spiritual life, but only by admitting this field through the side door of moral theology or ethics.[2] Using principles from dogmatic theology and scholastic vocabulary, ascetical and mystical theology emerged as subdivisions of ethics. The former studied the "purgative way" of ordinary Christians up to the phase of development known as "infused contemplation" or "mysticism." Mystical theology studied the spiritual life from the onset of "the illuminative way" of passive contemplation up to the "unitive way" characteristic of great sanctity. As all fields of study mirror the culture that nourishes them, so this forerunner of academic spirituality reflected its culture's assumptions about the hierarchy of spiritual stages, the elitism of Christian perfection available primarily to celibate religious, and certitude of dogmatic conclusions about God and "man."

With the Second Vatican Council's call to return to the sources in Scripture and tradition, the inadequacy of these earlier assumptions became clear. Out of the aftermath of the Council's impetus to renew Christian spirituality has come the young academic discipline that studies not only Christian but all spiritual experience, precisely *as experience.* That is, it aims to understand spirituality in all its concreteness, in all its complex interaction with its social, cultural, and cosmic setting.

Although spirituality as an academic field is young and its distinctive nature and methodology are still being debated, some consensus on these points is emerging. As a field spirituality is understood to be descriptive and critical rather than prescriptive and normative. Scholars agree also that the study of spirituality must be ecumenical, interreligious, and cross-cultural. One of its unique contributions to academic study is its focus on wholeness. Every aspect of human spiritual experience is integral to the discipline: bodily, psychological, historical, political, aesthetic, intellectual, social.

Turning from characteristics of spirituality to its practice involves attention to this particular *object*, its *methodological style*, an ideal *procedure*, and its *goal*. These distinguish it from other disciplines. The object of spirituality is spiritual experience in its uniqueness, in its messy particularity.

Methodologically the field of spirituality is interdisciplinary; tools from many disciplines, both religious and secular, are needed to address spiritual experiences both as spiritual and as experience. Methods of study that involve participation, not merely observation, are appropriate to spirituality for similar reasons that they are found in psychology and anthropology. Spirituality deals with material that cannot be understood—in the sense of being personally appropriated—except through personal experience or involvement with research data.

This participative style presents a problem regarding the "objectivity" of the discipline, and members of the academy have raised serious questions that reveal their mistrust of spirituality. They fear religious practice may substitute for research or religious commitment may lessen critical judgment or evangelization may be the hidden agenda. I suggest that the real issue behind these questions may not be religious commitment versus objectivity, but the myth of objectivity. The goal of fairness or objectivity in academic disciplines used to be measured by the researcher's distance from the subject matter. I suggest that only when a researcher is critically aware of her or his actual commitments and assumptions, and acts to make them assist rather than prevent insight, can the researcher be objective. This methodological style characterizes the best of contemporary research and scholarship in spirituality.

Regarding *procedure* in the study of spirituality, we find that all serious investigation tends to move in a pattern of three phases. Phase one is descriptive, bringing to our attention the data associated with the experience being investigated. Phase two is analytical and critical, leading to an explanation and evaluation of the subject. In this phase, theological, human, and social sciences are very important. A final phase is synthetic and constructive, leading to the kind of personal knowledge that deeply shifts the scholar's own horizon on the experience studied, as well as on the wider world.

For example, inquiry into strategies of spiritual survival for contemporary Catholic women would begin with a description of their frustration, alienation, and spiritual searching; phase two would explain reasons for these situations and evaluate these reasons according to criteria such as theological or psychological adequacy; phase three would construct creative strategies such as feminist liturgy or feminist reinterpretations of divine mystery or spiritual darkness.

Finally, spirituality as a discipline or field of study has a threefold *goal* or *aim*. Although most people associate spirituality primarily with practical assistance toward a life of greater self-transcendence, the first goal in the study of spirituality is knowledge about religious experience as experience. Only then can it helpfully move to the second and third goals: developing the researcher's own spirituality and fostering the spirituality of others. This triple goal, which includes the aim of changing self and the world, may not be shared by the hard sciences, but it is common to the social sciences, such as psychology, and to the humanities, such as art and philosophy, which aim to liberate humanity from a narrow horizon and free humans for mature relationships.

SPIRITUAL MATURITY

Most issues associated with Catholic spirituality as both experience and academic discipline come into focus by attending to a central question: How can we become spiritually mature? That is, how can we realize our spiritual potential? Assuming now that all subsequent discussion comes from a contemporary Catholic viewpoint, notice how reflection upon this one question of experience raises many other issues and suggests the comprehensiveness, complexity, and interdisciplinary nature of spirituality as an academic field. Spiritual maturity is inseparable from issues such as the relationship of grace and nature, growth in prayer, contemplation and action, the role of spiritual darkness. Understanding spiritual maturity is also inseparable from attention to theology, psychology, and history. For example, while all great spiritual teachers say that maturity requires discernment and contemplation rooted in self-knowledge, a psychological climate that insists on conformity to passive female roles allows a very different experience of self-knowledge than a culture that encourages critical questioning. Maturity is also a theological matter. Maturity understood as sharing the trinitarian life of divine persons who are equal in their sharing of life with each other and with all humanity differs from an experience of trinitarian life perceived as flowing in a hierarchical pattern from a patriarchal Father.[3]

An overview of the history of spirituality will afford a glimmer of the richness of the tradition on the question of spiritual maturity and indicate the promise of feminist research that remains to be done. In what follows I apply six tasks of the feminist scholarly agenda[4] to spirituality viewed from the perspective of Christian spiritual maturity. In order to liberate the spiritual tradition from its androcentric bias and make it as inclusive of women's experience as it is of men's, feminist scholars first point out that women have been ignored in the field. For example, Franciscan spirituality ignored Clare until only recently, when she began to be recognized as cofounder, with Francis of Assisi, of the Franciscans. Clare came to be appreciated as the first woman to write a religious rule.

Second, feminist scholars demonstrate that what we do know about women is often accompanied by a high level of diminishment, romanticism, or even hostility. For example, Margery Kempe, an illiterate, medieval woman who left her family to wander the world crying bitter tears, was judged a neurotic eccentric until feminist research disclosed her charism of repentant tears and her vocation to be a pilgrim in a world that assumed women traveling alone were either prostitutes or crazy.[5]

Third, feminist scholars search out and publicize the unknown women in the discipline, in order to add as many figures as possible to an otherwise male pantheon of pioneers and mentors.

Fourth, feminist scholars perform a revisionary reading of the old texts and traditions so that they lose their power to terrorize and exclude women. For example, feminist hermeneutics of Hebrew Scripture and the New Testament has already made a significant scholarly impact on biblical studies and increasingly on spirituality (as exhibited, for instance, in the work of Sandra Schneiders). Revisionist readings challenge the Bible's sexism by revealing its alternative tradition of inclusive language for the divine and its insistence on women's equal discipleship.

Fifth, the discipline of spirituality is challenged methodologically by feminists to redefine its borders, goals, and consequences. For example, Christian ascetical theology used to assume that its foundation rested on a Bible whose inspiration guaranteed its immunity from challenges of sexism and racism. This foundation is now profoundly challenged.

Lastly, scholars work toward a truly integrated field, one not reduced by its prejudices against women, lower classes, variant sexual preferences, or anything else. Future generations may see this accomplished; it is now only emerging. This commitment to integration contributes research on subjects such as the religious experience of poor Hispanic women whose spiritual resources come from "popular religion" (for example, processions, promises to God, concentration on devotion to Mary) and has been derided as superstitious by church authority and theological scholars.

One last word is important regarding assumptions. It is important that insights developed in the present time, such as feminist awareness, not be confused with the fallacy of "presentism." I do not blame the past for not seeing what the present sees as significant, nor do I claim that persons in the past regarded as significant what only recently has become a clear issue. For example, although writers in Christian antiquity almost totally ignored women's experience and generally believed women were inferior humans, the point is not to lay blame, as though they *could* have seen otherwise and freely chose to be blind. Rather, Christians now inherit assumptions about women's humanity that shape the possibilities for their spiritual maturity, and these assumptions require critical evaluation today. For another example, although Hildegard of Bingen used female images for God and was more accomplished in music and healing arts than many women or men in any age, it is inaccurate and inappropriate to call her a feminist. She accepted women's subordination to men and viewed the world as essentially hierarchical; thus she lacks the critical evaluation of patriarchy that is integral to feminism.

Having specified spirituality in terms of six tasks for feminist scholarship, I will apply these tasks to a single issue: spiritual maturity. I will explain maturity and evaluate conclusions about it through an overview of the history of spirituality on the question of Christian maturity. My aim is to clarify spirituality as an academic field by using a topic that integrates psychological issues of personal and social development with theological concerns regarding God's relationship with humanity.

Biblical Spirituality

Feminist biblical scholarship has now demonstrated that even the most basic resource for Christian spirituality, the Bible, must be approached with caution. For some feminists, women and men, the Bible is seen as so pervasively sexist that it can no longer be the revelatory text that grounds their spiritual tradition. These persons have concluded that to sustain personal integrity they must separate from Christianity and seek a spiritual path elsewhere. On the other hand, some feminists are convinced that the hermeneutics of suspicion can reconstruct a biblical theology in which revelation is seen to be a human experience of both sinful sexism and redemptive liberation from all that limits humans or blocks divine love.[6] I write this section from the latter perspective.

We begin our overview of Christian spirituality by looking at early Christian communities of Paul and the gospel writers. Paul's letters reveal that his own religious experience centered on seeing the risen Lord and feeling empowered by the Spirit to witness to God's re-creation of all women and men in Christ, taking down all spiritual barriers between Jew and Greek, slave and free. How this spiritual equality would be worked out in new social structures was a question that Paul's culture could barely grasp. Yet the subversion of that culture's patriarchal assumptions was latent in Christian teaching regarding the new creation.

Paul taught that the experience of daily life in Christ involves bearing one another's burdens, which fulfills the whole law; giving and receiving the Spirit's gifts that build up the body of Christ; eating the meal of unity and love and remembering God's re-creating action in Christ and in us; offering ourselves as living sacrifices of praise and thanksgiving for God's overwhelming love for us in Christ. This is the love that no suffering need separate us from, if we believe that in Christ our struggles continue redemptive love.

This appreciation for the way suffering can reveal that true power resides not in control but in love and relationship to all people is something Paul himself learned from experience. In the beginning of Paul's ministry, his experience of the risen Lord led him to concentrate on proclaiming the power of the resurrection. Later, his experiences of failure and persecution led him to shift his focus and appreciate more deeply the mystery of Christ's passion. His mature experience was one of moving ever more deeply into the entire paschal mystery, of loving trust even unto death so that the power of God manifest in Jesus' weakness might be manifest also in Paul's weakness and in ours.

The religious experience of Mark's community centers on Jesus as the suffering servant messiah because the disciples of Jesus were persecuted and asked, Why is this happening to us? The Gospel replies that if one is a disciple of Jesus, one must expect to follow the master's path of faithful love, giving one's last breath as Jesus did.

Mark portrays the male disciples as particularly fearful and very slow to learn that the true servant of God must love even unto death. Mark taught the community that they too will receive Jesus' patient mercy as they struggle in faith, even as Peter did. Women disciples are noted for their presence at the crucifixion, as well as throughout Jesus' ministry, and they receive the first announcement of Jesus' resurrection. Like all disciples in Mark's Gospel they are portrayed, in the end, as fearful.

Luke's community was a missionary church learning to expand its boundaries of sharing and concern. Only slowly and painfully did they realize that life in Christ called them to care for more than just their own family and friends. As Jesus was impelled by the Spirit to bring the good new of God's covenantal love to the poor and oppressed, so they are called to lives of generosity and service to all. Those in positions of authority were reminded of their responsibility to follow Jesus' path of serving others instead of being served. The story of the prodigal son reveals a divine father who, far from being a controlling patriarch, is prodigal in honoring human choices and in displaying faithful love.

Matthew's community experienced its identity as one of commitment to Mosaic teaching, honoring Jesus as the primary interpreter of the Law, in the face of challenges by other interpreters of the Law. The community meditated upon Jesus, the personification of wisdom, who embodies Israel's righteousness. Mercy, forgiveness, and trust in the midst of persecution come to expression in the Beatitudes. Living according to this teaching means cooperating with God, bringing into being God's new covenant by replacing relationships of domination with those of justice and peace.

John's community experienced unity as well as alienation. More than any other Gospel community, its members realized the depth of Jesus' unity with God and their own indwelling in God through rebirth as God's daughters and sons. They experienced themselves as friends of Jesus and as his sisters and brothers. They lived in relationship to the new Paraclete who lived in them and continued to teach the community the meaning of Jesus' words. Their sense of alienation, stemming from rejection by a very conservative segment of the Jewish community, was so misinterpreted by later generations of Christians that anti-Jewish attitudes came to be legitimated through (mis)use of this Gospel.

At the heart of the apostolic spirituality of the fourth Gospel is the experience of being sent even as Jesus was sent from the Father. Over and over this Gospel echoes the phrase, "As . . . me, so . . . you." All disciples experience, in their own way, the same relationship Jesus has to his Father, the same work as Jesus, the same Spirit, the same joy, the same life.

Finally, Paul and the communities of the Gospels understood their religious experience through Jewish Scripture interpreted in light of their experience of Jesus the Christ. Today, Christians must value their Jewish roots in a way that respects the continuing integrity of revelation in the Hebrew Bible on its own terms. To appreciate this integrity it is wise to include Jewish interpreters.

In summary, the biblical tradition reveals spiritual maturity as an experience of deep and inclusive love. Spiritual maturity is the loving relationship to God, Christ, the Spirit, and to all of humanity that is born of the struggle to discern where and how the Trinity is present in the community, in ministry, in suffering, in religious and political dissension, and in one's own sinfulness. Guidelines for "testing the spirits" do not eliminate the need to trust one's own sense of vocation in the absence of certitude. Maturity is understood primarily as a matter of relationship. Yet the attitudes we now call self-direction and adult freedom are also present in the biblical language of a call to conversion and to fidelity in the midst of spiritual confusion.

Early Christianity

Liturgical and theological texts indicate that Christians, insofar as we can make general judgments from sources that are written entirely by men, understood their lives as personal participation in the mystery of Christ, nourished by sharing in the Lord's Supper and expressed by inclusive love that bore witness to life in the Spirit and drew others to faith. This common faith was experienced in the complexity of the later Roman Empire: both Eastern and Western centers of culture and theology; hierarchical arrangements of gender, race, and class; assimilation and rejection of the dominant culture.[7]

Because Christian spirituality consists of a constellation of integrated elements (God-images, community, asceticism), rearranging one element affects all others, as the history of this period demonstrates. The Sunday Eucharist celebrated in house churches or in larger communities composed of poor and rich, illiterate and educated, women and men, reinforced certain insights, such as the acceptance of diversity, reconciliation, hope, and generous love. Conviction deepened that the community was the primary place to meet the risen Lord.

Initial emphasis on martyrdom also affected all later interpretation of Christian experience. Whereas Paul saw ministry as the imitation of Christ, early martyrs understood a painful death as the closest imitation of Jesus. Praising martyrdom, then, reinforced Greek culture's tendency to deny the body and the world. When martyrdom was no longer possible, complete self-denial was sought through asceticism and monasticism.

Asceticism arose as a countercultural movement against the church that was overly identified with political institutions. Primarily a lay movement, it had a solitary side that tended toward contempt for the flesh and a communal side that stressed simple prayer, that relished Scripture, and that promoted charity and purity of conscience as attitudes needed for proper interpretation of Scripture. Only through asceticism could women overcome men's identification of females with flesh, which was judged as subordinate to spirit, identified with males. That is, women could be equal to men on condition that they renounce the satisfactions of bodily life. Wise ascetics, such as Macrina and Benedict, attracted persons seeking spiritual guidance.

Desert mothers and fathers manifested a profound realization that tradition is not a set formula but a continuity of life lived according to the gospel. Desert wisdom is perennial, yet naturally it mirrors the authoritarian, patriarchal society from which it comes. Christian culture's absorption of ancient learning resulted in a model and method of promoting religious experience that idealized philosophical contemplation centered on the mind. Its method aimed to subject the passions to reason. Virginity, practiced by a minority of women and men, enjoyed a moral and cultural supremacy unchallenged until the Reformation. In ancient Mediterranean society, sexual abstinence was a social convention with negative and positive connotations foreign to modern persons. Negatively, virginity meant fighting against tensions of unfulfilled sexuality. Even more significantly, it meant struggling against the force of social convention that swept a person into her or his supposedly natural social role as a married person whose sexual life was directed toward perpetuating family and kinship. Positively, virginity committed a person to new grounds of social cohesion. For women it meant that what Eve lost through sin the virgin regained through a celibate life. She lived an angelic life that could mediate between the divine and the human. Although this theory was not always practiced, its symbolic power cannot be underestimated. Gradually this theory modified the Platonic ideal of the soul withdrawn from the body, so that the emphasis shifted to withdrawal of the body-self from society's claims regarding the primacy of family and kin. This made a certain type of autonomy possible for upper-class women and for many women in monasteries.

In summary, spiritual maturity in this era continued to be seen as union with God and love of neighbor. However, the influence of surrounding culture added conflicting ideals: love of neighbor was set alongside contempt for the flesh (and, consequently, contempt for women who were identified with flesh); purity of conscience accompanied unquestioning obedience to male authority. Virginity, as an ideal, had a double effect: renunciation of sex as a sacramental way to experience God, along with freedom to renounce the social conventions that restricted women to marriages arranged for the sake of property and family status.

Medieval Spirituality

While the medieval period was innovative in styles of religious life and art, it was not revolutionary because it remained firmly rooted in previous traditions.[8]

Popular spirituality could be distinguished from professional. Mass conversions, low levels of general education, and pastoral neglect promoted the cult of relics, magic under the guise of sacraments, pilgrimages simply for the sake of travel, and thinly veiled paganism. In contrast, the professional spirituality of nuns and monks was informed by study and guidance.

Professional religious life flourished in a variety of forms. While women and men continued to withdraw into solitude, there emerged an urban ministry of clerics devoted to including laity in cathedral liturgy. A central question became: What is the authentic experience of apostolic or evangelical life? Monks concluded that monastic life was the only place in which the image of God could truly be restored to humanity in this life. In contrast, mendicant women and men were convinced that genuine evangelical life was possible outside of monastic structures. Francis of Assisi, for example, believed that anyone could preach who was called by God's Spirit. Francis wandered the countryside, begged for support rather than relying on wealthy benefices, and called all to conversion using metaphors of trade drawn from the experience of the new merchant class. The rule written by Clare of Assisi, who was also attracted by evangelical poverty, reveals not only her originality in stressing women's discretion but also her insistence on radical poverty at a time when Franciscan men were far from this ideal. Her rule also reflects papal decrees that women be secluded.

Beguines were another type of lay group. Independent from men's authority, these women lived at home or in small communities in voluntary poverty and celibacy. With no formal church supervisors, they combined work, common prayer, and life "in the world." Eventually all mendicant preaching was clericalized and all women's religious communities were forced to accept strict cloister.

Although many medieval women and men conveyed their experience of God and of Jesus through maternal imagery, this symbol functioned differently for each sex. Although Julian of Norwich in her *Showings* may be best known for her theology of God's motherhood, she was hardly original since the Bible and patristic writers used feminine images of God. For women, divine motherhood conveyed primarily an experience of receiving unconditional love. For many Cistercian abbots, on the other hand, this image was associated with authority. Out of a need to supplement their male exercise of authority with attitudes such as gentleness and availability, which were considered feminine, they imaged Christ, their model of monk and abbot, as mother and midwife of souls. In the process of infusing authority with love, these men romanticized motherhood, repeated female stereotypes, and imaged Christ as a nursing mother even while they maintained their own separation from and even hostility toward actual women.

Medieval writers described "man" as the image and likeness of God. In *The Cloud of Unknowing,* for example, one finds patristic themes: grace as divinization, human faculties as reflections of the Trinity, the image of God as given from the beginning yet tarnished by sin, and asceticism as the way to develop the true likeness to God. For medieval women and men such as Clare and Francis of Assisi, one became one's true self by conforming to the model of true humanity: Jesus poor, humble, and entirely surrendered to God. Jesus' maleness was not significant; rather, it was his obedience and love that united him to God and to us.

Attachment to Mary was a striking feature of medieval religious experience. During this period the figure of Mary changed from the inspiring mother of Christ to the merciful mother of the people to the queen of heaven and earth who protected her faithful ones. At times her ability to rescue became the focus of exaggerated devotion. The cult of the Virgin reinforced an androcentric image of woman. It praised a woman surrendered to a male divinity, valued entirely on the basis of her abstinence from a sexual life and her devotion to a son's goals. The glorification of this one woman left unaffected the subordinate situation of real women.

In the midst of the wars and religious divisions of this period, some women heeded their inner voices urging them to redirect political affairs. Catherine of Siena admonished the pope and struggled to reconcile warring factions. Joan of Arc led armies to victory, then was betrayed into enemy hands. Joan chose fidelity to her vocation rather than escape, and she was burned at the stake. These saints demonstrate the inseparability of religious and so-called worldly experience.

Eastern Orthodox spirituality in this period is well represented in Gregory Palamas's teaching about hesychasm[9] (silent contemplation), which stressed a theme noted in Western as well as Eastern religious experience: silent prayer of the heart, understood as prayer of the whole person, including the body. Its aim was to be conscious of the grace of baptism already given yet hidden by sin. Its method was probably influenced by Islam's joining of the holy name to the rhythm of breathing. Its wider context was the Eastern understanding of the connection between active and contemplative life. *Active*, for Gregory, referred to the redirection, not suppression, of passions. *Contemplative* referred to silence of the heart, to complete openness and surrender to God. A cloistered nun could be active, while a busy mother could be contemplative if she had silence of heart. Prayer of the heart was considered a type of constant prayer possible for all persons, not just for monks and nuns.

In summary, medieval writers envisioned spiritual maturity as wholehearted conformity to Christ's love and care for all. This care was often conveyed in female images that symbolized different meanings for women and men. New forms of religious life revealed that while men could attain Christian maturity outside of monastic cloister, for several reasons women were presumed to require seclusion. First, unless women were directly attached to men by living in their households, women were defined as "loose," that is, immoral. Second, monastic cloister served in some cases to protect women from male relatives who wanted to force their return to family control. In more cases, however, it symbolized either the conviction that women's humanity was so flawed that it required enforced protective boundaries or it acted as an extension of family control when daughters were put into convents because a suitable marriage was not possible. Writers, both female and male, saw that maturity requires personal judgment in order to discern the appropriate response to new forms of apostolic life and in order to be faithful to contemplative and active aspects of interior development.

Reformation Spirituality

Protestant response to some aspects of medieval tradition led to a new understanding of spirituality. Monasticism was no longer perceived as a special way to experience God. Rather, God was seen as available in all aspects of life, especially where the word of God was preached authentically and the sacraments of baptism and the Lord's Supper were celebrated. Celibacy was no longer the privileged state of life in which to achieve union with God; instead, marriage was particularly valued and in some cases became almost an obligation for clergy. In this movement women lost the advantages of convent life, among them independence from patriarchal marriage and the opportunity for higher education; instead they received a new role expectation: serving as the pastor's wife, which involved total service to the congregation while receiving none of the reverence and rewards bestowed on the clergy.[10]

Catholics and Protestants tended to respond to each other's theology by emphasizing the differences and assuming the other's view had no merit. Contemporary Catholics, however, can now appreciate Luther's insights regarding the importance of Scripture and even notice parallels to the great Spanish mystics that neither Teresa of Jesus (of Avila) nor John of the Cross nor Luther consciously intended.

For Luther, speech about God is speech about absence; God is met only in the cross, in a kind of loneliness in which there are no signs of transcendence, no conceptual neatness, no mystical assurances. Teresa of Jesus and John of the Cross would agree with Luther's conviction that one can neither contain nor control God. Luther and the authentic Catholic contemplative tradition object to the perversion of contemplation into an experience that imprisons God in a set of human feelings or thoughts or impressions. Indeed, John of the Cross in *The Ascent of Mount Carmel* teaches the inevitability of the dark night in which human desire is transformed and human projections onto God eventually are surrendered in order to allow authentic union with God in Christ. John, Teresa, and Luther would agree also that knowledge of God is possible only on God's terms: when humans yield their self-assertive will and respond to God's total self-gift of undeserved love. The affinity between Luther and the great Carmelite reformers does not, however, discount their theological differences over grace, church, and human nature.

Carmelite reform, initiated by Teresa of Jesus and extended to the friars through John of the Cross, was intended to make religious life a community of loving friends, living in poverty and solitude. Its theology of spiritual and human development can assist persons to become completely disposed toward God's action for the sake of the needs of the church and the world. Contemplative transformation, according to Teresa's teaching in *The Interior Castle,* is directed toward one purpose only: "the birth always of good works, good works" (7.4.6).

Teresa's astute interpretation of her own process of religious development, explained first in the *Life* and revised and expanded in *The Interior Castle*, eventually made her a Doctor of prayer for the universal church. Using the "rhetoric of femininity," for example, referring to herself as a weak, ignorant woman to avoid the Inquisition's censure because she dared to teach about spiritual matters, Teresa communicated her experience of deepening prayer through the image of four waters. She explained how her efforts at self-knowledge and honest love (drawing water from a well) yielded a greater capacity for receiving God's love (a wheel turned by a donkey eases the effort of drawing water). Fidelity in the desert of love's purification allowed the full force of God's acceptance and love to inundate her (like a river) with abundant gifts (like rain) of intimacy with the Trinity and of leadership in the church. In the Carmelite tradition, another resource for current feminist concerns is the theology of equality, even with God, that permeates *The Spiritual Canticle* of John of the Cross. Here spiritual maturity is described as complete mutuality with God, as "equality of friendship" (stanza 28.1).

Ignatius of Loyola also distilled his religious experience into guidelines for spiritual growth. His *Spiritual Exercises* are an imaginative method of meditating on and contemplating Scripture. They were designed to assimilate one to the mysteries of Christ and facilitate discernment for a contemplative person in apostolic action. Although they use male-centered examples and military images, the *Exercises* are intended to be adapted to different needs. By expanding the biblical meditations to include women's discipleship and by substituting examples that are truer to women's experience, the *Exercises* can be made effective for women today.

In summary, Reformation spirituality valued what we now call self-direction and intimate relationships. Protestants and Catholics who desired reform called these values fidelity to one's interior call and surrender to God's love. They were considered necessary for both women and men. Religious upheaval reinforced the need to follow an informed conscience, as Martin Luther and Katharina (née von Bora) Luther did. In the midst of uncertainty reformers of this era developed the themes of personal discernment and critical self-knowledge that our own era needs in order to face profound changes.

Modern Spirituality

As the sixteenth century affected later Catholic spirituality through the Spanish mystics, so from the seventeenth century onward French spirituality was also very influential.[11]

Neither monasteries nor universities were the seedbed of this spirituality; rather, it was the parlor of Madame Acarie, known later as the Carmelite Marie of the Incarnation. Her discussion group included Benedict of Canfield and Pierre de Bérulle. They absorbed the Platonic perspective of Denys the Areopagite (sixth century) and reshaped it to support their own understanding of spirituality. Canfield's *Exercises of the Will of God* stressed holiness as accessible to all through an experience of self-emptying that permits participation in the passion of Jesus Christ. Bérulle also taught participation in the mysteries of Christ. In his *Grandeurs of Jesus* the goal of Christian life is imaged as the reproduction on earth of the adoration and servitude of Christ in heaven.

This era was influenced by the exceptional personality of Francis de Sales. A bishop best known for his warmth and sensitivity as a spiritual director, his *Introduction to the Devout Life* became a classic description of how the laity can become holy through the practice of love in ordinary life. Jane de Chantal, Francis's intimate friend, spiritual companion, and cofounder of the Visitation order, was also an outstanding spiritual director. Her *Letters* demonstrate great skill in promoting the integration of spiritual and human maturity. Her unique contributions to Salesian spirituality have become lasting influences.

Jansenism, a complex and controversial combination of theological, political, and economic issues, was named for Cornelius Jansen, whose rigorist presentation of Augustine's theology of grace reinforced certain practices. In confession a penitent should not be given the benefit of the doubt; one should sometimes give up Holy Communion as an act of humility or through mortification; moral life must be strict.

Nineteenth- and twentieth-century spirituality was, like all previous spirituality, a creative response to God's presence discerned in events and ideas. Responses to the Enlightenment, secularism, atheism, and political revolution ranged widely. Thérèse of Lisieux, for example, interpreted her experience of spiritual darkness as redemptive identification with modern struggles for faith. Pierre Teilhard de Chardin reconciled science and faith by interpreting his experience of cosmic unification as *The Divine Milieu*. The concern to restore biblical prayer, share monastic riches with the laity, and reunite spirituality and theology motivated the liturgical movement. Responses to industrialism included the social spirituality of Dorothy Day's and Peter Maurin's Catholic Worker movement in the United States. In Europe, Africa, and the Middle East Little Brothers and Sisters of Jesus, inspired by Charles de Foucauld, began a ministry of evangelical presence as poor workers among workers. Affective, sometimes sentimental, devotion to Mary tended to compensate for Jansenist rigorism and patriarchal religion by promoting Mary as the kind, approachable mediatrix of all grace.

In summary, modern spirituality continued to respond to dramatically new perspectives on faith and doubt, on mission, science, social structures, and world religions. Maturity remained a matter of loving relationships and fidelity to one's vocation. Radical new possibilities for women to found religious congregations, and the Enlightenment critique of religious authority, reinforced the need for a kind of spiritual discernment that demanded one both trust and evaluate personal decisions. Foundresses such as Elizabeth Seton and Cornelia Connelly exemplify the challenges and continuities of modern Catholic spirituality.

Contemporary Spirituality

Western culture is now in the process of a paradigm shift more profound than any since the modern era began. In every field of study and endeavor the standards of "authentic reality" are beginning to change from individualism, hierarchy, and male centeredness to a new paradigm of interdependence, mutuality, and inclusiveness. Yet tremendous pressures resist the emerging paradigm, and Catholic feminism is embedded in this tension as it tries to understand and reach spiritual maturity.

Exploration of this tension will move in three steps: (1) a definition of Catholic feminism; (2) integration of this view with spiritual maturity; and (3) a consideration of the difference it makes to have this perspective.

Recently, a woman who was asked why she was joining the Catholic church when she knew its pervasive sexism replied, "I'm not drawn by the tradition of authority and administration that stays in union with Rome; I'm coming to belong to the great mystical and theological tradition that is still bearing fruit in good works all over the world." Catholicism unites these two aspects that Catholic feminists experience as inseparable yet often in tension.

Catholic feminists also struggle to reconcile two aspects of secular feminism. Individualist feminists argue for the moral equality of women and men whose shared humanity deserves equal rights. Relational feminists also affirm equality yet stress the difference it makes in our culture to be socialized as a woman rather than as a man. They insist that society value the qualities and skills that culture develops in women and grant the same status and rewards to women's contributions that are given to men's.

Catholic feminists desire an integration of these two aspects: realization of women's equal human dignity and capacity for all roles in life and church ministry, and just reward for women's unique contributions rather than restriction and abuse. Feminists who identify as Catholic believe they can still find a "usable tradition" within the church.[12]

How is spiritual maturity understood from a Catholic feminist perspective? Because Catholic theology maintains that grace (the Trinity's loving presence) and human nature are intrinsically related, Catholic feminists presume that human and spiritual maturity can be integrated. However, knowing that the tradition has presented a double standard for women and men, they wonder *how* this can be done when women's spiritual maturity is seen so often as self-denial and submission, while men's maturity is presumed to be the standard of human maturity and is described as leadership and heroic resistance in the face of challenge. Given the feminist principles explained above, integration of human or psychological maturity with Christian maturity is possible, then, if and only if the paradigm of maturity is the same for women and men and the same for psychology and spirituality. Everyone strives for maturity in her or his own unique way, so "the same" paradigm means the absence of conflicting values and ideals.

This integration is possible in both theory and practice when a feminist model of psychological development is related to a feminist theology of spiritual development and shown to be identical.[13] In brief, a feminist theology of spiritual development notices that the classical spiritual tradition defines maturity as intimate relationship with the Holy Mystery (ineffable yet named as Source, Word, and Spirit) and with all persons and the cosmos, an intimacy made possible by increasing independence from attachments that block deeper relationship. The desire to affirm women's experience as much as men's leads feminist theologians to notice how both autonomy (traditionally denied or restricted for women) and attachment (culturally reinforced in women) are essential for Christian maturity. In the tradition, autonomy for the sake of relationship is described in the language of detachment for the sake of union with God. That is, the autonomy valued in psychology for its ability to free people for deeper relationship, is spoken of in spirituality traditions as detachment that makes possible union with God. Different cultures have interpreted this detachment in different ways, from renunciation of any pleasure, especially sexual, to letting go of all images of the divine in prayer. Likewise, the language of union with God has been interpreted in immature images of fusion or self-annihilation. Feminist theology finds that the negative connotations of the religious language of detachment and union can be overcome by using feminist structural developmental psychology.

Developmental psychology that gives equal value to women's and men's experience maintains that every phase of human development involves both autonomy and attachment. Greater maturity is a matter of ever greater independence from *fusion* with family, friends, religion, and culture, precisely for the sake of relationships of intimacy that are deeper, more complex, more inclusive of diversity. The self develops through a complex process that includes dying to the old way of interpreting the meaning of oneself and others in order to relate in ways that are ever more authentically intimate and mature. Autonomous persons are free to give themselves in truthful love not only to those who are "like them" but also to those who are different. In order to live from inner self-direction rather than from compulsion or role conformity, one must "die" to fusion with social roles or to identification with unexamined ways of living. This developmental transformation is a kind of death because it requires facing the radically unknown that is part of facing the fear of failure, anxiety over accepting new ideas, or insecurity in relationships that are more mutual and thus less controlled and predictable. Out of this death comes freedom for relationships that are deeper and more inclusive. In this developmental perspective, autonomy is detachment from restrictive ways of being and relating, precisely so that unbounded love and care for all can arise from ever freer self-donation. Thus union with God and others, in this view, integrates independence with relationship at every phase of development. Unlike models of maturity based on male socialization seeing independence as the goal, this feminist model values independence precisely in terms of its potential for allowing deeper relationship. Thus differentiation for the sake of deeper relationship is the meaning of maturity for both men and women.

This feminist model of human maturity enables the integration of Christian and psychological development in both theory and practice. The Christian language of growth through detachment and spiritual darkness for the sake of union that is more mutual can be recognized as a matter of gaining psychic freedom in order to relate with the intimacy born of equality. In one phase of development it would be freedom from immersion in unexamined relationships to others (including God) in order to *have* relationships rather than simply *be* relationships (women's traditional socialization). In another phase it would be freedom from the need to control relationships (men's traditional pattern and the temptation for feminist individualists) in order to welcome the vulnerability necessary for intimacy and mutuality between equals. The transition from one phase of development to another may feel like death because it is the death of one entire way of being oneself. No wonder spiritual tradition calls this a "dark night" of the senses and the spirit. No wonder, either, that a Catholic feminist would notice how the feminist desire for equality is echoed in the Christian tradition viewing friendship as the school of the spiritual life. As many mystics describe it, using the analogy of friendship, it includes God putting us in God's self, making us God's equal.[14]

What difference does it make to have this feminist perspective? It makes every issue of Catholic spirituality, which is the same as every aspect of life, a struggle for conversion, for a complete change of heart and mind. When feminists desire to identify themselves as Catholic, they face a religious situation of contradiction and conflict. While affirming women as baptized into Christ as fully as men, official church teaching and practice also ignore, demean, and even oppress women. Even while being trivialized or restricted, Catholic feminist women and men (including some bishops) are thinking and acting in creative and courageous ways to convert themselves and others toward the Christian maturity described above. This experience of the patriarchal religious situation in the process of conversion is studied and promoted by the academic study of Catholic spirituality. When we grasp the enormity of this task of transformation in both experience and academic endeavors we may feel frustrated, exhausted, and tempted to quit. Even more, when the feminist critique results in losing past certitudes people feel a profound loss of existential meaning. At times, maintaining a feminist Catholic spirituality feels like a matter of survival. Living with oppressive church structures and male-centered theology is torture, but rejecting Catholic spiritual riches is starvation.[15] Maintaining faith, fidelity, and feminist integrity while the church is converted to genuine inclusiveness requires validation from the spiritual tradition.

How does our Catholic spiritual tradition help us interpret and respond to this contemporary situation? It offers resources that speak directly to the connection between this experience of darkness and the Christian maturity described thoughout this chapter. When Catholic spirituality seems profoundly inadequate and therefore our very identity is at stake we have John of the Cross's advice to those struggling with faith: "Because the gold of the spirit is not purified and illumined . . . Wishing to . . . clothe them with the new . . . God leaves the intellect in darkness, the will in aridity, the memory in emptiness, and the affections in anguish, by depriving the soul of the feelings and satisfactions it previously obtained from spiritual blessings."[16]

This "intellect in darkness" well describes the perspective of feminist women and men who must relinquish the entire male-centered theology of God, acknowledge the significant problems with Goddess theology,[17] and labor toward a complete reconstruction of the tradition about the Holy Mystery. Surely, a "memory in emptiness" fits the experience of those whose memory of traditional Christology and sacramental theology brings emptiness at the realization of their profound inadequacy or brings pain when they are used to restricting or oppressing women. Knowing that maturity requires letting go of all that blocks wider truth and deeper union, feminists are invited to believe that "although the [person] has not the support of any particular interior light of the intellect or of any exterior guide . . . love alone . . is what guides and moves [the person] and makes [her or him] soar to God in an unknown way. . . ."[18] The creative love manifest in this book is just one witness to the spiritual energy working to liberate the world for a still unknown spiritual maturity.

NOTES

1. For a fuller historical treatment of this term, see Sandra M. Schneiders, "Spirituality in the Academy," *Theological Studies* 50, no. 4 (1989): 684–87.

2. Schneiders has made the most original contribution to defining spirituality as an academic field and to specifying its methodology. See, for example, "Spirituality in the Academy," 676–97. Schneiders's position is represented here.

3. See Catherine Mowry LaCugna, *God for Us: The Trinity and Christian Life* (San Francisco: Harper San Francisco, 1991).

4. These six tasks were first named and developed by Mary Jo Weaver, *New Catholic Women* (San Francisco: Harper & Row, 1985), 154–55.

5. Clarissa W. Atkinson, *Mystic and Pilgrim: The Book and the World of Margery Kempe* (Ithaca: Cornell Univ. Press, 1983).

6. For a concise treatment and further resources see Sandra M. Schneiders, *Beyond Patching* (New York: Paulist Press, 1991), 37–71.

7. Useful resources for this period include Peter Brown, *The Body and Society: Men, Women, and Sexual Renunciation in Early Christianity* (New York: Columbia Univ. Press, 1988); Elizabeth A. Clark, *Women in the Early Church* (Wilmington, DE: Michael Glazier, 1983); Douglas Burton-Christie, *The Word in the Desert: Scripture and the Quest for Holiness in Early Christian Monasticism* (New York: Oxford Univ. Press, 1993).

8. Useful resources for this period include volumes in the *Classics of Western Spirituality* series, such as Julian of Norwich, *Showings* (New York: Paulist Press, 1979); Francis and Clare of Assisi, *The Complete Works* (New York: Paulist Press, 1982); *Clare of Assisi: Early*

Documents, edited and trans. by Regis J. Armstrong (New York: Paulist Press, 1988) benefits by the collaboration of Margaret Carney; Carolyn Walker Bynum, *Jesus as Mother: Spirituality of the High Middle Ages* (Berkeley and Los Angeles: Univ. of California Press, 1982).

9. *Westminster Dictionary of Christian Spirituality,* s.v. "hesychasm," by Kallistos Ware.

10. Resources for this period include primary sources in translation from the Institute for Carmelite Studies (Washington, DC) and volumes of *The Classics of Western Spirituality* on Luther and Ignatius of Loyola; Rowan Williams, *Christian Spirituality* (Atlanta: John Knox Press, 1979), and *Teresa of Avila* (Harrisburg, PA: Morehouse Publishing, 1991).

11. Resources for this era include volumes from *The Classics of Western Spirituality* such as *Bérulle and the French School;* Francis de Sales and Jane de Chantal, *Letters of Spiritual Direction;* Louis Dupré and Don E. Saliers, eds., *Christian Spirituality: Post-Reformation and Modern* (New York: Crossroad, 1989); Jill Raitt, ed., *Christian Spirituality: High Middle Ages and Reformation,* vol. 17 of *World Spirituality: An Encyclopedic History of the Religious Quest* (New York: Crossroad, 1987).

12. For further development see Joann Wolski Conn, "New Vitality: The Challenge from Feminist Theology," *Proceedings of the Catholic Theological Society of America* 46 (1991): 70–74.

13. Joann Wolski Conn, *Spirituality and Personal Maturity* (New York: Paulist Press, 1989).

14. Constance FitzGerald, "A Discipleship of Equals: Voices from Tradition—Teresa of Avila and John of the Cross," *Proceedings of the Theology Institute of Villanova University,* ed. Francis A. Eigo, O.S.A. (Villanova, PA: Villanova Univ. Press, 1988), 63–97.

15. Mary Jo Weaver, *Springs of Water in a Dry Land: Spiritual Survival for Catholic Women Today* (Boston: Beacon Press, 1992), p. xii.

16. "The Dark Night," bk. 2, chap. 3, no. 3, in *The Collected Works of St. John of the Cross,* trans. Kieran Kavanaugh and Otilio Rodriguez (Washington, DC: Institute of Carmelite Studies, 1973).

17. Contemporary Goddess religion is a complex phenomenon that claims its roots in primal matriarchal societies that were centered on Goddess worship. Its practitioners sometimes describe it as a foreshadowing of feminism. Problems with it include (1) no written evidence for the existence of primal matriarchies or the Great Goddess; (2) reliance on secondary literature for overstated conclusions; (3) reliance on the psychic reality for its adherents while ignoring historical problems; (4) a focus on a utopian poetic and a theology untested by even one generation; (5) an uncritical attitude toward its own tradition while dismissing traditional Christianity as unredeemably sexist. These issues are explained in Rosemary Radford Ruether, *Gaia and God: An Ecofeminist Theology of Earth-Healing* (San Francisco: Harper San Francisco, 1992) and Mary Jo Weaver, *Springs of Water in a Dry Land.*

18. "The Dark Night," bk. 2, chap. 25, no. 4.

FOR FURTHER READING

Classics of Western Spirituality. New York: Paulist Press, 1980. A library of original texts translated and introduced by outstanding scholars associated with each author or tradition. Some introductions include feminist concerns.

Conn, Joann Wolski, ed. *Women's Spirituality.* New York: Paulist Press, 1986. An anthology of essays integrating feminist theology and psychology; explains how women's spirituality may be feminist, feminine, or neither.

Conn, Joann Wolski, and Walter E. Conn, eds. *Horizons on Catholic Feminist Theology.* Washington, DC: Georgetown Univ. Press, 1992. Explains and illustrates six tasks of feminist theology.

Fischer, Kathleen. *Women at the Well.* New York: Paulist Press, 1988. A discussion of spiritual direction from a feminist perspective; includes attention to issues of power and violence.

McGinn, Bernard. *The Foundations of Mysticism.* New York: Crossroad, 1991. The first of three projected volumes; the appendix on theological, philosophical, comparative, and psychological approaches to mysticism outlines all the controversies of the twentieth century.

Meehan, Brenda. *Holy Women of Russia: The Lives of Five Orthodox Women Offer Spiritual Guidance for Today.* San Francisco: Harper San Francisco, 1993. Against the rich backdrop of nineteenth-century Russia, the author—a leading expert in Russian history and especially the history of religion in Russia—charts the forgotten lives of five holy women who each modeled a distinctive spiritual path and inspired the vibrant spirituality that lived on underground among communities of women in our century.

Miles, Margaret. *Practicing Christianity.* New York: Crossroad, 1988. Critical perspectives for an embodied spirituality.

New Dictionary of Catholic Spirituality. Edited by Michael Downey. Collegeville, MN: Liturgical Press, 1993. Uses contemporary scholarship, incorporates feminist perspective.

Plaskow, Judith, and Carol P. Christ, eds. *Weaving the Visions: New Patterns in Feminist Spirituality.* San Francisco: Harper & Row, 1989. Explains new patterns in feminist spirituality, but has an uncritical view of research on Goddess religion.

Ruether, Rosemary Radford. *Gaia and God: An Ecofeminist Theology of Earth Healing.* San Francisco: Harper San Francisco, 1992. Examines patriarchal and ecofeminist religious visions of creation.

Sheldrake, Philip. *Spirituality and History.* New York: Crossroad, 1992. A full-scale contemporary exploration of the role of history in the study of Christian spirituality.

Weaver, Mary Jo. *Springs of Water in a Dry Land.* Boston: Beacon Press, 1992. Gives strategies for spiritual survival for Catholic women today. It includes a clear, balanced critique of Goddess religion.

World Spirituality. General Editor, Ewert Cousins. New York: Crossroad, 1985. An encyclopedic history of the religious quest. Women are vastly underrepresented.

Contributors

LISA SOWLE CAHILL is Professor of Moral Theology at Boston College. She is the author of several books, including *Between the Sexes: Foundations for a Christian Ethic of Sexuality* (Philadelphia: Fortress Press, 1985).

ANNE E. CARR is Professor of Theology at the University of Chicago. She has published several books and articles on various Catholic thinkers and on feminist theology, including the landmark *Transforming Grace: Christian Tradition and Women's Experience* (San Francisco: Harper & Row, 1988).

JOANN WOLSKI CONN is Professor of Christian Spirituality in the Pastoral Counseling and Spiritual Direction Program at Neumann College (Aston, Pennsylvania). She is the editor of *Women's Spirituality* and author of *Spiritual and Personal Maturity* (New York: Paulist Press, 1989).

MARY CATHERINE HILKERT is Associate Professor of Systematic Theology at Aquinas Institute of Theology in St. Louis. She is co-editor of *The Praxis of Christian Experience: An Introduction to the Thought of Edward Schillebeeckx* (San Francisco: Harper & Row, 1989), and she has published many journal articles.

MARY E. HINES is Professor of Theology and Chair of Graduate Programs in Ministry at Emmanuel College (Boston). She is the author of *The Transformation of Dogma: An Introduction to Karl Rahner on Dogma* (New York: Paulist Press, 1989).

ELIZABETH A. JOHNSON is Associate Professor of Theology at Fordham University (New York) and author of various articles and books, including *She Who Is: The Mystery of God in Feminist Theological Discourse* (New York: Crossroad, 1993).

CATHERINE MOWRY LACUGNA is Professor of Theology at the University of Notre Dame (Notre Dame, Indiana). She has written many articles on theology and liturgy and is the author of *God for Us: The Trinity and Christian Life* (San Francisco: Harper San Francisco, 1991).

MARY AQUIN O'NEILL is Founder and Director of the Mount Saint Agnes Theological Center for Women in Baltimore, Maryland. She has written various articles on theological anthropology.

SUSAN A. ROSS is Associate Professor of Theology and Director of the Women's Studies Program at Loyola University (Chicago, Illinois). She has written on women and the sacraments in various journals.

SANDRA M. SCHNEIDERS is Professor of New Testament Studies and Christian Spirituality at the Jesuit School of Theology and the Graduate Theological Union (Berkeley, California). She is the author of several articles and books, including *The Revelatory Text: Interpreting the New Testament as Scripture* (San Francisco: Harper San Francisco, 1991) and *Women and the Word* (New York: Paulist Press, 1986).

Index

Abortion, and ethics, 212–13
Androcentrism, 15–16, 19, 35, 71, 72; of the Bible, 19, 34–35, 73, 141–42, 146–47; of Christology, 118–20, 131; medieval, 248, 249; of sacramental system, 153; and sexuality, 201; of theology, 13, 156. *See also* Patriarchy; Sexism
Anointing, sacrament of, 200
Anthropology, 155–57; and Christology, 120, 130; dual, 120, 146–51, 163; of mutuality, 146, 151; theological, 84, 94, 120, 139–60
Aristotle, 7, 89, 90, 188, 214
Arius/Arianism, 75, 85–92 passim, 98, 100, 112n.46, 130
Asceticism, 241, 246–48
Athanasius, 85, 98
Augustine of Hippo, 7–8, 88–90, 154, 188, 214, 252
Authority: biblical, 37, 39, 46–47; governmental war, 227, 229; to interpret tradition, 72–73; of magisterium, 33, 61–62, 64, 68, 75–76; religious (general), 7, 14; and spirituality, 244, 248. *See also* Hierarchy

Baptism, 99, 106, 187, 199, 200
Bible, 31–57; androcentrism in, 19, 34–35, 73, 141–42, 146–47; apostolic witness in, 22; authority of, 37, 39, 46–47; canonicity of, 40–44, 73–74; Catholic use of, 31–37, 51, 52n.6; and ethics, 220–22, 230; and feminism, 18, 20, 31–57; as human discourse, 39–40, 51; inerrancy, 37, 39, 44; infallibility, 37; as inspiration, 40–44; Jewish, 41; normativity, 17, 20–21, 45–47, 51; and patriarchy, 12, 17–21, 34–36, 46, 49, 73; as revelation, 32, 36, 49, 51, 72–73; sexism in, 35, 36, 242–43; and spirituality, 241, 242–45, 251; theology of, 31–57, 243; tradition and, 32, 69, 74; as word of God, 37–40. *See also* Early Christianity
Biblical interpretation, 19–20, 24, 31–57, 220–22, 243
Bishops: *Challenge of Peace*, 226; and consultation process, 80n.40; theologians' relation with, 169–70. *See also* Magisterium
Body: asceticism and, 246; in Eucharist, 189; God's, 185–209; of Jesus, 155–56; of Mary, 152, 155–56; sanctification in, 152–55, 157; sex as language of, 223; women's, 22–23, 153–55, 157, 189. *See also* Humanity; Sexuality
Bynum, Carolyn Walker, 189, 193

Cahill, Lisa Sowle, 211–34
Cappadocians, 85–88, 90, 91, 93–94, 98

Carmelites, 250–52
Carr, Anne E., 5–29, 150
Catherine of Siena, 189, 248–49
Catholicism, 3, 21, 148, 253; Bible use, 31–37, 51, 52n.6; and body, 155, 157; dual anthropology, 148, 150; ecclesiology, 161–84; ethics, 211–34; feminist theologians, 2–3, 6, 9–29, 61–82, 99–100; and Marian dogmas, 152; marriage, 155, 201–2, 223–25; and ordination of women, 2, 35, 54–55, 61, 148, 150, 163, 170, 186–87, 192, 202; and theology of revelation, 61–70; and sacraments, 186–209; spirituality, 237–57; theological methods, 7–8, 24; and Trinity, 83–114; on war and peace, 226–30. *See also* Church
Christ, 115–37, 152; biblical testimony to, 46, 51; centrality and finality of, 14, 22; Jesus distinguished from, 17, 128–29; as revelation, 32, 60, 65–66, 77; in Trinity, 36, 85–86, 92, 94, 98, 100, 104–5, 106. *See also* Jesus
Christianity: communal-historical identity, 18; ecumenical, 11; and nature religions, 194–95; recovery of women in, 10, 14, 19–21; spirituality, 236; tradition, 14–16, 59–82, 187–90; women at center of, 18, 19, 21, 24–25. *See also* Catholicism; Early Christianity; Patriarchy; Protestantism; Theology
Christology, 115–37, 152; cross in, 115–16, 125, 126–27; doctrine, 129–31; wisdom, 120–34
Church, 161–84; Bible's special status in, 40–47; from description to image, 171–73; egalitarian, 20, 174–78; history, 176–77; loyal opposition, 76; as mystery, 172; nature of, 171–73; as People of God, 162, 172, 192; teaching and learning, 169–70, 180n.22; and women's spirituality, 253, 256–57; in world, 164–67, 176–77. *See also* Christianity; Hierarchy; Liturgy
Clare of Assisi, 241, 247, 248
Clergy: celibate, 188; feminist base communities and, 167–68; laity divided from, 166–67, 169–70, 180n.22, 188, 192, 201; Reformation and, 250; and sacraments, 188, 202–5; and spirituality, 246–48. *See also* Bishops; Magisterium; Ordination of women; Papacy
Collins, Mary, 71–72, 80n.33, 193, 204
Communion, Trinity and, 87–92, 98, 108
Community: base, 167–68, 173; church, 161–84; of dialogue, 169–70; and ethics, 216, 221; image of God reflected in, 141; and language for God, 106–8; spiritual, 243–44, 250
Complementarity: men-women, 84, 94–99, 110–11, 149, 150, 198–99; and Trinity, 84, 94–99, 110–11